Black Roy W
Va Beach

St. Mary's in June 1 PM
1st 2nd Sat
area 804
424-5638

The Tombstone Hills, from Fifth and Toughnut Streets: 1—Grand Central and Contention Mines over this hill, third and richest of Tombstone strikes. 2—Toughnut Mine, second big Schieffelin strike. 3—Tombstone water tank, fed by reservoir. 4—Tombstone reservoir, fed by springs in Huachuca Mountains twenty miles away, via a seven-inch iron pipe laid in the early eighties. 5—West Side Mine. 6—Lucky Cuss Mine, first big strike by Schieffelin. 7—Huachuca Mountains.

This Book

is the book to end books about Tombstone and the quick-triggered gentry who made it "the toughest town in the West"—Wyatt and Virgil and Morgan Earp, Doc Holliday, Buckskin Frank Leslie, Curly Bill Brocius, and the rest. Here, in print for the first time since the Tombstone Epitaph *printed it, is the* Epitaph's *own on-the-spot account of the most famous gunfight in Western history, the fight in the OK Corral, and the running news stories (including the verbatim testimony) of the trial that followed.*

Here are facts hidden for over seventy years behind the hearsay, the conflicting partisanships of one of the Southwest's bitterest controversies. For these are the Tombstone Epitaph's *own news stories, unretouched from the long-lost, recently discovered files thought to have been destroyed in one of Tombstone's famous fires.*

Here is frontier news reporting and editorializing at its rich, rare, racy best. Here are stories of "sporting men" like Johnny-Behind-the-Deuce and "sporting women" like Diamond Annie—stories of "the town drenched in silver and sin"—printed shoulder to shoulder with stories of church socials and family picnics. Historic homicides, Boot Hill burials, and stagecoach robberies share space with birth and wedding notices and cutting editorials. For Editor John Clum printed the truth as he saw it, mincing neither words nor opinions, even in a time and place where epithets were frequently answered with bullets.

Here is the heart-stirring, heart-breaking truth about the discovery (and loss) of silver mines so rich that their ore would take the imprint of a silver dollar. Here is the true story of the fire started by a keg of exploding whiskey—of the other fires and other disasters which

Tombstone weathered to earn the title of "The Town Too Tough To Die." And here, in its own words, is the "autobiography" of the Tombstone Epitaph, *the newspaper that kept the town alive and that lives today in much the same frank, fearless tradition.*

Ninety per cent of this book is simply the news as you would have read it had you lived in Tombstone in the '80's. The rest is the skillful, unbiased correlation of that news by Pulitzer Prize Winner Douglas Martin, former Managing Editor of the Detroit Free Press, *now head of Journalism at The University of Arizona. Martin it was who, with a newspaperman's tenacity, unearthed the long-missing files of the* Epitaph. *And it is Martin's unerring, veteran newspaperman's sense of "what is news" that has panned these nuggets out of this new bonanza of evidence to prove or disprove what has heretofore been Western legend.*

A new high in Southwestern Americana.

Tombstone's Epitaph

Tombstone's Epitaph

DOUGLAS D. MARTIN

Third printing, 1955

To Cecyl

who has lived the uncertain life of a newspaper man's wife with understanding and without complaint for more than thirty years.

Preface

Many books have been written about Tombstone, Arizona, and one thing is common to them all. Every author borrows from the old files of the *Tombstone Epitaph*.

This is always true when historians seek to present accurately the story of a place or an era. Where else can they turn with the assurance of such a wealth of material as they get from the pages of its newspapers, if such records exist?

Yet the references to the *Epitaph* have, at the best, been brief, and too often there has been no credit given.

The men who reported for the *Epitaph* are worthy of better treatment than this. They were "the working press" during one of the most colorful periods of our history and there is richer color, sharper flavor, and greater detail in what they wrote than those who rewrite their work can ever achieve.

It would have been far easier to have rewritten their principal stories and woven them together than to carry out the tedious task of checking the details and dates through the years. But this is their book, and the real story of Tombstone.

I have added only such explanatory material as seems essential if the reader is to follow the dramas unrolled in the files, and only such dates as are necessary for chronological clarity. Capitalization and punctuation of the *Epitaph* have been followed here, as has also, so far as possible, the general style of headings. No attempt has been made to correct errors appearing in *Epitaph* quotations.

One wishes the *Epitaph* had been generous with by-lines and we could use the names of the old reporters today. But I salute them all and credit them with a job well done.

I would be ungrateful if I did not acknowledge the friendship and assistance of Clayton A. Smith, present editor and publisher of the *Epitaph,* and sparkplug of Tombstone. He trusted his files to my care for many weeks. Nor can I overlook the assistance of Mrs. J. H. Macia, pioneer resident of Tombstone and historian of Cochise County. Her marvelous memory for names, dates, and facts saved me many hours of research.

I appreciate also the help extended by the Arizona Pioneer Historical Society, the University of Arizona Library, and the University of California Library at Berkeley.

DOUGLAS D. MARTIN

Contents

1 Tombstone's Epitaph

The car with eastern license plates draws up in front of an adobe plastered building and the occupants get out and stare at the painted sign which reads, "Crystal Palace Bar—The Most Historic Bar in Arizona."

They are standing on Allen Street in Tombstone, Arizona. Once this piece of national highway was the vortex of the gaudiest, richest, and most lawless mining camp in the West. Huge, mule-drawn ore wagons carrying fortunes in silver rumbled down its three short blocks, and hundreds of miners milled about the doors of its saloons and gambling houses. Scarcely a square yard of its dust but was stained with the blood of men who fought with six-guns and fists over mining claims, cattle, liquor, women, or the colors of a shirt.

Now the street drowses under the burning Arizona sun, deserted save for a few loafers who squat on their haunches in the black shadows of the tin awnings which shade the fronts of some of the stores.

Despite the silence there is no feeling that this is a ghost mining town. The walks and pavements are in good repair and the one-story buildings are well painted. One has a strange sensation of waiting for a new play to begin on an old stage.

To the east stand black, rocky hills which bristle with weathered shaft houses and hoists, and the hills too seem to be only temporarily silent as though the mining crews had knocked off for lunch.

The tourists drift into the Crystal Palace, where they stand at the famous old bar and scan the framed paintings and lithographs of the past, study the bullet hole in the mirror of the backbar and eventually ask, "Where is the *Tombstone Epitaph?*"

The directions are brief, for the *Epitaph* is just around the corner on Fifth Street in an old adobe building which is half-hidden in the circling arms of a whispering cottonwood tree.

High above the doorway is the Old English lettering which, for over seventy years, has decorated the masthead of the newspaper from whose columns American editors clipped such wild tales of border life that its name and fame have never died.

This is one of journalism's shrines, home of the faithful recorder of Tombstone's wild days of sin and silver and unfaltering keeper of the faith through the town's lonely years of incredible disasters.

Without the flame which burns within these walls there would be no Tombstone today. The desert greasewood bushes would have taken over its streets.

One will read many pages of Western history without finding another town which has lived through such agonizing misfortunes as have been the lot of Tombstone. Nor will one find another newspaper which can match the record of the *Epitaph's* devotion to its community.

Many men helped make the *Epitaph,* just as many nameless men help to make every newspaper. They are gone, but their stories are preserved in the yellow, brittle pages of *Epitaph* files which are stacked on unpainted wooden shelves inside this doorway.

Scores of historians and writers have read these files and painstakingly scanned the thousands of pages for original news reports of the events which made Tombstone famous, only to come upon the fact that the years 1880, 1881, and 1882 are missing. Unfortunately, these were the colorful years when the Earps and the Clantons, Curly Bill and Johnny Ringo wrote their names in blazing gunfire on the history of the Southwest.

It seems strange so many earnest researchers have accepted the old tale that the earliest files of the *Epitaph* were destroyed when a keg of whiskey exploded and burned up the town. As a matter of fact, the *Epitaph* escaped both that fire and a second equally destructive blaze, and the early files are safe in the

University of California Library at Berkeley and the library of the Arizona Pioneer Historical Society at Tucson.

Only in these issues do you get the eyewitness accounts of early Tombstone, although to bring the first character on stage one must go back three years before the *Epitaph* was born and follow the story of a prospector known as Ed Schieffelin.

Schieffelin was a wandering miner of the 1870's, who had prospected in Nevada, Utah, Colorado, Idaho, and California. He was accustomed to working alone in wild country and as the record of his wanderings shows, he was a restless man whose eyes turned often to far horizons.

Somehow he stumbled over the information that a force of United States cavalry was to leave San Bernardino, California, for a new post known as Fort Huachuca, in the Territory of Arizona, and he decided to ride along with them for protection until he could reach the mountains of the Southwest.

The five-hundred-mile journey, much of it through lands dominated by savage tribes, was made safely, and for a while Schieffelin tried to prospect while following the scouting parties sent from the fort. He soon decided that he could accomplish little this way and, despite many warnings that he would meet death at the hands of the Apaches, he gathered an outfit and went out into the deserts alone in the summer of 1877.

The last words Schieffelin heard as he left the safety of the fort were the warning, "All you'll ever find out there will be your tombstone." He never forgot it, and he lived to ridicule it again and again.

The time spent riding with the troopers had not been wasted, for Schieffelin had learned the geography of the desert and the surrounding mountains. He had been particularly fascinated by a line of black hills which flanked the San Pedro Valley on the east and he made these his first objective.

For weeks Schieffelin prospected in these hills and finally he found two ledges which his experience told him showed signs of rich silver. In ironic humor he named the first discovery "Tombstone" while the second he called "Graveyard."

Backtracking to the old pueblo town of Tucson, Schieffelin showed his pieces of ore to a rancher who had helped stake him, but his benefactor was unimpressed and wanted no part of the claim. There was no assayer in Tucson at that time and the prospector decided to try to interest his brother Al, who was working in Signal Mine, near Globe, over two hundred miles away.

It was a rugged and lonely journey but the determined Schieffelin made it and was rewarded beyond his hopes.

Richard K. Gird, assayer at the mine, agreed to test Schieffelin's samples, and when he had finished the job he made an exciting report. The ore ran $2,000 to the ton.

Gird was so certain Schieffelin had made an extremely rich strike that he agreed to furnish an outfit for a one-third interest in the claims. Schieffelin accepted and although the agreement was never put on paper, it was never broken.

Working secretly, the three men got together a buckboard, a team of mules, and a saddle horse, and in February of 1878 they set out. Once back in the San Pedro Hills, Schieffelin found his monuments and began working the claims. They proved disappointing but Schieffelin was not discouraged. He felt certain from the formations and the colors of the rocks that there was silver on this hill.

Al went out one day to shoot a deer for meat, and Ed shouldered his rifle and his pick and followed. Al got his deer and was packing the meat back to camp when he heard his brother hail him. "Come here and see what I've found if you don't think there is rich ore in this country."

Schieffelin's pick stood upright with the point buried in an outcropping. It was the claim that was to become famous as the "Lucky Cuss," with silver so pure the impression of a half dollar could be imprinted in it.

"I was considerably excited," Ed Schieffelin wrote in his memoirs, "when we found that the samples assayed fifteen thousand dollars to the ton. We were now perfectly satisfied that we had all we wanted."

But it was not Schieffelin's nature to be satisfied. Within a week he was prospecting again, and again he made a rich discovery. This time the claim ran $2,200 to the ton and he called it the "Tough Nut."

The Lucky Cuss Mine

Schieffelin's faith was justified a thousand times over. He had picked the lock of a fabulous treasure chest which men were to know as "Loma de Plata," the hill of silver.

Gird and Al Schieffelin hurried across the desert to Tucson to record the claims, and news of their strike leaked out. Other prospectors followed their return trail and in less than a year men were swarming over the black hills, while at the foot of the slopes there sprang up the sheds and tents of a settlement bearing the magic name of "Tombstone."

One rich strike was followed by another and still another and from all over the West men started moving towards the new camp. Miners led the way across the desert, and in the clouds of thick dust raised by their wheels and the hoofs of their mules and horses came gamblers, lawyers, merchants, saloon keepers, laborers, thieves, doctors, murderers, madams, ranchers, and newspaper men.

By 1880, five hundred roofs had been raised and two of them sheltered pioneer newspapers. The *Nugget* began weekly publication in 1879, and the *Epitaph* followed a year later as a daily and weekly.*

It was a wild country into which those early newspaper men brought their Washington hand presses and their cases of type. Seventy-five miles of desert, shimmering in the blow-torch heat of the region, separated them from the nearest town to the west. Across the mountain trails lay the Mexican border and between the two, Indians rode the warpath, ambushing and killing small parties or descending on a lonely rancher as he prepared his evening meal. Sometimes they killed him outright. Sometimes they tied him to his own cookstove and left him to fry.

Life was scarcely safer in the town of Tombstone than it was outside. The only laws were the pistol, the shotgun, and the rifle. Yet newspapers lived and some even prospered. In all, ten newspapers were launched in the town's first seven years, in which the hills gave up $18,000,000 in treasure and men picked another million from a stope under one city street.

Officially christened Tombstone at the first general meeting

* University of Arizona Bulletin; "Newspapers and Periodicals of Arizona, 1859-1911," by Professor Estelle Lutrell, gives the following information concerning Tombstone's famous newspaper:

Tombstone Epitaph, established May 1, 1880, daily and weekly.

Consolidated with *Tombstone Republican* as *Epitaph and Republican,* 1884-85.

Cochise Record and *Epitaph* consolidated under name of *Daily Record-Epitaph* in 1885.

Resumed name of *Tombstone Epitaph* in 1887.

Weekly edition published as the Sunday edition of the *Tombstone Prospector* until the *Prospector* ceased publication March 7, 1924.

Other newspapers which tried the Tombstone field and discontinued publication there were, *Tombstone Daily Nugget,* 1879-May 5, 1882; *Evening Gossip,* 1881; *Independent,* 1882, discontinued some time that same year; *Daily Tombstone,* 1883, merged with the *Epitaph,* 1886; *Arizona Kicker,* 1892; *The American,* March to June, 1903.

of miners, in 1879, the camp had two thousand inhabitants when the *Epitaph* came off the press early in 1880, and by the close of 1882 it claimed ten thousand, although there is no official record of such a population, and boasted that it was second only to San Francisco in the West. Homes went up wherever there was a piece of level ground, while for those who had no yearning for family life there were boarding houses and hotels. The most famous of the latter were the Occidental, Grand, and Cosmopolitan.

The stores and shops were fond of advertising that they sold the latest fashions for men and women as well as complete lines of foods and wines. Saloons and gambling houses, heavy with plush furniture and dripping with velvet drapes, imported bartenders from St. Louis, Chicago, and New York and guaranteed they could mix any known drink. As for the restaurants and hotel dining rooms, the menus published by the *Epitaph* show that no better meals could be found from coast to coast.

The final brand which marked the town as metropolitan was its new daily paper, the *Tombstone Epitaph*. Tombstone approved the name and the accepted story was that Ed Schieffelin had suggested it on the theory that newspapers, like epitaphs, were generally a collection of lies.

But John P. Clum, who founded the paper, wrote an article fifty years later in which he said the idea was his own. He declared he chose it because he thought any town named Tombstone should have an epitaph and because "the name would yield to the paper a million dollars worth of advertising in six months."

The editor and publisher of the *Epitaph* was by no means an unknown figure or a Johnny-Come-Lately to the territory. He had served with distinction and success as Indian agent at the San Carlos Apache Reservation until convinced that the Government treated its wards with stupid indifference and unfairness. No man to dodge an issue, he carried his protests to Washington, and when he was overruled he resigned from the service.

A chance to buy the Tucson *Citizen* presented itself and Clum acquired the paper. It was a good property in a growing and prosperous community and Clum was successful. But the news of rich strikes in the Tombstone district, seventy-five miles to the south, kept rolling in, and the Tucson editor was attracted by the opportunity to launch a paper there and share in the wealth of the hills. So he sold out in Tucson, ordered a Washington hand press, type, and supplies from San Francisco, and hurried off to the new camp to buy or build an office.

He found the town in the midst of such a building boom that he could not hire carpenters at any price. Weeks passed and he got news that his new equipment had reached the end of the railroad in Tucson and would be shipped across the desert in a few days.

Clum met the emergency by persuading workmen to erect a framework measuring twenty by forty feet. Back he went to Tucson, where he bought canvas, had it cut and sewed to fit his frame, and freighted it back to Tombstone. When the press and type cases arrived he set them up in his canvas-covered shed, and with two printers began working from early daylight until the oil burned out in the kerosene lamps at night.

They worked around the clock on the last day of April, and, on the morning of May 1, the first edition of the *Epitaph* came off the new hand press. Featured on the front page was a two-column editorial which was captioned "The First Trumpet," in which Clum declared, "Tombstone is a city set upon a hill, promising to vie with ancient Rome upon her seven hills, in a fame different in character but no less in importance."

One may think Clum was merely employing the editorial privilege of boosting the home town to woo its support for his new paper. But succeeding editorials prove he meant what he wrote. He believed implicitly in the future of the town and he fought fearlessly for the policies he thought would advance the growth of the community.

What was even more important was the fact that he established an editorial policy from which no *Epitaph* editor has departed and which has repeatedly rallied the spirits of an almost beaten people and renewed their faith in the ultimate greatness of their home town.

Like any civic-minded editor, Clum noticed the needs and the shortcomings of the community and his editorial pen often sketched indelible little scenes of the Tombstone of his day. One catches something of the ebullient spirit of the people as well as a glimpse of Allen Street in this brief admonition:

"The practice of fast riding or driving through the principal thoroughfares is one that should be summarily stopped," he wrote once. "We noticed a couple of horsemen making a quarter stretch of Allen street between Fourth and Fifth last evening, endangering the safety of any child who might have been in the way."

Then he added severely, "This is the second time we have had occasion to call attention to this breach of the ordinances, and we trust it will be the last."

Mayor as well as editor, Clum kept his eye not only on the ordinances, but on chances to improve conditions in Tombstone. An editorial of May 10, 1881, presents one of the camp's discomforts which must have been obnoxious. The first water encountered in the mines was being taken out in a big bucket and tossed down a draw. Clum saw a use for it and wrote this editorial:

"In the past," said Clum, "with water at one and a quarter cents a gallon, street sprinkling has been a luxury too costly to be indulged in, but with the strike of water in our mines, which, at the present moment, is allowed to run to waste, street-sprinkling becomes entirely possible and within reach of the city authorities. With the vast teaming constantly going on within the city the friable calcarious soil has been ground to an impalpable powder, several inches deep, notably on Fremont street, which with every breath of wind is set afloat in such stifling clouds that to be abroad becomes almost intolerable. The penetrative power of this dust is something to be compared only to the Bakersfield Simoons, which penetrate to the innermost sanctuaries everywhere and of everything. That the effect of inhaling this lime dust is injurious to health in a large degree cannot be doubted for a moment when the fact is stated that in a half-hour's time it will completely destroy the best coat of polish on boots or shoes. If its effect is so potent in that respect how can it be otherwise than deleterious when inhaled into the lungs. There is no doubt but what water in sufficient quantities to thoroughly sprinkle Allen and Fremont streets, between Second and Eighth, can be obtained in the mines for the nominal cost of hoisting it to the surface, which the mines are obliged to do whether they will or not. We understand a petition is being circulated among the business men asking the City Council to take immediate action in this matter. As the conservators of the health of the city, as well as law and order, we call upon the City Council, whose regular meeting will be tomorrow evening to take immediate action upon this matter. Columns might be written upon this subject, but giving the gentlemen who have the comfort and convenience of the citizens of Tombstone as much in charge as their protection in other directions, credit for good sense and judgement, we trust this brief notice of the subject, together with the petition that will be presented for their consideration on Wednesday evening will be sufficient."

Tombstone was not long in discovering that its new editor was not only a booster but courageous and able as well. It elected him mayor in the first city election, held January 4, 1881, and he was soon made postmaster. These posts and his editorship of the *Epitaph,* made him the most important figure in the most promising town in the West.

It was an honor which many editors would have avoided, for Clum was elected by the votes of the Law and Order League and naturally the *Epitaph* became the organ of law and order in a community which was dominated by gunmen, rustlers, and those business men who fattened on their trade.

But Clum earnestly believed there was a job which had to be done if Tombstone was to continue to prosper and he said repeatedly in his editorials that the town must be made safe for its law-abiding inhabitants, because capital would not come in where it could not feel secure.

Five months before the *Epitaph* was founded, Wyatt Earp, a famous peace officer who had served with distinction in Wichita and Dodge City, came to Tombstone as a shotgun messenger for the Wells, Fargo & Co. stagecoaches. He was appointed a deputy sheriff and aspired to be appointed sheriff but lost out to Johnny Behan, a Democrat. Earp, a Republican, then resigned and was appointed a United States deputy marshal for the district.

The *Epitaph* saw in Earp an honest and fearless law officer who had broken up many hard crowds in the cow towns of Kansas, and whose reputation and speed in drawing a gun were in themselves a deterrent to crime. The paper became his champion and when Clum was elected mayor he made Wyatt's brother, Virgil, his chief of police. Morgan, another brother, served under Virgil as a special officer.

The deputy sheriff's star had scarcely been pinned on Wyatt Earp's coat before he clashed with the "cowboys," as the *Epitaph* called the "lawless crowd," and the war was on.

The Democratic *Nugget,* which had watched unhappily the rise of Clum and the Republican *Epitaph,* took up the cause of the rustlers and robbers. It ridiculed Clum and the Earps, and the battle which began at this time has lasted for nearly three-quarters of a century. Tempers still have a low boiling point in and around Tombstone when the Earps and the Cowboys are discussed.

The *Epitaph's* files should settle some of the old differences of opinion. For, granting that the *Epitaph's* editor was undoubtedly prejudiced, a reading of his news stories should convince anyone that Clum was a good, factual reporter. He never wrote a sensational lead or a sensational head. He told his stories calmly and chronologically, stopping now and then to put in some background. The worst that can be said of his news writing is that he often editorialized, but it should be remembered that this was common among editors of his day.

And what material he had from which to fashion his news reports! Stagecoach holdups, street killings, posses riding the desert trails behind fleeing bandits, the theft of Wells, Fargo shipments of bullion, the Earp-Clanton-McLowry battle at the OK Corral, in which three Cowboys died in thirty seconds, the shooting of Virgil Earp, the murder of Morgan Earp, and at the end the final act in which Wyatt Earp killed three of his enemies and disappeared in the desert, to leave Tombstone forever.

A few weeks after Wyatt Earp disappeared, Clum, too, left Tombstone. The paper was sold late in April, 1882, and on May 1, exactly two years after Clum brought it out, the *Epitaph* changed owners and policies.

Various reasons are given for the editor's departure from the town in which he had felt great faith and for which he had fought so many valiant editorial battles. Those who disliked him passed on the word that he feared assassination. This is most improbable for Clum was no coward.

Myers Myers, in his late book, *The Last Chance,* says Clum was sold out by his two partners, Charles Reppy and Tom Sorin. This too seems unlikely for when Clum finally wrote the story of his experiences on the *Epitaph* he spoke of both these men with respect and affection.

A story one hears in Tombstone is that the Clums lost a baby daughter there and Mrs. Clum insisted on leaving. But Woodworth Clum says in *Apache Agent* that Mrs. Clum died in Tombstone. Mrs. J. H. Macia confirms this and adds that when Clum visited Tombstone in 1930 he searched for his wife's grave on Boot Hill but was unable to find it.

Whatever his reason for going, Clum left Tombstone at the height of its boom. For the second successive year the mines had produced five million dollars in ore. Some water had appeared at the five-hundred-foot level in the shafts in March, 1881, but the *Epitaph* had hailed it as a great boon which "would tend to bring more capital to the Tombstone district than would a dozen 'Big Strikes' in the upper levels."

It is possible, of course, that in the next year Clum may have sensed coming events, or, because of his connections, he might have learned there was disaster ahead. This is pure conjecture. The known facts are that, a year after he left, the water forced the richest and deepest mines to close and the five million dollar production fell off 50 per cent. Nor was that figure ever to be even approached again.

Pumps were installed and the mines re-opened but operated under difficulties. There was a strike, during which the mines were flooded again and in 1886, when fire destroyed the pump house and hoisting works of the largest mine, the boom exploded, and Tombstone collapsed. Hundreds sold their homes for the price of a stagecoach ticket or a horse and wagon. Others merely walked away and abandoned their homes and belongings.

Once again the clouds of dust hung heavy above the desert trails and campfires flickered in the chill winds of the mountain passes, but this time Tombstone and hope lay behind.

The *Epitaph* survived and its voice never faltered. It will seem fantastic to any journalist, and it might well have seemed fantastic to the people of Tombstone, but, so far as the paper was concerned, the trouble in the mines was minimized. Once it did say darkly that those who had lost faith in the camp would live to be sorry. Why they should lose faith was something the *Epitaph* did not discuss.

On the whole the paper seemed somewhat justified in this observation, for the mine owners were a long way from surrender, and the town was still the most important community in that section of the Southwest. From the pages of the *Epitaph* it is difficult to see that there was much change in the affairs of the community. Life went on and much of it was rugged.

The Earps were gone and so were many of the more notorious cowboys. But enough remained to keep the community from being dull. Profanity was forbidden on the streets but there were killings, holdups, and robberies in the town and the district. The number of saloons, bawdy houses, and gambling establishments was reduced, but those that remained kept on doing business. Men still carried six-shooters on their hips or stuck inside the waistbands of their trousers and Boot Hill kept on growing.

Though the yield of the mines dropped steadily the *Epitaph* kept the hopes of the town up with stories of the progress being made in the efforts to pump them dry again. Like a good cheerleader it refused to stop shouting because the going was tough and its pages show dozens of such news notes as these:

"The water problem is no longer a problem."

"The pumps maintain a mastery over the immense body of water."

"The mammoth pumps continue their task of unwatering the depths."

Twice the deep shafts were pumped clear and the *Epitaph* could say, "We feel the good old days of Tombstone are about to come soon." But the price of silver was dropping; the cost of operation was increasing, and the day came when the operators gave up, discharged their crews and shut off the pumps.

That stopped the *Epitaph* only long enough for the editor to write two paragraphs on the fateful news, to which he added the promise that this was not the end. There would be a reorganization, the *Epitaph* said, which would mean "the ultimate rejuvenation of the district."

Thirty-one years of Tombstone history had passed by this time without a break in the *Epitaph's* editorial policy and another nineteen years were to come and go before it was to come close to admitting "the dear old camp" was finished. The words must have been written with a heavy heart for they followed the day of the paper's greatest triumph; the observance of its fiftieth birthday with a celebration which it named "Helldorado."

Helldorado—the name was apparently taken from the title of Breakenridge's book on the district—was a three-day Western festival, with a program featuring re-enactments of the famous killings of the past, a hanging and the Earp-Clanton-McLowry battle at the OK Corral. Thousands of visitors came to Tombstone and spent so much money that the hungry populace demanded the show be made an annual affair.

For almost half a century the town had lived on hope. Now it had hope and Helldorado and the *Epitaph* had provided the nourishment in both cases.

But there was still another disaster around the corner. Scarcely were the street decorations removed when the people of Cochise County held an election and the guests who had danced in the streets, drunk at the bars, and gambled at the tables voted to move the county seat from Tombstone to Bisbee.

This blow knocked Tombstone to its knees. Families moved away by the dozens. Stores locked their doors. The bank failed, and many of the citizens lost everything they owned.

The whole state of Arizona mourned for the town, and the newspapers of Tucson said, regretfully, that this was the end. Tombstone, they added, would now join the dead mining camps of the West.

Dazed though it was, the *Epitaph* struggled to its feet, started its press and threw back the answer that Tombstone would live on. "Henceforth," said the *Epitaph,* "let it be known that we are 'The Town Too Tough To Die.' "

The courage behind the boast caught popular fancy so completely that it advertised Tombstone across the nation as nothing else had done since the days of the Earps, and made it one of the tourist meccas of the West.

Fifteen more years drifted quietly by, and then the *Epitaph* dusted off Clum's old trumpet and, in 1945, sounded the familiar old call, "Tombstone stands at the threshold of a new era."

This time its faith seemed justified, for there was every prospect that the town might become a great health center. The Rev. Fr. Aull, a retired priest, founded a clinic there for the treatment of asthma and arthritis, and so glowing were the stories of apparently authenticated cures of responsible and intelligent people that the streets of the town were crowded with parked automobiles from every state. Four hundred patients a day breathed chlorine gas from tubes leading to little black boxes.

Once again the name of Tombstone spread across the nation and once more the town boomed. The population doubled. Homes and courts went up. Old adobe walls were pulled down to furnish blocks for new buildings. Real estate prices jumped and so did the prices of everything else.

This hope, like all the others, failed to materialize. The Rev. Fr. Aull decided his chlorine gas machines should be available the country over and offered them for sale everywhere. In city after city there began to appear advertisements which said, "Why Go To Tombstone? Take the Tombstone Treatment at Home."

That checked the boom and when stories that the treatment brought no permanent cure began to spread, the period of prosperity faded out.

This was the hour when many finally gave up hope and said, sorrowfully, that Tombstone had dreamed its last dream of greatness. But not the *Epitaph!*

Down in the paper's old, dark building, which was once the town's biggest dance hall, Clayton A. Smith conceived the idea of a drive to restore the original fronts of the buildings on Allen Street and make Tombstone the historical attraction in the West that Williamsburg is in the East.

It is an ambitious project which calls for capital and unlimited faith. But if the capital can be interested there can be no doubt of the faith, for the *Epitaph* was born with "the faith that sees the ring of hope around nature's last eclipse."

Who knows, but that the *Epitaph* will live to justify John P. Clum's boast that Tombstone would vie with Rome upon its seven hills? How can one measure the possibilities of such faith as the *Epitaph* has shown and shows today?

It still believes the time will come when the mines will be recaptured and the apparently inexhaustible supply of water will be sought by parched Arizona for irrigation and even for the mains of Tucson, seventy-five miles away. It has no doubt that some day hard rock miners will go down again to the one-thousand-foot level to reopen the promising old drifts and sink their drills into the ore which modern mining authorities say is still there.

Perhaps it is this fighting faith, or maybe it is only the glamor of the paper's old days, but something draws the modern generation of newspaper men to the *Epitaph's* doors. A skeptical and scornful clan they may be, but they come hundreds of miles to stand like pilgrims in the office.

There are no mahogany desks, rugs, or concealed lights. There is only an old flat desk, a battered roll top, a square of faded linoleum on the floor, and a naked bulb hanging by a fly-specked cord from a rusty, tin ceiling.

Yet this is the place where working newspaper men, now forgotten, wrote in longhand the colorful day-to-day record of a fascinating era.

Wednesday is publication day and when the hour comes to start the press the editor throws on the power and the pressman tugs at the flywheel. Under the two impulses the ancient Campbell erupts suddenly in a series of roars, each one opening with a thunderous crash that can be heard on Allen Street. The moment is as important and as vibrant as the press start on the greatest of metropolitan dailies, and the *Epitaph* shares it with the community.

Citizens within earshot of the familiar uproar wander in through the front office and read the headlines over the editor's shoulder and no one objects, because the staff feels the paper belongs to the people of Tombstone, just as it feels the people and the town belong to the *Epitaph.*

The files, for which many a library would pay well, are stacked in the front office where any visitor may see them. These are the past. But the roar of the old Campbell in the back room is the voice of the present and the hope of the future—the living *Epitaph* of Tombstone.

2 Local Brevities

Just as one can create a picture in his mind of any small town today by reading the local brevities in its weekly newspaper, so can he re-create early Tombstone by scanning the brevities in the *Epitaph*.

In this chapter and in others it has been necessary, in a few instances, to supplement *Epitaph* stories with notes from the *Prospector*. There was a period when the two papers were consolidated, with the *Prospector* as the daily and the *Epitaph* publishing the weekly and Sunday editions. They were under one management and their policies were identical.

It is not necessary to read of "Death's Doings" or stories of famous holdups and murders to learn that life was rough in Tombstone. The locals reflect faithfully the spirit of the day. One finds stories of hardships and strange deaths, of rough men and loose women, but one also finds reports of church bazaars and of concerts and other entertainments.

These local items were used without regard for length or subject matter. The report of a church social might be sandwiched between the announcement of the opening of a new saloon and a note about a cockfight.

One may contend that this is not the whole picture, but he must also admit that there is no whole picture without the local brevities.

In this chapter one learns much about the life that went on at the foot of the hills of silver; what the people talked about, what disturbed them, what made them laugh.

• The chairs, tables, etc., belonging to the Public Library Association have been moved from the building in which they have been stored on Fremont street, to the one near the express office where it will be reopened in a short time. There is no reason why this should not be a successful public enterprise if carried on properly. To make it so however the first idea should be to make the rules governing it not so obnoxious to those who will patronize it that they will be driven away by hanging the walls with such chromos as, "Keep off the grass," "No Smoking Allowed," "Don't spit on the floor," etc. A man who has to walk a tightrope to get to a newspaper or book will naturally pull back from the undertaking.– (Aug. 3, 1889.)

The Epitaph Office as it looks today

• The attention of the city marshal is called to a disagreeable nuisance in the shape of a roaming band of goats owned by someone on Eighth street near Safford. They destroy everything green within their reach, and they should be rounded up by the owners or the authorities.

• Miss Josephine Randall has started a physical culture class among Tombstone young ladies and already 12 residents have joined and are taking up the work under the efficient tutorage of Miss Randall.

• That a roulette game can't be beaten was disproved yesterday morning at Naco. The scene of the play was at Deel's saloon when, about three o'clock, two masked highwaymen entered from the rear, and in stentorian tones which left not the slightest doubt as to their meaning, ordered everybody present to throw their hands up and get into line. There was a great scramble to obey orders. One attendant sought safety behind the bar and while in his retreat snapped an unloaded revolver at the robber who stood guard; he was found later on compressed into the sink, from which it was with much difficulty that he was extricated. One of the bartenders produced a cut-off shotgun and slipped behind those in line from which place of vantage he was wont to massacre the marauder, but his legs trembled, his nerve deserted him, and he handed the gun to one of the linemen, Deputy Sheriff Ellis, who shot the robber dead while he was in the act of putting the games money into a bag. It developed at the inquest that the dead robber was well connected, his people being reputed as quite wealthy. Constable Hudspeth immediately organized a posse and started in pursuit of the escaped robber.

• A miner who was arrested for striking his brother-in-law over the head with a six-shooter, because the latter persisted in blowing himself in against faro, was yesterday fined $2 and costs by Justice Easton.

• Full moon last night—also some other things in the same happy fix.

• Lovers of the festive beans and the succulent pork are notified that at Tom Walker's Wine Rooms tonight those tempting viands will be spread. Tom places but one restriction on patrons, that no matter how much they may like the beans, they must not go out and blow about them.

• It won't do any harm to go to church today. Try the experiment anyhow.

• A carload of beer received this week by the Cochise H & T Co., one received by Hoe Hoefler, and one of keg beer by Martin Costello last week, will indicate that we will not suffer for something to eat or drink for a short time to come.—(April 24, 1889.)

• About noontime yesterday the remains of the late Kiv Phillips were taken from the undertaker's room on Allen street and started on the journey to San Francisco. The body was not well embalmed and the stench was beginning to get so great it was feared the express company would not ship it.—(July 10, 1882.)

• A Tombstone citizen fainted twice in a chair at Baron's barber shop yesterday. He had just returned from Crittenden and after riding through the hot sun took a glass of cold beer which is thought to have caused the attack.

• A woman known as Shoo-fly was arrested and locked up by officer Weiser. She was booked for being drunk and disorderly.

• Pete Rude, for threatening to kill Annie Watson (Diamond Annie), was yesterday bound over in the sum of $500, by Justice Reilley, to keep the peace. Failing to give the bond he was committed to the county jail. The justice notified him that he really thought the better plan would be to send him before a lunacy commission for an examination. Pete it appears, has become enamoured of the fair but frail Annie, and has, it is stated, squandered considerable money on her. His means being exhausted, and he not being cut out for a lover, wrecked his chances, and was the cause it is stated of his assault on Annie.

• It was reported at the time of Pete Rude's committment to the county jail in default of a bond of $500, to keep the peace, that his incarceration was intended as a safeguard against his probable attempt to wreak bloody vengeance on a well known cyprian named Diamond Annie, who had been as he claimed bleeding him. Annie took her departure today for fresh fields and the presumption is that Pete, who by this time must have come to his senses, will be discharged from custody.

• A new attraction will be at the Crystal Palace concert hall tomorrow night. . . . The band is well versed in thorough [*sic*] base, as well as popular music of the day, although not capable of leading the great orchestras of the world. If they were as fine as some of our local talent thinks it is, they would have no need to reside in Arizona and play occasional pieces.

• Will Bayless is suffering from a wound in the thigh made by a novel weapon in the hands of a young lady of Tombstone. Will was playing polo, mono, loco or some such high flying game and making a high jump to capture a ball, he in some manner became intangled in a bonnet pin which pierced his leg causing a very severe and painful wound.

• James Fair, Jr., is dead. It was the same old story of heart failure, which is another name for alcoholism.

• The Elite Theater Company gave a torchlight parade last night on Allen street.

• Several complaints have reached us lately from merchants on Allen street, stating that it was impossible for ladies to visit their stores to do their trading from the amount of empty beer barrels on the sidewalks. The city tax collector should see that the obstructions are removed.— (July 13, 1887.)

• Johnny Nobile, the popular mixologist of this city, now dispenses the liquid fluid at the Crystal Palace. John is a dandy at his business.

• Henry Campbell recently received several casks of fine table wines, including white and claret, from the Los Angeles Vintage Company which he was busily engaged today in bottling.

• The ice cream vendor made a mistake a few days since which nearly ruined his trade and came near ending the lives of several people. He bought a bottle of vanilla and one of horse linament, better known as XX. He took them both home but failed to label them in his native language. Next morning he made up his usual quantity of ice cream. Not being able to discern the difference between the two bottles he emptied the contents of one into the cream, and shortly afterwards started out on his mission of selling the same. The first parties investing in the cooling article lived on Seventh street. They still live but the man who flavored their ice cream with horse medicine is liable to climb the golden stair if he ever appears in that section of the city again this season.

• A squaw gave birth to a child boy in the brush this side of the San Pedro yesterday. She was unattended, but she managed to get along nicely, also she attracted a number of interested spectators. The child is said to be exceptionally light and doing remarkably, and was named Pedro by its several bystanding godfather witnesses.

• Sam Small says there are four degrees of drunkenness—the sociable degree, the money degree, the lion degree and the hog degree. Sam shows a suspicious knowledge of drunkenness.

• At the raffle at Blewett's store Monday night, No. 45 won the parlor set. John Blewett was the lucky man.

• Lovers of vocal music will miss a rare treat if they fail to drop into the Elite theater tonight and hear the exquisite rendering of La Paloma by one of the Ulms sisters.

• The putting of a steam wagon by the Copper Queen Mining Company on the road from Bisbee to Fairbank has already been noted in these columns. Several trials were made without success and it looked at one time as though the venture would not prove a success. Nothing daunted however, the management sent to England and had sent out from the manufactory of the wagon an expert in the manipulation of the machine. The move has proved eminently satisfactory, the new man making the thing work to a charm. The last trip was made from Bisbee to Fairbank and return in three days, the steam wagon hauling 27,000 pounds. The distance is about sixty miles, and the runs made entirely by day.—(March 11, 1887.)

• Miss Minnie Rafferty was quite severely wounded yesterday by the falling of a hatchet from the top of a step ladder onto her head.

• Joe Curby was arrested yesterday and will interview the court today. He claimed that his store had been robbed and used violent means to search a lady who had made a purchase at his store. The stolen goods were not found in her possession and she had him arrested.

• W. C. Monk has gone to California, not the judge but his brother.

• Fresh buttermilk at the Can Can.

• Services at the Catholic church at the usual hours today.

• Tombstone, from its inception, has been noted for its fair and courteous treatment of strangers and the villainous actions of a few disreputable hoodlums last night at the entertainment, do not, in any sense, tend to discredit our people. Whilst the Rev. G. H. Adams was giving his stereopticon entertainment, a few blackguards, among whom was Sol Israel, sought by indecent insinuations and discreditable remarks to bring discredit upon Mr. Adams, who is known far and wide in Arizona as a generous, public-spirited gentleman. There were several others who imitated Israel, but none so bold and brazen as he. A man who has lived and thrived upon the generous patronage of a decent community, ought at least to respect its churches and citizens. The darkness in the hall gave these vandals an opportunity to display their blackguardism to great advantage. The Epitaph is of the opinion that if James Coyle [Chief of Police] had been present he would have landed some of those rowdies in the cooler, there to meditate at leisure upon the propriety of their actions.

• Among the outgoing passengers yesterday were two Chinamen bound for their native country, they having accumulated sufficient wealth to leave the land of the Melican man. Fewer natives can say the same yet they will persist in giving their patronage to the Mongolian in preference to those who would retain the money in our own country instead of carrying or sending it to the heathen nation.

• One of the jurors selected Monday in the Hambleton case was taken violently ill with visions of snakes and was in such a condition yesterday morning as to render his excuse only a matter of request.

• A sporting man known as Portuguese Joe fell in a fit in front of the Crystal Palace saloon last night.

• Mr. McLean, Jr., of Huachuca siding came into the city yesterday. He says that apricots in Ramsey's Canyon are unusually large, some of them measuring eleven inches in circumference. Arizona is certain to be a great fruit country in a few years.

• The body of Hugh J. Brawley was recently exhumed from its burial place in Prescott and shipped east to his relatives. The Courier says people who viewed them said his features were quite natural.

• A hair-pulling match occurred on Fifth street yesterday between two parties of the weaker sex. For a few moments the scene would have made a picture for the brush of Dore, but the combatants were finally separated. During the melee various and numerous articles of feminine wearing apparel were flying wildly through the air and the total annihilation of everything present seemed imminent. The only intelligible expression heard was "How dare you interfere with my husband!" and the balance of the fracas would have given John L. Sullivan some exceedingly valuable points in the way of prize slugging. The combat was declared a draw as it was interrupted before either of the contestants had been knocked out.

• An accidental shot caused by the careless handling of a pistol caused quite a little commotion in the Occidental bar last night.

• The wise man who laid in a supply of wood last summer now pats himself on the back for his foresight. The man who didn't lay in a supply also pats himself but a little lower down.

• A young devil who ought to be in a reform school and who is a curse to the community, amused himself this afternoon by throwing rocks at a Papago Indian baby, cutting its face in a shameful manner. The infant had been left by its mother in a shady place near the city hall while she disposed of her ollas.

• An editor has invented an infernal machine, which he places in an envelope and sends to those who "refuse" the paper after taking it five years without paying for it. The machine explodes and kills the whole family, and the fragments that fall in the yard kill the dog. Glory certainly awaits that editor, and when he gets into the sanctum that awaits him above he will have an upholstered chair and be allowed to sit with his feet on the table.

• Pat Holland says that since leaving here he has had a siege in the Territorial prison and also a term in the insane asylum but that he came out of both institutions in fine health, and that he now feels content to spend the rest of his days in Tombstone.

• Great improvements are noticeable on Fremont street. A pane of glass which was broken out of the front window of this office is being replaced and a door which has been swinging on one hinge near the postoffice has been propped up.

• The City Recorder yesterday fined the Chinaman arrested on a charge of cruelty to animals sixteen dollars which he paid and went on his way rejoicing.

• A lady wants to say a few words to the grocery merchants and really it is a delicate subject to handle. She says: "You know it is about time for the grocerymen to set their vegetables outside on the walk and—and you know there are a good many tall dogs in town—and, and they drink so much water and—and it operates as though they drank from Siloma springs. Now, Mr. Editor, you must know what I want to say, and if you will help me out you will do the public a favor." At this point she bowed herself out and we came to the conclusion that she wanted the vegetables put on taller boxes, or, in other words, put above "high water mark." For the good of the woman and mankind the grocers will please attend to it. Those wire screens they use over baskets and barrels are not water tight.— (May 26, 1887.)

• The attractions at the concert hall are worth going to see. Piano, banjo, violin, bones, one lady singer and three song and dance men make a combination that attracts a large crowd every night. The proprietor is determined to amuse the patrons of his house and is succeeding.

• If you want to get fresh telegraphic (no grapevine) news read the Epitaph. Boston baked beans at the Fashion tonight.

• James Olsen came in from Ross' mill, on Sunday last minus two fingers on his right hand. He had charged a hole with frozen powder which did not go off. The next morning he attempted to clean the hole out with the pointed end of his spoon, when the blast went off shattering his hand as above stated.

• As near as can be learned there has been a serious disagreement between Brother Donnelly, leader of the Holiness Band here and about four-fifths of the band. The matter has gone to such lengths that the majority refuse to attend his services and it looks now as if he would be compelled for lack of moral support to abandon his crusade against Satan in this city.

• A little episode not down on the bills occurred at the close of the programme last Saturday night at the Bird Cage. A couple of female attaches had a hair pulling contest for a few seconds, which but for the promptness of Joe Bignon, might have ended in a general row.

• The seduction law recently passed, is quite a gem in its way. It provides that if the victim is under the age of eighteen, her seducer can escape the penitentiary by marrying her. If however the wronged woman has passed the eighteen year milestone on life's journey, her betrayer has not the choice between marriage and the bastile, but upon conviction goes to the penitentiary will he nil he.—(March 19, 1887.)

• Beautiful day yesterday.

• Stevenson & Walker of the Willows saloon on Allen street, placed in position today a patent beer cooler. This new arrangement keeps the beer as cold as ice and always fresh. Drop in and try a glass.

• Another crank has been toying with a Gila monster, with the result that he is likely to die.

• A Mexican lad having six fingers on each hand and six toes on each foot was an object of much curiosity on Allen street yesterday.

• Miss Bertha Parce appeared at the Episcopal church last evening and delighted a large congregation with the solo, "Jesus, I My Cross Have Taken," to the music of "The Last Rose of Summer." If Miss Parce could be engaged for the season by the Episcopal church the seats would not be empty ever afterwards.

• The Bisbee stage, preceded by a pair of horses much in earnest, rushed wildly around the block three times yesterday morning. On the fourth round the stage became tired and rolled over, stopping the team. The horses were not damaged, but the stage was laid up for repairs. Another one was procured and the usual trip proceeded with.

• A rattlesnake measuring five and one half feet in length and having ten rattles and a button was killed yesterday in the vicinity of Tenth street by Archer Grew and George E. Millar. The latter took the rattles.

• Dr. John Sullivan, the well known dentist, is the inventor of what is called "the Dental Electric Vibrator," an instrument which, to judge from the character of its work, promises to become not only extremely popular but remunerative to its inventor and patentee. In appearance it looks like an ordinary electric battery, with the positive and negative poles. When a tooth or root is to be extracted the poles are placed in the hands of the patient. Another electric cord is attached to the forceps, establishing a complete current of electricity, which causes the tooth, when touched by the forceps, to spring from the jaw without any perceptible effort on the part of the dentist, and without causing the patient any greater pain than would be caused by the prick of a pin. The machine, which has only been patented two months, is a credit to the inventive ingenuity of Dr. Sullivan, and as they are coming rapidly into use in the East and on the coast, cannot but prove a source of revenue to him.—(June 13, 1888.)

• A great deal of just indignation is expressed by those persons who have planted trees in front of their dwellings, at the running at large of stock on the streets. A man should not be blamed if he takes the law into his own hands, when his property is being destroyed.

• John Slaughter came up from his ranch on the line today. He sold 400 steers delivered at Deming for 2 cents, which is considered a little above the ruling price.

• A Sixth street Cyprian was fined $20 and costs in the City Recorder's court yesterday, for soliciting prostitution. The complaining witness was a next door neighbor, in the same line of business.

• It is supposed that all good people will go to church to-day as usual and that all good children will go to Sunday School. And yet picnics, hunting parties and baseball will get their share of patronage. We guess we'll take in the ball game.

• If you want ice cold St. Louis draught beer out of a genuine German pump call on Julius Ceasar at the Crystal Palace.

• Constable Fred Dodge arrested Joe Doe (alias the Bodie Kid) this afternoon and lodged him in the county jail. Our reporter did not learn on what charge he was arrested, but from hearsay it is thought to be in connection with some woman at the Quijoyoas.

• There appears to be an epidemic of sickness visiting Tombstone at the present time. Several deaths have recently occurred and a few cases of illness are reported. If some of the fossilized, pessimistic anti-statehood cranks were to die off it would probably do the country some good.

• City Attorney Swain brought a cluster of apricots to this office last evening which were as thick as what we have heard of the inmates of a Mormon harem in Utah.

• Miss Bertha Marie Parce will, at the earnest solicitation of the ladies and pastor, render a solo at the Methodist church tomorrow morning providing she is feeling well, and will also render one of her choicest selections at the Episcopal church in the evening by request.

• A tenderfoot from New Jersey named Markley while playing cowboy at Crittenden a few days since, undertook to show his skill with a pistol. The result was that he shot the horse he was riding through the neck, killing it, and in falling it broke Markley's leg.

• Godfrey Tribolet says that in all his travels he never saw a more efficient fire department than that of Tombstone, and he has witnessed fires in the principal cities of this and other countries.

• A fallen angel was arrested last Wednesday on a charge of using profane and indecent language and had a hearing before Justice Hawke in the afternoon. The said angel vehemently denied the charge in terms so strong that His Honor turned pale and nearly fainted. Restoratives were applied and the court was able to gasp "twenty dollars!" The necessary coin was put up and His Honor is thinking seriously of taking a week off and fumigating the courtroom.

• Steve Wolsley won the gold watch and chain raffled off at Jack Martin's saloon last night by Wm. Dabb by a throw of 47 and Tom Allison the house and lot by a throw of 15, that being the lowest.

• Miss Lillian McAllister, aged about 12 years, killed a rattlesnake on Sunday last with a riding whip, which measured over five feet in length, and had thirteen rattles and a button.

• The time is near at hand when pestilence and disease are liable to arise from filth and garbage collected in back yards and out-of-the-way places during the past winter and we urge the necessity of having such places cleaned and purified at once. Don't wait until disease has taken a fatal hold upon a loved one but act at once. Keep your own premises clean and have your neighbor do the same and you will not have the burden of a broken heart to lay at the feet of divine providence. Providence has already too much to bear from the wilful negligence of mankind.

• In spite of all the hilarity of St. Patrick's day, there was no one very badly drunk yesterday.

• Chinatown was enlivened yesterday afternoon by the racket of Chinese musical instruments, the beginning of the funeral ceremonies of Too Yen, who was bitten by a hog. The funeral celebrations were finished today and were gorgeous as such affairs usually are.

• A novel sight was witnessed at a faro game in this city last night, in the person of one of the players who, refusing a proffered seat, fell upon his knees and in that position played through several deals. He positively refused to take a seat and as if in answer to his petition he won.

• The show windows of the Can Can restaurant this afternoon presented a beautiful sight. In one window was presented to the public gaze fish of all kinds, and in the other the choicest of meats. If our citizens desire a first class meal let them drop into the Can Can this evening.—(July 27, 1887.)

• There is talk of putting on a horse and buckboard to carry the mail between Tombstone and Prescott. The distance can be made in five days which will beat the railroad by five weeks.

• Dan Simon pulled a gun on Joe Russell at Bisbee yesterday, but the weapon was knocked out of his hand before he could fire. No particulars as to the cause.

• The fakirs who accompany a circus came up in full force to ply their games on the Tombstone suckers. Their program was interrupted by the local authorities. Four-Paws circus itself was the biggest fake of them all, but it was permitted to run.

• The Chinese residents of Tombstone made life miserable for our inhabitants yesterday. They were commemorating the birth of some ancient woman. Mankind always makes a fool of itself when a woman is the question and the Chinese are no exception to the rule.

• Ed Ferris' little white dog got canned this morning and Ed is looking for the party who did it with a six-shooter.

• The ladies of the M. E. church will give an oyster supper at Mining Exchange Hall next Wednesday evening. All are cordially invited.

• Miss Ella Gardiner, a serio comic vocalist, made her bow to a Tombstone audience at the Bird Cage last night and made a very good impression. She has a pleasant face and shapely form and a voice considerably above the average. She received several encores and the gratified audience like the preacher's daughter kept crying for more.— (July 12, 1887.)

• A candy pull at 7:30 this evening for and by the children of the Methodist church will be given at the rooms adjoining the store of F. Wolcott on Fremont street. The children voted as to whether they would have a candy pull or a Christmas tree and the former carried by a large majority.

The Bird Cage Theater, built in 1881

• "Napa Nick" is running the San Jose house in the absence of the proprietor. He requires the strictest references from persons desiring accommodations. Ladies and gentlemen of sporting proclivities will not be received upon any terms. Terms, cash in advance.— (July 15, 1887.)

• Another wedding is on the tapis. The cool nights are having the usual effect.

• A 10-year-old son of Henry Waters and another boy about 15 years of age concluded last Sunday that Tombstone was too small for them, and packed a burro with a sack of flour, a side of bacon and a few other articles and quietly stole away in search of adventure. Monday morning the families of both boys were much alarmed, and employed Antonio Rodriguez to trail the youngsters. They were found at South Pass, about 12 miles from town. They had lost their burro and were in a quandary.

• A monte game is now in full blast at the Crystal Palace.

• If anyone doubts that the soil in and about Tombstone will grow vegetables he or she is invited to inspect a squash now growing in the garden of J. B. Miano on Seventh street, which measures 6 feet 3 inches in circumference.

• An amusing story is related of the examination of a witness before the grand jury last week. Allen Potter, the beardless youth, was having his case examined and the landlady from whom he had stolen the money was giving her testimony. After telling the tale she made a plea for the boy by saying: "Gentlemen, don't be hard on the poor little fellow. He robbed me but I forgive him. He is young and inexperienced, and besides that gentlemen, he could not help it gentleman, for he comes from Texas."

Several of the grand jury men who hailed from the same state are said to have fainted, with the exception of Uncle Billy Plaster, who jumped over the table in his endeavor to find a nail to bite on.

• A Washington telegram says that General Sheridan does not believe in the scheme suggested by Congressman Lair, of Nebraska, to enlist a regiment of cowboys to fight the Apaches. He says that cowboys fight pretty well when they are drunk, but does not think they would be of much service on a long, tedious campaign in which discipline has to be preserved.

• Some years ago Tombstone went through the throes of an anti-Chinese excitement. The head and front of this agitation was C. N. Thomas. But times have changed and now this anti-Chinese agitator has come to the conclusion that the Chinese are a very fine people—at least good enough to go into business with. Last week, Hop Lee, a well known Chinaman of this city, received a letter from Mr. Thomas, who is wrestling with a prospect hole near Mammoth, wanting Hop Lee to go into partnership with him in a restaurant at Mammoth. But Hop Lee declined. For a high toned agitator and Mayor of the Tombstone city water works it is considerable of a comedown to be refused a favor by a Chinaman.

• The large bull snake killed in the house of a Mexican woman, last Sunday, has been stuffed by Joe Clark, and is on exhibition at the saloon of Fred Clark on Allen street above Fifth.

• The examination of G. W. Buford on the charge of unlawfully branding a heifer was continued in Justice Easton's court yesterday to give an expert time to go to the ranch and examine the brand on the cow.

• A jew was traveling in the holy land. He wanted to cross the sea of Galilee, which is very narrow, and was shocked at the enormous price asked by the ferryman. "Mein Got," he cried, "If you beeple wanted to charge him a price like dot, it's no wonder Jesus walked."

As do all newspapers, the *Epitaph* made errors. It handled these departures from the paths of truth promptly but casually. Three examples from *Epitaph* pages are enough to show how briefly the *Epitaph's* editors made corrections.

• The report came from Bisbee last evening that Joe Martinelli of that city got into difficulty with another man Sunday night, and shooting by both parties was the result. Martinelli is in jail. No further particulars.

We learn that it was not J. Martinelli who did the shooting at Bisbee last Sunday, but a man named Dawson. Mr. Martinelli had nothing whatever to do with the shooting.

• Another divorce suit was filed in the district court yesterday. Hattie B. Harris wants the court to free her from her husband because he won't support her.

Through an error yesterday's Epitaph stated that Mr. Harris had been sued for divorce by his wife on grounds of non-support. It is Mr. Harris who has entered suit for abandonment. His wife is at present in California.

• Ambrose S. Lyall died in this city yesterday morning of abscess of the liver.

The statement that Ambrose Lyall died of abscess of the liver was an error. It was cancer of the liver.

3 Society, Churches, and Culture

When one reads the record as it is written, day by day, in the pages of the *Epitaph,* he understands why Tombstone was known as the toughest mining camp in the history of the West. But the same record also shows the town had a happier and a finer life than that of Allen Street.

Four churches had been organized by 1880. The Methodists and Catholics built, the Presbyterians let bids, and the Congregationalists started services. That same year the *Epitaph* promoted the building of a new school house because the school children were "cooped up in a little bird cage about large enough to accommodate a man and his wife."

Standing today and sheltering a congregation is St. Paul's Episcopal church, oldest Protestant church in Arizona in which services are still being held. It was built under the leadership of Rev. Endicott Peabody, who was later to become famous as head master at Groton.

All the churches were active and all contributed to the social as well as the spiritual needs of the community. The *Epitaph* was conscious of the importance of churches and saw to it that the socials, bazaars, dances, and concerts which they sponsored were well advertised.

Fraternal and military orders were extremely popular. The *Epitaph* names the G. A. R., Knights of Pythias, King Solomon Lodge of Free and Accepted Masons, Cochise Lodge of the Independent Order of Odd Fellows, Daughters of Rebecca, and some organizations unknown today.

The volunteer fire companies must be included in the social register. Membership in these was a mark of distinction. Dues were charged and fines were levied for failure to attend meetings.

St. Paul's Episcopal Church

The firemen's masquerade balls and holiday dances were what the *Epitaph* called "social triumphs."

Tombstone celebrated every holiday and the fire department, the uniformed fraternities and the G. A. R. always staged a parade. The streets were deep in dust but the wooden awnings were brightly decorated with flags and bunting.

Unlike many camps, Tombstone knew luxury. The parlors of the hotels were lavishly furnished and so was the men's club, which was "carpeted with rich Brussels carpet, large pattern and yellow the predominating color."

Weddings were considered important and the *Epitaph* usually reported them in detail. The brides could join the Women's Club, the Terpsichorean Club, and the Shakespearean Circle.

As Mrs. J. H. Macia, cultured pioneer, puts it. "Tombstone was not without religion, culture, or polite society. We built churches and schools and we took time, here on the desert, to plant, nurture, and grow the largest rose tree in the world."

All this one finds in the *Epitaph,* and from its hundreds of stories these have been selected.

Wedded for Life

Milton, the most gifted of English poets, wrote, "Hail love, mysterious law, true source of mysterious love, hail," and in so writing he truly expressed the source of all earthly happiness. For in the joining of hands and the blending of hearts, in the uniting of two futures into one, we find the solving of all that is sweet or bitter in life. These truths are brought forcibly before us in the wedding of George Bravin and Miss Mary E. Butler, two young people who will henceforth together face the future for weal or woe. They were united in the holy bonds of matrimony at the residence of the bride's parents, on Ninth street, by the Rev. G. L. Pearson. Mr. Richard Vincent acted as best man for the groom and Miss Emma Butler as bridesmaid. After the ceremony the guests sat down to a sumptuous repast, during which they were surprised by a brass band. The house was thronged with friends and acquaintances and the festivities of the occasion extended into the early hours of the morn.– (April 29, 1888.)

At 12 o'clock yesterday, Edward Warren Perkins and Miss Gertrude Dean Howe were married at the residence of the bride's parents in this city, Rev. Pritchard of Bisbee performing the ceremony. The wedding was strictly private, only a few friends of both parties being present. A reception was held from 12:30 to 2:30 o'clock after which the newly married couple departed for California, where they will remain about three weeks. Mr. Perkins is a valued employe of the Grand Central Company, well liked by all who know him. The bride is the daughter of Mr. and Mrs. H. G. Howe and is an accomplished and charming young lady. The reception room was elaborately decorated with flowers, the couple being married under a canopy of ivy and geraniums, surmounted by a large "wishbone" of choice roses. A large number of invited guests attended the reception, and the presents were useful and costly.– (Aug. 27, 1889.)

When the Terpsichorean Club gave a dance it was a social function of importance. One mask ball seems to have impressed the editor. Perhaps because he got a quart of whiskey for his staff he saw it as rivalling anything in the largest cities. This is the way he wrote the story.

THE MASK DANCE

A Joyous Event and Proves a Grand Success

The mask ball by the Terpsichorean club last night was indeed a carnival of pleasure and was a howling success. The hall was crowded with spectators and persons in disguise; standing room was at a premium, and the whole affair rivaled many more pretentious masquerade dances of the larger cities.

The diversity of costumes embraced everything that provoked merriment and laughter from the ludicrous, burlesque, comic and unique impersonations to admiration of the beautiful and artistically gowned characters. The imitations and antics of each of the representations and the striking contrasts of the intermingling maskers heightened the effect. Forty-four couples were in the grand march. So complete were the disguises that it took a more critical eye than ours to solve them.

The first prize for best dressed lady was awarded Miss Ella Blackburn who represented "Silver Queen" in a handsome and tastily trimmed costume. The gentlemen's prize for best dressed character was won by Ellery Butler as Spanish Cavalier in a handsome suit. Charles Langnaap of the Prospector force carried off the consolation prize—the bottle of whisky, much to the delight of the office force who have sampled the bottle and pronounced it OK. (More of the same brand is to be had at the Tombstone Pharmacy.) Charlie impersonated a hermit and sustained his part well. Ray Swain as the devil elicited many favorable comments.

At 1 o'clock refreshments were held at the Can Can. There was no pause in the dance which continued until six o'clock in the morning. The Terpsichorean club can well feel proud of the grand success achieved.—(Feb. 23, 1900.)

No New Year's Eve was allowed to pass without a dance, and the fire fighters of the town were usually the hosts. This story speaks of the large attendance.

The New Year

The New Year ball of the Rescue Hose Co. was a grand affair. It was a social triumph and one of the brilliant events which always attend a Fireman's dance in Tombstone. The hall was decorated in gala colors intermingled with garlands of foliage. On the front wall, over the musician's stand, were the figures,

"1900" and Welcome ever smiled to the large and joyous assemblage. Fully 250 people were present and seven sets found room for dancing. Many visitors from the surrounding country were present and comforts and enjoyment of none were overlooked. The music under the leadership of Charles Wiser, was excellent and dancing, with the exception of the intermission for supper, continued uninterrupted until 3 a. m., closing one of the most successful and by far one of the most enjoyable dances held in Tombstone for years.—(Jan. 1, 1900.)

Important as he was in the community, the editor sometimes missed invitations to dinner parties and he was not above speaking about it, as he does in this report of a formal affair.

An Enjoyable Affair

On Thanksgiving Day Mr. and Mrs. Bradley maintained their reputation for hospitality in a manner highly appreciated by those who were so fortunate as to enjoy it. They served an elegant dinner to nineteen invited guests whose enjoyment was only equalled by their appetites, and the good things set before them.

Dinner commenced at five and continued until eight o'clock, during which time mirth and the satisfaction of appetites were the order of the evening. The host and hostess spared no pains in their efforts to please and the table fairly groaned beneath the good things with which it was burdened. Mr. Tracy delivered an eloquent toast to the "host and hostess" which was responded to in an equally eloquent manner by Major Stebbins, after which the guests were treated to some happy and witty remarks by Miss Diamond. Messrs. Ritter and Taylor in their usual elegant and happy manner, contributed to the enjoyment of the company by well timed and appropriate speeches. Lack of space and an opportunity of personal observance forbid a more detailed account of the evening's enjoyment, but the Prospector deems it sufficient to add that all present enjoyed themselves highly, and departed feeling that Thanksgiving Day in 1887 with them, was one of social enjoyment long to be remembered, and the hospitalities of the host and hostess, will no doubt remain a bright spot in their memories, long after many such occasions have passed into history.—(Nov. 24, 1887.)

One of the many stories of holiday celebration found in the *Epitaph* will serve for all, since all were of the same pattern. The following is the report of the program on Memorial Day, 1888.

MEMORIAL DAY

A Day Held Sacred By All American Soldiers
How the G. A. R. and their Friends Honored the Occasion

Even the heavens favored the day sacred to the surviving soldiers of the Union army. The sun draped his face in fleecy clouds of ashen gray, while a gentle breeze cooled the air and held aloft in its arms the floating ensigns of liberty. At the hour appointed by Grand Marshal Coffman the various societies were in the positions allotted them and at a signal the bands began to play and the procession started on its march to the cemetery. The order of march as designated by the committee was strictly followed. After the cavalry band came Burnside Post No. 2, G. A. R., and the old heroes stepped as lightly to the music of the military band as they marched in days of yore to the deadly music of shot and shell. The uniform rank, K. of P. presented a fine soldierly appearance as did also the Select Knight's A. Q. U. W.; after these came the P. O. S. of A. and the president of the day and the orator. In the second division the Tombstone band preceded Engine Co. No. 1 followed by Rescue Hose Co. No. 1. Both fire companies carried an abundance of flowers, wreaths, etc., particularly the floral offerings of the first named company, prepared by Mrs. Curby, were handsome and artistically arranged. The United Order of Honor, Knights of Pythias, Ancient Order of United Workmen, Daughters of Rebecca and mayor and city council followed, which with the large number of citizens on horseback and in carriages and afoot made one of the largest and most imposing processions ever witnessed in Tombstone. The ceremonies at Schieffelin hall in the evening were interesting and entertaining. The large building was crammed to its utmost capacity.

One of the notable features of the evening was the splendid singing of the Tombstone Glee Club. After this Col. L. F. Eggers, of Prescott, was introduced and ably sustained his reputation as an orator in the delivery of the following fine oration.—(June 1, 1888.)

The complete address followed in one and one-half columns of agate type. One week later the paper reported a strange discovery, as follows:

A Coincidence

After reading the oration delivered by Mr. Miller at Flagstaff, on Decoration Day, we are more than ever impressed with the singularity of coincidence, insomuch as a large portion of it is word for word the same as that delivered at this place by Col. Eggers. We do not know whether Peter robbed Paul or Paul robbed Peter, or somebody sold out them both. It is possible, however, that that class of orations was disposed of in the outside districts of large territories in large quantities at jobbers' rates.—(June 7, 1888.)

A Grand Success

The high esteem in which the German population of Tombstone's population is held by our citizens generally, was amply evinced by the huge attendance at the inauguration ball of the Tombstone Turn-Verein last night given in their new hall on Fourth street. The very best of Tombstone's people were present, and it was generally conceded that the affair was the greatest social success ever witnessed in Tombstone. In honor of the occasion the Turners had decorated their hall in a very unusual manner, the walls being hung with paintings surrounded with flags, while festoons of red, white and blue made graceful curves to the sides and ends of the room and robbed the ceiling of its bareness. The unwonted sight of flowers also greeted the eye, the resources of Mr. Fuller's conservatory having been brought into requisition. . . .

During the dancing the scene from the galleries was a most enjoyable one. "Brave men and fair women" there were in plenty, and the handsome toilettes of the ladies, as they were whirled through the various dances did much to make up a picture which no pioneer of this ambitious little city would have dared predict a year ago. There were present a number of people from the different towns and camps in the vicinity of Tombstone, even Camp Huachuca adding her quota of guests. An eastern gentleman present expressed the utmost astonishment at the beautiful and elegant costumes of the ladies present and it was indeed hard to realize at times that the bright scene was really in Tombstone.—(March 11, 1881.)

The musicale given at the residence of J. A. Rockefellow yesterday afternoon was a delightful affair. The musical and critical element of the city was well represented in the audience which was not large but thoroughly appreciative. The occasion not only netted quite a sum for the Congregational Building Fund, but also indicates the fact that Tombstone is alive to musical talent. We are pleased to say that the standard of the recitals given by Miss Kerwin and her assisting artists are of a high artistic order and we hope that these occasions will occur frequently as they give a fine musical tone to our community.

Pleasant Party

By invitation a pleasant party met last evening in the dining room of the Cosmopolitan Hotel. Dancing was the order of the evening, and until the wee sma' hours the devotees of Strauss, led by the strains of Lee's quadrille band, drove care to the winds. Love looked love to eyes that spoke again, and all went merry as a wedding bell.—(Aug. 11, 1880.)

A Delightful Party

On Friday evening Miss Maggie Fisher gave a most delightful party at the residence of her father on Fourth street. The veranda was illuminated by Japanese lanterns and the appointments were all that good taste and experience could suggest. There was good music for those who cared to dance and cards and tables for the votaries of whist. At 12 o'clock a most sumptuous repast was spread, and it was in the wee hours before the guests thanked the charming young hostess for one of the most delightful evenings of their experience.—(April 29, 1888.)

St. Patrick's ball was a great success as the Epitaph predicted it would be. The speech at the presentation of the Irish and American flags, by the Hon. T. J. Drum, as also the reception speech on behalf of the Land League, were as elegant bits of oratory as have been heard in Tombstone for many a long day. The thanks of an oppressed and kindred people are due to Miss Nellie Cashman, whose every heart beat throbs in sympathy with suffering humanity the world over. Long and prosperous may her days be is the prayer of her friends here, which means the entire population of Tombstone.—(March 18, 1881.)

• All ladies attending the Leap Year Reception to be given by the ladies tomorrow night are asked to "bring a man and a cake." Refreshments are to be served and the combination is presumably for that purpose.

• A very pleasant entertainment was given last evening by the Misses Herring at their residence on Toughnut street. The principal feature was an interesting game of Lotto.

• The members of the Turnverein Society held a meeting last night in their new hall and exercised themselves upon the new apparatus. Joints were discovered to be a little stiff, but the stiffness will soon come out. The Society is now in a flourishing condition, and bids fair to become one of the largest and most influential in the camp. Our German fellow citizens do nothing by halves.– (Dec. 14, 1880.)

Editor John P. Clum allowed the town four months in which to do something about churches after he launched the *Epitaph,* and then he gave it a piece of his mind. It may or may not have been due to the power of the press, but two churches were built and two others under construction shortly after this editorial appeared.

THE CHURCH

We presume there is not another town of the same size and age of Tombstone in the United States that does not contain at least one church. Here, right in the heart of the richest mining country on earth stands the unfinished walls of an edifice for church purposes, that has been in course of operation for months. It can't be that Tombstone differs so much from the ordinary mining camp in California, where a hat passed to raise money to build a church would almost have the bottom knocked out by the contributions of all classes of citizens. We don't know who has the matter of raising funds for the purpose in charge but we do know that if a committee of business men would take the matter in charge, they could raise money enough in one day to build and handsomely furnish a church. It's a burning shame that the only place of worship in town is had through the courtesy of Mr. Ritchie, himself not a church member, nor particularly religiously inclined.– (Sept. 1, 1880.)

Once established, the churches were important contributors to the community life of Tombstone. Their concerts, bazaars, ice cream festivals, picnics, and dinners were popular events.

BENEFICENT BAZAAR

Church Charity Catches the Contributions of the Chosen as Cleverly as Those of the Wicked.

The bazaar inaugurated at Schieffelin hall last evening for the benefit of the Episcopal church was certainly one of the most successful, socially and financially, ever given in Tombstone, and for elegance of appointment and refined taste would compare favorable with similar scenes in California or the eastern states. The booths were cleverly arranged on either side of the hall with decorations emblematic of the nationality which they represented. The attendants of these pretty pay-your-money-before-you-look-in-places were attired in the national costumes, and the mingling of the many bright colors, of sparkling eyes and rosy cheeks, formed a most charming and delightful picture. . . . In every respect the affair was most ably conducted and reflects great credit upon the ladies and gentlemen in whose hands the arrangement of the details was entrusted.

The bazaar will continue this evening and possibly tomorrow, concluding with a dance.– (Dec. 9, 1882.)

The Catholic Festival

Last evening at Schieffelin Hall, one of the most enjoyable festivals ever given by a church society took place under the auspices of the Catholic denomination. The hall had been tastefully decorated and served as a pretty background for the many pretty faces and handsome toilettes which abounded on every hand. Tombstone society people turned out in full force and from the opening hour to the closing at three o'clock, enjoyed an uninterrupted flow of enjoyment. Considerable interest was manifested in the chances of Messrs. Ward Crane and Neagle to carry off the elegant gold mounted cane which was presented to the candidate receiving the largest number of votes, and this, no doubt, added considerable zest to the enjoyment of the evening. Dancing to the music of Vincent's band was inaugurated at nine o'clock and continued until three with little interruption.

The receipts from admission, voting and booths and refreshment stands are estimated at $1,000, and as the expense will be comparatively light, a handsome sum will be added to the church treasury.— (Oct. 7, 1882.)

Grand Concert

As already noticed, a grand concert will be given at Gird's building, corner Fourth and Fremont streets this evening for the benefit of the Presbyterian Church. The ladies and gentlemen engaged in its preparation and production embrace the best musical talent in the town. The programme has been selected with great care and cannot fail to give satisfaction. A novel feature of the entertainment will be the production of an original song entitled TOMBSTONE CAMP. Words by Ed. Schieffelin.— (Oct. 1, 1880.)

The Ice Cream Festival

The festival last evening at the Masonic Hall under the auspices of the Baptist society, was a most enjoyable and successful entertainment. Tombstone has seldom seen a more happy and congenial gathering. The ladies' committee are deserving of great credit for the faultless arrangements which assured the harmony and success of the evening. The welcome song, "Here Again We Meet You," by the teachers of the Sunday school was rendered with most agreeable melody and received with hearty applause by the audience. A duet by Mr. S. A. Taylor and Mr. Stewart was sung with much expression and met a full appreciation. The trio, by Mrs. Taylor and Messrs. Burke and Stewart, was rendered with most happy effect and was marked a feature of the evening. The recitation of Barbara Fritchie, by Mr. Fred Brooks was given with excellent modulation and so pleased his hearers that they would not be content until Mr. Brooks gave Mark Twain's description of the coyote, which, as a humorous production, was a success. The band was out in full force and discoursed several selections in excellent time and harmony, adding greatly to the enjoyment of the evening.— (July 16, 1881.)

Sunday School Picnic

Yesterday the Sunday School of the Methodist Church of Tombstone had a picnic for the children and their friends—the first picnic of any kind known in this region. They went in wagons and carriages, leaving town between eight and nine, and went to Granite Springs, northeast of town near the foot of Dragoon range. There were over one hundred in the company, principally children, and the occasion will long be remembered, not only as being the first of its kind, but as in every way pleasant. The ride itself was pleasant on account of the mild temperature of the day. All went in for a good time and no unpleasant thing occurred, nor personal injuries, though the front axle of one of the small wagons broke down on the return trip. The children were made happy for which the officers, teachers, committee and school are truly indebted to Brown & Taylor, O. K. Corral, Mr. Bullock, Smith & McMean, Danfort and J. O. Dunbar, for their liberal contributions of teams, wagons, harness, etc., to whom hearty thanks are hereby extended.— (May 8, 1881.)

The Church Dinner

The Thanksgiving dinner given by the ladies on Thursday evening, in the new Methodist church was a decided success in every particular—not only satisfying the social and financial expectations of its projectors, but also the keen appetites of the cheerful throng who gathered there to eat, chat and be merry, as well as thankful. As early as half past five the guests began to assemble and at six the first tables were spread with every delicacy that the combined genius of ancient and modern times could suggest. The inevitable turkey was there in all his glory with great urns of cranberry sauce to tempt the appetite and enhance the relish. Then there were mince pies, pumpkin pies, frosted cakes, jellies, jams and fruits and great kettles of steaming coffee, and pots of strong tea for the spinsters and—but why proceed? It is enough to know that the bounties of that board have vanished forever—and we are much mistaken if some who feasted there did not quietly steal away, forever a victim of chronic dyspepsia. We have not learned the exact amount of the net proceeds but it cannot be less than $150, which will go far toward seating the new church.— (Nov. 27, 1880.)

The School Christmas Tree
Two Hundred and Fifty Little Ones
Made Happy by Santa Claus

Yesterday will be a long remembered day by the school children of Tombstone. By half-past-one there was a perfect blockade around the entrance of Schieffelin Hall and when the doors were thrown open the children rushed in with an ardor begotten of long continued expectancy of what the fabled God of the Christmas tree would bring them. Later many ladies and gentlemen came in and by 2:30 the hall was comfortably filled with old and young. When the curtain was rung up a beautiful picture was revealed upon the stage. Upon the right and left were the trees, loaded with the gifts, and in the center, slowly descending from the Heavens, came old Santa Claus clad in his robes of fur and a shower of snow, the whole scene illuminated by a red light from the wings of the theater. There was a furious burst of applause from the audience at the revelation before them. Santa Claus made an amusing address to the children and distributed the hundreds of beautiful gifts, every child receiving something. The value of the presents exceeded $300. Mr. Sherman received an elegant gold pen with pearl handle, gold mounted, presented by his pupils. Each of the other teachers received gold pens but less costly than the principal's. The school directors received presents both comical and useful. Mr. Billcke, senior, was the recipient of a nice china doll, and went away disgusted at the little thing's nakedness; this was unkind for such things seldom if ever come into the world dressed, which fact, from his age, he ought to have taken into consideration. The affair was not only a success but a credit to the generosity of the citizens who contributed to the happiness of the little ones.–(Dec. 25, 1881.)

It is difficult to understand why, but the *Epitaph* slighted the Bird Cage Theatre. It did not mention the building or opening of this famous vaudeville house and bar and the available files provide only occasional brief comments on the artists. The paper gave considerable attention, however, to the Elite Theater and to Schieffelin Hall.

Miss Jeffrey-Lewis and Miss Nellie Boyd were two of the camp's favorite actresses as these theatrical notes show.

Forget-Me-Not

There is no actress on the American stage who has more talent in the delineation of the stronger passions than Miss Jeffrey-Lewis. Beauty of face and form, combined with rare dramatic power, enable this talented artist to arouse and retain the sympathy of her audiences wherever she performs. It would be superfluous to attempt any elaborate criticism of a play so well known as "Forget-Me-Not" or an actress so world renowned as Miss Lewis. Suffice

Schieffelin Hall, built in 1881

it to say that the play gives the actress full scope to display her histrionic powers and that she more than fully came up to the expectations of the audience.

There was a very large house which was quite an agreeable surprise to the company. So fearful were they that they had almost decided to give Tombstone the go-by. The result is only another proof of the fact that Tombstone never fails to patronize a first-class company.

Miss Lewis will appear tonight in "Diplomacy," which she has kindly consented to give for the benefit of the cemetery fund. There will no doubt be a big audience, as this is a most interesting play and given for a worthy object.– (Nov. 30, 1880.)

Fanchon, the Cricket

. . . Much has been and always will be said by some, derogatory to the stage and its effects, and while this theorism resolves itself into fact as regards a certain class of performances, we contend it does not hold good concerning the legitimate drama.

In this connection it gives us pleasure, not only to chronicle the admirable manner in which Fanchon was given last night as the initial performance rendered by the Nellie Boyd troupe, but also the warm reception given them by the Tombstone public. When the curtain rose last night it was not to half-filled benches, but a crowded house standing room being at a premium and many being turned away from the door. Those who failed to gain admission lost a treat, as, excepting the fact that stage room was too contracted for proper apportionment of scenic effects, the renowned play of Maggie Mitchell was almost faultlessly rendered. Tonight, "Case for Divorce," at which, after the cordial greeting of last night and the merit of the troupe, it is needless to say there will be a good house and a sterling performance.

East Lynne

The audience last night was not what it ought to have been to witness the pathetic drama of East Lynne, as presented by the Nellie Boyd Troupe. Those present made up in appreciation for lack of numbers. The play was well rendered throughout: the music good, and the audience well pleased. Tonight closes the season in a fitting manner with the most dramatic of all dramas, Wilkie Collins' "New Magdalene." The house ought to be filled to its utmost capacity tonight.—(Dec. 14, 1881.)

Lecturers and magicians were popular entertainers in Tombstone and the *Epitaph* usually spoke well of their performances and urged the public to attend. One Prof. McDonald—the *Epitaph* was often weak about using initials—seems to have lectured on interesting topics.

Special Lecture

This afternoon at three o'clock Prof. McDonald will lecture to ladies only on How to Acquire Health, Retain Youth, Augment Beauty and Enhance Happiness. This lecture is chaste and refined and imparts so much valuable knowledge that no woman can afford to miss it. In the evening he will lecture to gentlemen only on Manhood, the Secrets of Nature, the Mistakes of Life and their Remedies. Look out for a large audience of men tonight. Boys under 15 admitted free but to hear only the first part of the lecture. On Monday night he will lecture to both sexes and at the close will perform amusing experiments with boys, money, water and electricity.

He is doing a lively business daily at the ante-room in front of Schieffelin Hall, giving phrenological examinations in regard to making the most of life in every respect, with advice pertaining to health.

• Prof. E. G. Taylor's performance of defined illusions, magic and sleight-of-hand last night was witnessed by an audience composed mainly of the best people in Tombstone. The ladies graced the entertainment with their presence and seemed to enjoy the strictly first class affair. The Professor employs no cheap clap-trap accessories in the production of his illusions. Every article used by him is exposed to the critical examination of the audience, and astonishment succeeds astonishment as inanimate articles are made to take to themselves wings and fly from place to place at command. There is no attempt at concealment in anything he does and one is almost forced to believe in the truth of "the black art."

In spite of the purpose and the name of their club, the ladies of the Shakespearean Circle sometimes discussed subjects other than the plays of the immortal bard, as they did at their March meeting in the year 1900.

The ladies of the Tombstone Shakespearean Circle are proving delightful entertainers as the series of receptions tendered by members of this literary club have become notable social events. Last night another of these pleasant social entertainments was given by Mrs. C. B. Tarbell at her home, the circle members and guests numbering over 35 invited. Several novel features were presented which afforded pleasant diversions and productive of instructive and entertaining enjoyment. A departure in line with the literary feature which contributed in no slight degree to the success of the evening was a debate on the subject "Is woman intellectually equal to man." Much enlivenment was created by the speakers and the arguments developed a revelation of research which won for the ladies the affirmative contention of mental equality of the sexes. Instead of reproach and contumely for the men who defended their sex the ladies granted smiling and gracious indulgence and all resolved in friendly converse. The evening's interspersed with music, singing, recitations, engaging games, etc., indeed made it most enjoyable. Refreshments were served and sociability reigned until long past midnight when all took leave of the hospitable hostess and carried with them pleasant recollections of the evening.

The list of cultural groups seems to have been complete in November, 1881, when a debating and literary club was formed.

Tombstone Literary and Debating Club

This club has been organized for the purpose of mutual improvement in elocution, composition and debate. Considerable enthusiasm was manifested by the members present, and our new society promises to be a perfect success as well as a delightful source of recreation these coming winter evenings.

LUXURY

If citizens and visitors were half as impressed by the Grand Hotel as was the reporter from the *Epitaph* they must have entered it with awe. It was apparently no mean hostelry for a mining town. Not the least of the attractions was the fact that every room had an outside window.

There were about 3,500 people in Tombstone in the summer of 1880 and the town was growing in true boom fashion. New hotels and saloons went up rapidly. Most of the buildings were shells of raw lumber but here the similarity to structures in the ordinary mining camp stopped.

The town felt it had a great future and it wanted only the best, which meant that interior furnishings and decorations must be gaudy and expensive. Always ready to promote Tombstone, the *Epitaph* ran a series of stories that summer in which it described the most popular places of entertainment. These eyewitness accounts actually surpass anything the authors of features and fiction have written about the city of silver. Here are the paper's stories on the Grand Hotel, the Tombstone Club, and the Alhambra and Oriental saloons.

The Grand Hotel

Through the courtesy of Mr. H. V. Sturm an Epitaph reporter yesterday paid a visit to and made a brief inspection of the new hotel christened the Grand which will be formally opened for dinner this evening at five o'clock. The general size and character of the structure have been mentioned so often during the course of construction that further mention would be superfluous and we will confine ourselves to a description of the interior appointments of it. Passing into the building by the front entrance the first thing that strikes the eye is a wide and handsome staircase covered by an elegant carpet and supporting a heavy black walnut balister. Thence upstairs to the main hall, and turning to the right we are ushered into a perfect little bijou of costly furniture and elegant carpeting known as the bridal chamber. This room occupies half of the main front and is connected with the parlor by folding doors through which the reporter passed, and entering the parlor was more than astonished by the luxurious appointments. A heavy brussels carpet of the most elegant style and finish graces the floor; the walls are adorned with rare and costly oil paintings; the furniture is of walnut cushioned with the most expensive silk and rep, and nothing lacks, save the piano which will be placed in position shortly. On down through the main corridor peeping now and then into the bedrooms, sixteen in number, each of them fitted with walnut furniture and carpeted to match; spring mattresses that would tempt even a sybarite, toilet stands and fixtures of the most approved pattern, the walls papered, and to crown all, each room having windows. All are outside rooms thus obviating the many discomforts in close and ill-ventilated apartments. Returning we pass down the broad staircase and turning to the left are in the office and reading room. Here we met Mr. R. J. Pryke, the polite and affable clerk, so well known to Yosemite tourists in California. The office fixtures are as is common in first class hotels and fully in keeping with the general character of the house. The dining room adjoining next invites inspection. Here we find the same evidence of good taste in selection and arrangement that is so marked a feature of the whole interior. Three elegant chandeliers are pendant from the handsome centerpieces; walnut tables, extension and plain, covered with cut glass, china, silver castors and the latest style of cutlery are among the many attractions of this branch of the cuisine.

Thence into the kitchen where we find the same evidence before mentioned; an elegant Montagin range 12 feet in length, with patent heater, hot and cold faucets, in fact all the appliances necessary to feed five hundred persons at a few hours notice are present. The bar occupies the east half of the main front and is in keeping with the general furnishings. Want of space prevents more than this cursory glance at the Grand and its appliances for the comfort and convenience of guests. A Grand (no pun intended) invitation ball will take place this evening.—(Sept. 9, 1880.)

The Tombstone Club

The elegant rooms of the Tombstone Club, in the second story of the Ritchie building were thrown open to the members last evening. A casual glance at the rough unplastered walls and crude stairway on the exterior, would not lead one to believe that such taste and elegance reigned within. The main sitting room of the club is 19 x 45 feet, tastefully furnished with writing and card tables, easy chairs and reading tables. The floor is carpeted with rich Brussels carpet, large pattern and yellow the predominating color. The unity of color in the furnishing of the room immediately attracts attention. The chairs, cuspadores and curtains are of the same general color as the carpet, which has the effect of making the appearance more pleasing to the eye than hetrogeneous blending of hues. A magnificent sideboard, well ladened with choice liquors and cigars is not the least attractive portion of the furniture. A spacious apartment in the rear of the reading room will be subdivided in card, store and wash rooms in a few days. The club has about sixty members, and is in a very flourishing condition. More than seventy publications, comprising all of the leading American and foreign, newspapers, magazines and periodicals are received. To Mr. Richard Rule, who has had charge of furnishing the rooms and arranging them, the club is indebted for a display of elegant taste and good judgment.—(Sept. 29, 1880.)

The Alhambra

Mr. Tom Corrigan, the gentlemanly and courteous proprietor of this well known Tombstone saloon should have been more than pleased at the crowd that greeted his reopening on Saturday evening last. His friends, and they are legion, crowded the spacious apartments from early eve until far into the morning, and over beakers of foaming Heidsick welcomed his re-entre. To the old habitues of the Alhambra the change is a marked one. The first thing greeting the eye is the new bar, of black walnut, handsomely embossed in gold. Behind the bar stand two elegant side boards of walnut handsomely mounted with birds-eye maple. The glittering array of decanters and glasses ornamenting the same, presents a scene of artistic beauty that must be seen to be appreciated. On the walls of the bar and reading room are tastefully arranged many elegant paintings and engravings, copies of the great masters. The chandeliers are of bronze and gold, and when lit cast such a flood of dazzling light over the surroundings as to lead to the impression that Alladin's cave had been rediscovered and we were in the midst of it. The ceiling has been raised also and the walls covered with paper of elegant design. An orchestra of three pieces discusses the latest and most fashionable music. The gambling tables, three in number, are surrounded by crowds eager to tempt the fickle goddess. Behind the bar, pleasant and smiling stand Andy Robertson and L. A. Greary supplying with their well known skill the thirsty throng, while ever and anon Tom's good natured face can be seen as he greets with a friendly hand shake some old time friend. The stock of liquors and cigars cannot be excelled in Arizona. Everything in this line has been procured regardless of expense and with an eye single to the taste of his numerous patrons. The opening was in every sense a grand success and argues well for the Alhambra again resuming the place it occupied prior to Tom's visit east.— (Sept. 14, 1880.)

The Oriental

For several weeks past the spacious corner building of the Vizini & Cook block has been undergoing numerous finishing touches preparatory to its occupation by Messrs. M. E. Joyce & Co., the genial proprietors of the soon-to-be-famous Oriental. Last evening the portals were thrown open and the public permitted to gaze upon the most elegantly furnished saloon this side of the favored city of the Golden Gate. Twenty-eight burners, suspended in neat chandeliers afforded an illumination of ample brilliancy, and the bright rays reflected from the many colored crystals on the bar sprinkled like a December iceling in the sunshine. The saloon comprises two apartments. To the right of the main entrance is the bar, beautifully carved, finished in white and gilt and capped with a handsomely polished top. In the rear of this stand a brace of sideboards which are simply elegant and must be seen to be appreciated. They were made for the Baldwin Hotel of San Francisco, but being too small Mr. Joyce purchased them. The back apartment is covered with a brilliant body brussels carpet, and suitably furnished after the style of a grand club room, with conveniences for the wily dealers in polished ivory. The selection of the furniture and fixtures displays an exquisite taste, and nothing seems to have been forgotten—even to a handsome stock of stationery. Tombstone takes the lead and Messrs. Joyce & Co. our congratulations.— (July 22, 1880.)

FEASTS

Tombstone loved to eat and it ate well. *Epitaph* advertisements and news columns spoke constantly of the menus offered at the Can Can, the Russ House, the Elite Restaurant, or the Maison Doree. The camp had no railroad, but fish and oysters arrived in ice from the Gulf of California.

As an illustration of the dishes enjoyed, and the courses served, this 1887 Thanksgiving menu has been taken from the news columns. Who will question the news judgment of the editor?

MENU

Thanksgiving Dinner—Maison Doree Restaurant

SOUP

Chicken Gumbo

FISH

Tenderloin of Sole—Tartar Sauce

ENTREES

Buffalo Tongue — Papillote
Saddle of Lamb a la Milanese. — Pate Financiere

VEGETABLES

String Beans — Corn — French Peas

ROAST

Turkey, Cranberry Sauce
Sucking Pig, Apple Sauce
Beef — Lamb

SALAD

Celery — Lettuce

ENTREMETS

Queen Fritters, a l'Israelite
Cream Puffs, Vanilla

PASTRY

Custard Pie. — Mince Pie. — Apple Pie.
Cranberry Pie.

DESSERT

Fruit. — Walnuts. — Almonds. — &c. — &c.

POETRY

Throughout many of its years the *Epitaph* catered to its more cultured readers by printing poetry clipped from *Harper's Magazine* and sometimes with verses from the classics. Occasionally it used contributions from subscribers or picked up something from an exchange.

This poem undoubtedly attracted the attention of the editor because of the local touch in the last verse.

THEY HAD NO POET AND SO THEY DIED

In the dim waste land of the Orient stands
    The wreck of a race so old and vast
That the grayest legend cannot lay hands
    On a single fact of its tongueless past.
Nor even the red gold crown of a king
    Nor a warrior's shield nor aught beside,
Can history out of the ruins ring—
    They had no poet—and so they died.

Babel and Nineveh, what are they
    But feeble hints of a passing power
That over the populous East held sway,
    In a dream of pomp for a paltry hour.
A toppled tower and a shattered stone
    Where the satyrs dance and the dragons hide,
Is all that is known of the glory flown—
    They had no poet and so they died.

Down where the dolorous Congo slips
    Like a tawny snake through the torrid clime,
Man's soul has slept in a cold eclipse,
    On the world's dark rim since the dawn of time.
And if ever the ancient Nubians wrought
    A work of beauty, or strength, or pride,
It was unrecorded, and goes for naught—
    They had no poet and so they died.

In the lonely southwest, by the tropic seas,
    In the land of summer, and sun, and gold,
'Tis said that a nation as grand as Greece,
    Up grew in the glorious days of old;
But Time, the leveler, came at last,
    And scattered its splendors far and wide,
And the marvelous Aztec empire passed—
    They had no poet and so they died.

And even here in the sun-crowned West,
    In the land we love, in the vales we've trod,
Where the bleeding palms of the world find rest,
    On Freedom's lap at the feet of God—
Even here, I say, ere the earth waxed old,
    A race Titanic did once abide,
But ah! their story is left untold—
    They had no poet and so they died.

Exchange.

4 Death's Doings

All newspapers have what they call standing heads, such as "Weather," "Chicago Grain," and "Vital Statistics." The *Epitaph's* standing heads covered the kind of news it carried. It used, "On the Hill," for weekly reports from the mines, "Arrivals," for the daily list of stagecoach passengers, and "Death's Doings," for brief reports of homicides and other violent endings. Certainly it is the only newspaper in the world which ever used this heading, but it had a good reason for the caption.

The editors were busy men and death called frequently in Tombstone. Life was what counted. Twenty-mule ore-wagons rumbled in an endless train down Fremont Street. Rich strikes were reported weekly in the mines. New buildings were rising. Homes went up by the hundreds. Saloons and gambling houses spent thousands of dollars on royal furnishings and decorations and got it all back from the payroll of the hard-rock miners. The town was young, reckless, and excited by its wealth.

What time was there for writing a head on the news that an unknown man had been murdered, when the Contention Mine had just brought in a new lead? Why bother about the name of a Mexican who was shot for being caught with stolen horses, when the Oriental was having a grand re-opening?

Of course, if death's victim was a camp personality and the manner of his taking off was interesting, the story was worth considerable type and a head. But if it were just another death the *Epitaph* often wrote a brief story, dropped it under "Death's Doings" and forgot it.

Surely no other paper in the history of American journalism ever carried more reports of crime than the *Epitaph* published in its first ten years.

Even though the stories were written in the stilted style of that day, and violate all modern rules of newswriting, when collected they tell a fascinating story of how Tombstone earned its reputation as the toughest town in the West.

One of the accounts should be of particular interest to historians because it challenges a favorite legend built up around Marshal Wyatt Earp. It is the story of John O'Rourke, alias "Johnny-Behind-the-Deuce" and has been told many times—but not this way.

While Earp figured prominently as the hero of the popular legend, and a marker shows the spot where he presumably held off the mob, he is not mentioned in the *Epitaph* account, although the paper was his advocate, his protector, and his friend, and it seems improbable that it could have overlooked so heroic a moment in his career. Perhaps the answer is that a local legend grew until it was accepted as a fact and that neither romancers nor recorders found this account in the files of 1881.

SLAUGHTERED

Brutal Murder of an Upright Citizen at Charleston by a Desperado

Again, the bloody hand of a murderer has been raised against a peaceable citizen; again the law is scoffed at and Justice derided. Yesterday's sun rose bright and cheerful over our neighboring village of Charleston, mellowing the crisp night air with its rays. Once more her toilers began their daily avocations with renewed energy, little dreaming of the damnable deed that, in the glowing light of noonday, was to await one of their number.

Sometime since the cabin of Mr. W. P. Schneider, chief engineer of the Corbin Mill, was entered and robbed of several articles including some clothing. Circumstances pointed very strongly to two parties, one of whom is so well known by the cognomen of "Johnny-Behind-the-Deuce" that we were unable last night to obtain his real name, but direct proof not being sufficient, no arrest was made. Yesterday at noon Mr. Schneider left his duties and went to a restaurant where he was accustomed to take his meals, and on entering approached the stove and, noticing a friend standing by, entered into conversation. Having just left the heated engine room the air without felt cool which brought from Mr. S. a remark to that effect. "Johnny-Behind-the-Deuce" who was also in the room, then said, "I thought you never got cold." Not desiring to have anything to do with one of his character, Mr. Schneider turned and said, "I was not talking to you, sir." This raised the lurking devil in the diminutive heart of "J-B-the-D.," who blurted out, "G—d d—n you I'll shoot you when you come out," and left the room. After eating his dinner Mr. Schneider passed out the door, and was proceeding to the mill, when, true to his promise, the lurking fiend, who had secreted himself with hell in his heart and death in his mind, drew deadly aim and dropped his victim dead in his tracks.

Immediately after the shooting the following telegrams were sent to Mr. Richard Gird, the superintendent, who was in the mine here at the time:

Charleston, Jan. 14, 1:30 p. m.

To Richard Gird; Schneider has just been killed by a gambler; no provocation. Cow boys are preparing to take him out of custody. We need fifty well armed men.

Charleston, Jan. 14, 1:35 p. m.

To Richard Gird; Prisoner has just gone to Tombstone. Try and head him off and bring him back.

Charleston, Jan. 14, 1:50 p. m.

To Richard Gird; Burnett has telegraphed to the officers who have the murderer in charge to bring him back to appear at inquest. See that he is brought back.

Considerable delay occurred in getting these dispatches to Mr. Gird, who at the time was in the mine, and just where was not known; but as soon as he received it, prompt action was taken, and a number of the miners were ordered to report to the officers, to resist any attempted rescue of the prisoner. Owing to some delay in delivery at the office of the company, and subsequent loss of time in finding Mr. Gird, over an hour elapsed, we are informed, after transmission before the dispatches were opened, and during this time the murderer was flying over the road toward the city, reaching the corner of Fifth and Allen a few minutes after the dispatches had been read. It is asserted that the officers, fearing pursuit, sent the murderer, who was on horseback, on ahead. However, this may be, it is certain that he came in ahead, his horse reeking with sweat, and, dismounting in front of Vogan's saloon asked for protection, acknowledging that he had killed his man. In a few minutes Allen street was jammed with an excited crowd, rapidly augmented by scores from all directions. By this time Marshal Sippy, realizing the situation at once, in the light of the repeated murders that have been committed and the ultimate liberty of the offenders, had secured a well armed posse of over a score of men to prevent any attempt on the part of the crowd to lynch the prisoner; but feeling that no guard would be strong enough to resist a justly enraged public long, procured a light wagon in which the prisoner was placed, guarded by himself, Virgil Earp and Deputy Sheriff Behan, assisted by a strong posse well armed. Moving down the street, closely followed by the throng, a halt was made and rifles leveled on the advancing citizens, several of whom were armed with rifles and shotguns. At this juncture, a well known individual with more averdupois than brains, called to the officers to turn loose and fire in the crowd. But Marshall Sippy's sound judgement prevented any such outbreak as would have been the certain result, and cool as an iceberg he held the crowd in check. No one who was a witness of yesterday's proceedings can doubt that but for his presence, blood would have flown freely. The posse following would not have been considered; but, bowing to the majesty of the law, the crowd subsided and the wagon proceeded on its way to Benson with the prisoner, who by daylight this morning was lodged in the Tucson jail.

Scarcely had the outfit got out of sight until stories of all descriptions regarding the killing and attending circumstances grew rife. One was to the effect that Schneider had chased "Johnny-Behind-the-Deuce" out of the restaurant with a drawn knife. This grew and brought forth a revolver in the other hand. Then it was reported that Mr. Gird had turned his mine loose for the purpose of lynching the prisoner. Again it was said by some of the pals of "Johnny-Behind-the-Deuce," that he was an honorable citizen, etc. etc. With regard to the knife story the facts given by an eye-witness and borne out by the character of the deceased, prove them to be false. Concerning the charge that the miners were turned out to defeat the law, we have it from Mr. Gird himself that they were ordered to report to the officers, in keeping with the tenor of the dispatches received by him, to sustain the law. In view of the diabolical and unprovoked crime committed, it is not to be wondered at that some of them should have joined the crowd that followed, desiring vengeance. As to the honorable character of the martyred kid who sails under the banner of

"Johnny-Behind-the-Deuce," it is a well known fact that he was driven out of Tiger District by the best element of that camp, about a year ago, and tonight he will repose at the county expense in a jail on whose walls are inscribed horrid mockery of justice blazoned in the names of other murderers who have partaken of county refreshment to be turned loose again to fasten themselves on the Tombstone public, a living curse. Today the clods will fall over his victim, silent in his last long sleep, no more to be a staff to parents who having passed the summit of life's divide with whitened locks already stand beneath the descending scythe of Time. Mails will come and go, anxious hearts with eager beat will note perhaps the postman's knock. No news from day to day until at last the sad tidings will cross the threshold, and bending under the weight of woe two more souls will gladly welcome death.*—(Jan. 17, 1881.)

Famous among Tombstone legends is the story of the shirt which caused a killing. There are some variations, as might be expected after seventy years, but the facts as the *Epitaph* printed them are essentially the same as those told today. Here is the *Epitaph's* report.

A FATAL GARMENT.

About 7 o'clock last evening the pistol was again used with fatal effect on Allen street, resulting in the death of T. J. Waters from gunshot wounds from a weapon in the hands of E. L. Bradshaw. The causes which led to this unfortunate tragedy are brief. Waters was what is considered a sporting man, and has been in Tombstone several months. He was about forty years of age, powerful built, stood over six feet in height and weighed about 190 pounds. When sober he was a clever sort of man but quite the opposite when under the influence of liquor. Yesterday he won considerable money and had been drinking a great deal, hence was in a mood to be easily irritated. Bradshaw was an intimate friend of Waters but a very different character, being a man of medium size, over fifty years of age and very reserved and peaceable in his disposition. We understand that these two men had prospected together and when Waters first came to Tombstone he lived in Bradshaw's cabin. Yesterday morning Waters purchased a blue and black plaid shirt, little dreaming

* "Johnny-Behind-the-Deuce" escaped from the Tucson jail and was never recaptured.

that the fated garment would hurl his soul into eternity before the sun had set. It so happened that several good natured remarks were made about the new shirt during the day until Waters had taken sufficient liquor to make the joking obnoxious to him, and he began to show an ugly resentment and was very abusive, concluding with, "Now, if anyone don't like what I've said let him get up, G–d d–n him. I'm chief. I'm boss. I'll knock the first s— of a b— down that says anything about my shirt again." This happened in the back room at Corrigan's saloon and as Waters stepped into the front room Bradshaw happened in, and seeing the new shirt his friend was wearing made some pleasant remark about it, whereupon Waters, without a word, struck Bradshaw a powerful blow over the left eye which sent him senseless to the floor. Waters then walked over to Vogan & Flynn's, to see, as he said, "if any s— of a b— there don't like this shirt." He had just entered the street when Ed. Ferris made some remark about the new shirt, which Waters promptly resented in his pugilistic style. After some more rowing Waters went back to Corrigan's saloon. As soon as Bradshaw recovered from the knockdown he went into the back room, washed off the blood, went down to his cabin, put a bandage on his eye and his pistol in his pocket. He then came up to Allen street and took his seat in front of Vogan & Flynn's saloon. Seeing Waters in Corrigan's door, Bradshaw crossed towards the Eagle Brewery, and walking down the sidewalk until within a few feet of Waters, said: "Why did you do that?" Waters said something whereupon Bradshaw drew his pistol and fired four shots, all taking effect, one under the left arm probably pierced the heart, two entered about the center of the back between the shoulders and one in the top of the head ranged downward toward the neck, any one of which would probably have resulted fatally. Waters fell at the second shot and soon expired. Bradshaw was promptly arrested and an examination will be had in the morning before Justice Gray.—(July 25, 1880.)

There seems to have been nothing glamorous about Jerry Barton unless it was his great physical strength. He killed men with his bare hands. Some reports say the law finally put him away for a few years in the territorial prison, but the *Epitaph* does not mention it. This is the first story on Barton's deeds. It broke in October, 1881, when the camp was young.

Shooting Scrape at Charleston

About eight o'clock on Sunday morning last, Jerry Barton who keeps a saloon in Charleston, shot a Mexican named Jesus Gamboa, inflicting a very ugly though not necessarily fatal wound.

From the Mexican, who was brought to the hospital here today, an Epitaph reporter learned the following version of the occurrences: Jesus and several friends of his had been carousing and drinking around for several days, spending between them about $40 in Barton's saloon. On the morning referred to the party, having spent nearly all their money, broke up, each going his own way. Jesus went into Jerry's saloon and sat down, when the proprietor came up to him and said, "You can't have anything to drink here," at the same time striking him on the back of the head with a glass. Jesus made no resistance, but laid his head on his arms which rested on the table. A moment later the saloon keeper fired at him, the ball entering just behind the left shoulder, ranging clear across the back close to the skin and lodged near the point of the right shoulder blade. The ball has been extracted and the wound is now looking as well as could be expected.

Later.–A special dispatch from Charleston to the Epitaph states that Barton struck the Mexican on the head with a pistol, and that the weapon was discharged by the concussion. The saloon keeper was arrested and placed under $700 bonds to appear before the grand jury. Barton is also under bonds for the murder of one Merrill, committed some months since.–(Oct. 11, 1881.)

Five years later Barton killed E. J. Swift, 60, on Allen Street, with a blow of his powerful fist. Apparently this was not popular, because Swift was a member of the volunteer fire department. It may have been the mistake which put Barton back of the bars. Judging from the coverage, the *Epitaph* thought it was a good story as killings went.

NECK BROKEN

A Man Killed by a Blow From the Fist
A Tombstone Tragedy Ending in Death

Yesterday evening, E. J. Swift and Jerry Barton, both well known in this city, met in front of the Fashion saloon and had a disagreement in relation to the settlement of a liquor bill which Barton claimed was due from a party of firemen of whom Swift was one. Said debt was said to be contracted at Barton's saloon in Fairbank, at the time of Chief Engineer Tribolet's departure for Europe. From angry words the men finally came to blows, with the result that Swift was finally knocked down. He subsequently caused the arrest of Barton who was taken before the City Recorder and fined $8 which he paid. About one hour later, the two men met again in front of the St. Louis Beer Hall, and the quarrel was renewed. It has been impossible for the reporter to find any one who knows how the second quarrel started, although the Coroner's jury which is now in session may discover. Suffice it that Barton, it is said, caught Swift by the beard and struck him two or three blows in the head and neck, winding up by throwing him from him into the street. Several parties who saw the latter end of the difficulty, ran over and picking up Swift, carried him into Macneil, Moore & Co.'s store on the opposite side of the street. Attempts were made to resuscitate him, but without avail, and in less than two minutes from the time he was struck he was a corpse.

Chief of Police Oaks, who had also seen a brief portion of the difficulty, had in the meantime arrested Barton and conveyed him to the County Jail. The body of Swift was in the meantime taken to the dissecting room of the County Hospital, and an autopsy made by Dr. Dunn.

The result showed that the neck of the deceased had been broken in two places. Barton's victim had been a resident of Tombstone about eight years, having been in the employ most of the time of Tasker & Pridham and their successors Macneil & Moore. He was a trifle over sixty years of age, and has, in addition to a wife residing in the city, several grown children elsewhere to mourn his loss. The old gentleman, although somewhat eccentric, had but few enemies, and his death caused a very general feeling of sorrow in the community. The funeral will take place tomorrow at 2 p.m. under the auspices of the Fire Department of which he was one of the oldest and most honored members.

Jerry Barton, his slayer, is a saloon keeper at Fairbank. He has a record of two other killings on his hands in Arizona, having killed a man at Phenix by striking him in the neck some years since, and also the killing of his partner, Merrill, by shooting him at Charleston about six years ago. The Grand Jury now has his case under consideration, and as it will undoubtedly find an indictment, his trial will be a speedy one.

Since the above was written the Coroner's jury has concluded its labors. Beyond the fact, as previously stated, that Barton was seen to strike Swift several times, nothing was elicited to throw any light on the question as to how the second quarrel started, or who began it. The jury rendered a verdict that deceased came to his death from a blow or blows administered by Jerry Barton.—(March 17, 1887.)

• The funeral of E. J. Swift who was killed on Tuesday last by Jerry Barton, took place today from the house of Engine Co. No. 1, of which the deceased had been a member since its organization. The body which was enclosed in a handsome casket, the latter being embowered in flowers, laid in state some time prior to the funeral. Dozens of those who had known and loved the old man in life, came to pay the last sad tribute of respect to his memory. At the time appointed the procession formed: First came the officiating cleryman, Rev. G. L. Pearson; following was the band, Rescue Hose Co., Engine Co. No. 1, and the hearse in the order named. Six pall bearers, three from each company acted as an escort of honor. A long line of carriages closed the procession. Arriving at the cemetery the body was laid to rest according to the ritual of the Methodist church. Fare well old comrade. Green be the grass above the grave that shelters thee.—(March 19, 1887.)

• A watch which was raffled off at Allan Walker's saloon on Tuesday evening last was won by a party named Smith with a throw of 42. The watch was the property of the late E. J. Swift and was raffled off for the benefit of his wife.

• The widow of the late James Swift, living between Seventh and Eighth streets, is reported to be in a very precarious condition. It is said she is without the necessary food to keep her from starving. Somebody ought to look into the matter.

The story which follows is the only recorded instance of a man killing himself for love in Tombstone, and that may explain why the editor gave the story the full editorial treatment.

ALL FOR LOVE

An Infatuated Youth Attempts to Kill His Sweetheart He Blows His Brains Out and Dies at the Doorstep of Her House

At twenty minutes past two yesterday afternoon five pistol shots rang out clear and deadly, startling all who lived in the neighborhood of Second and Safford streets. Before the sound of the last shot had died away or the smoke from the pistol passed into the air, half a score of people had rushed to the scene of the shooting and there beheld a tragedy of unrequited love and death. The principals in this sad affair were George Daves and Miss Cleopatra Edmunds, a 17-year-old daughter of a former well-known citizen, Eugene (Stockton) Edmunds, who died here several years ago. From all that could be learned it appeared that Daves had for a long time been an ardent admirer of the young lady, and when he left here several months ago to better his position in life, it was, so he informed several of his intimate friends with the understanding that upon his return they were to be married. He went to a mine about forty miles from Casa Grande and worked there steadily for some months, until he believed he had accumulated sufficient to begin married life with. With this intention he returned to this city last Tuesday and immediately went to the residence of his intended, whose reception

Gave Him No Doubts

of her continued affection. Thursday evening they together visited a neighbor and in company with several others had a pleasant time until the hour of departure, when to his surprise and mortification she rejected him and accepted the escort of another. After returning home he told his father, "It's all over. I want nothing more to do with that girl." What cruel doubts and maddening thoughts racked his brain during the vigils of the night no one will ever know, and when his father left him early in the morning he yet tossed on his bed with sleepless eyes, saying he had not closed them all night. When his father returned at noon he said his son acted as if he had the blues, and he concluded he would not go to work but would stay with him the remainder of the day. A few minutes before the shooting the boy walked to the front door, then immediately stepped back and saying "goodbye father," picked up a revolver and quickly stepped out into the street. Before his father could reach the door to call or halt him he heard the shots and stepped into the street only in time to see his unfortunate son place the revolver to his head and send a bullet crashing through his brain. The following account given by

An Eye Witness

a prominent and reputable citizen is not without interest. He said: "I was walking up Third street with a friend, and as we passed Edmunds' house I saw a young man standing on the outside of the fence talking with Cleopatra Edmunds: she being on the inside near the gate. We had not gone more than 100 yards when we heard a woman scream, followed by a pistol shot. Turning I saw a young woman running across the street from the direction of Daves' home which is situated on the corner about 80 or 90 feet diagonally across the street from Edmunds followed by a young man who was firing at her as he ran. When she reached the front door of her house she fell, and he raising the pistol to his head fired, and fell just outside and in front of the gate." Another party who was also an eye witness corroborates the above statement, adding, however, that the young women walked across the street to the corner of Daves' house with the young man who was talking with her at the gate. That there she left him, and as she turned to return home, Daves came out of his house. Seeing him with a pistol in his hand she ran toward home, he following, firing four shots at her and taking his own life with the fifth. Of

The Four Shots Fired

at Miss Edmunds, one made a slight flesh wound on the top of the right shoulder, another entered the back just to the right of the lower point of the shoulder blade, passing through the right lung and body and coming out at the left margin of the right arm pit, making a dangerous and possibly fatal wound. Immediately after being shot she was attended by Dr. Goodfellow and at 12 o'clock last night was resting easy.

George Daves placed the pistol to his right temple when he fired the suicidal shot, the bullet entering the head at that point and coming out at the crown, causing almost instant death.

George Daves was 21 years old. He was born in Santa Clara Co., California and had lived here for the past five years. He has always been known as a quiet, peaceful and industrious boy. The deed he committed was the act of an irrational, frenzied brain, his life and probably that of an innocent woman paying the penalty of his madness.– (April 14, 1888.)

One frequently finds stories of Indian depredations in the *Epitaph.* Raiding parties of red men came up from Mexico or broke out of the San Carlos Reservation and went on the warpath. The *Epitaph* was Indian-minded in its first years because Clum had been an Indian agent, so it is not unusual to read such stories as this in its columns.

Devilish Doings
The Apaches Kill a Couple of Prospectors in Sonora

From H. W. Russell, acting superintendent of the San Pablo mine, in Sonora, it is learned that a man named Brown, better known as "Woodchopper" or "Big Brown" arrived in this camp near Nacosari, a few days ago and reported that while returning from a prospecting trip in the Sierra Madre, a party of four men, himself included, had been attacked by a band of Apaches about ninety miles southeast of Nacosari, on or about Christmas day. The names of the other parties Mr. Russell could not remember other than that one was Jake Offer, whom it will be remembered was severely wounded when Jim Kirk had his fight with the Apaches some months ago; the third a man named Jacobs and another man named Gus. The attack was made about two hours after sunrise while the party was in camp and as usual was an ambush. At the first fire Jacobs was killed outright and Offer mortally wounded. Neither of the others was hit and taking cover they managed to stand the Indians off until they could make their escape. Brown reported that Offer, finding himself wounded to the death, and determined not to fall into the hands of the Apache fiends, deliberately broke his rifle so as to render it unserviceable and then drawing his six shooter shot himself through the brain. The only plunder obtained by the Indians was a few burros a small amount of provisions and what they secured from the bodies of their victims. Brown and his companion after their escape came into Nacosari and reported the massacre, subsequently accompanying a party who went out and buried the remains. The band, Brown says, consisted of four Indians and one white man; on the latter point he is positive he cannot be mistaken. The Indians are no doubt those who escaped from Geronimo's band in Sulphur Spring valley after the surrender to Captain Lawton and returning to Sonora have been killing and pillaging since.—(Jan. 10, 1888.)

From here on the *Epitaph's* accounts of "Death's Doings" need no interruption or explanation.

Dastardly Murder at Pearce Camp
Ben F. Smith Found Weltering in His Own Gore

About 10 o'clock last Wednesday morning, Ben F. Smith, an Arizona pioneer, and the proprietor of a livery stable at Pearce, was found dead in his business office.

Mr. Smith laid upon his back; in his right hand he grasped a revolver and his hat was upon his head, leading the public to the conclusion that the unfortunate man had suicided. When the coroner's inquest was held, however, it was ascertained that a foul murder had been perpetrated; a bullet hole was found in the back of his head and one side of the skull had been crushed in by the blow of a hammer, which implement was found nearby and was an exact fit of the indentation in the skull. There was no evidence of a struggle in the room nor were there any powder marks about the body, which fact leads to the belief that the shot was fired from a distance, after which the murderer finished his victim with a blow of a hammer. What furnished the incentive for the villain to commit the crime is a mystery.

There is not yet any clue as to the identity of the perpetrators of the heinous crime. Elsewhere in this issue will be found an advertisement offering a reward of $1,000 for the arrest and conviction of the perpetrators of the crime.

COLD BLOODED MURDER

Our citizens were startled Monday morning by the announcement that Deputy Sheriff Phillips had been killed while attempting the arrest of a disorderly character. The facts elicited by the Epitaph reporter are as follows: About seven o'clock in the morning a Mexican whose name was subsequently learned to be Filomono Orante entered the saloon of Moses and Mehan, corner Fifth & Fremont streets and called for a drink. He was evidently partially intoxicated and soon drew a revolver which he flourished in a threatening manner. The barkeeper, James Hennessey, remonstrated with the Mexican, and endeavored to have him put up the weapon, but without avail, the latter being evidently in a dangerous humor. Hennessey then dispatched a messenger for an officer, fearing violence from the swarthy desperado. The messenger started in the direction of the Oriental corner where he chanced to meet Phillips who was en route to the sheriff's office, to attend to his official duties. Phillips immediately proceeded to the scene of the disturbance, and Hennessey explained the situation of affairs to him, telling him that the Mexican who had meanwhile stepped out, was armed and evidently desperate, and that he should be careful in approaching him. Phillips then went outside with the intention of arresting and disarming the Mexican. As the former approached the latter stepped backward and stumbled, at the same instant drawing his revolver and firing, the bullet, with deadly accuracy, striking the doomed officer in the right shoulder, and passing through the wind-pipe, lodging in the vitals. Simultaneously with the firing of the murderous shot, Phillips drew his own revolver, and after the deadly missile had accomplished its fateful mission and the death film had dimmed his eyes, fired a shot at his slayer. The shot from the dying man's weapon took effect in the thigh of the murderous wretch bringing him to the ground. With marvelous tenacity of life the mortally wounded officer then turned and retreated into the saloon, the blood gushing in spasmodic jets from his mouth, passing through and out the back door, a distance of some thirty steps, falling dead on the threshold. Officer Harry Solon appeared at this juncture and procuring an express wagon conveyed the Mexican to jail. Dr. Goodfellow dressed his wound later in the day and found that the bullet had broken the hip bone, passing through the rectum and inflicting a dangerous and probably fatal wound. When the facts of the murder became generally known, much excitement prevailed, and muttered imprecations and threats of lynching were freely indulged in. Senor Corella, the Mexican consul at this place, hearing of the threats of lynching notified Sheriff Behan who, as a precautionary measure, placed extra guards at the jail. A post mortem examination of the murdered man by Dr. Goodfellow, showed the nature of the wound to be as follows: The bullet entered the upper part of the right arm, passing through the pectoral muscles in front of the armpit, entered the chest cavity between first and second ribs; thence passing through the upper lobe of the right lung; thence through the upper left lobe of the lung, in the left side of which it lodged. Death occurred from hemorrhage into the windpipe and plural cavities. A coroner's jury was impaneled yesterday afternoon and after hearing some testimony adjourned until 10 o'clock today. – (July 8, 1882.)

A Justifiable Homicide

On Sunday evening about seven o'clock a tragedy was enacted in the Chinese restaurant on Allen street whereby one man is dead and another is at death's door with a bullet hole through his lungs. The dead man is Stephen Ruff, a well known cattleman and the wounded man Sam Chung, the proprietor of the Chinese restaurant. The particulars of the affair as learned and also adduced at the coroner's inquest is that Ruff was indebted to the Chinaman for four meals and was denied further meals until he paid his account. . . . Ruff, who had been drinking somewhat, became angried and left the restaurant. He arranged to leave town and returned shortly afterward to the restaurant with his Winchester and six-shooter. A few minutes after his appearance in the restaurant he was heard to ask the Chinaman gruffly for a meal and the latter expostulated because of the previous debt. The shooting began immediately. Five shots were fired and it was found that Ruff was dead, having three wounds on his body and one through the heart. His hand still clutched his pistol, having fired one shot and the pistol was half cocked when he received the fatal wound through the heart. The Chinaman named Sam Chung, was shot through the left lung the ball entering his chest and the exit near the spinal column. The wounded Chinaman is in a precarious condition and may die though up to the present writing he is alive.— (Oct. 22, 1900.)

Green Bush Kills Jake Baker

Last Wednesday a tragedy occurred near the San Bernardino ranch in this county, resulting in the death of Jake Baker at the hands of Green C. Bush. It appears that bad feelings had existed between the men for some months, and during that time Baker had on several occasions abused Bush and threatened his life. On the day of the killing he rode up to Bush's house and shot his dog and asked if "he wanted some of it." After again abusing Bush he rode off, but only went a short distance when he returned to the house. Seeing him do this Bush went to the house and got his gun, and when Baker rode up the fight began, resulting in the latter's death. Bush came in here last night and gave himself up to the sheriff. He has the reputation of being an extremely quiet well tempered man who during the eighteen months he had resided in that vicinity, where he has a ranch, has never had a difficulty of any kind. Baker also owns a small bunch of cattle in that section and leaves a wife and three children, who, however, are not in this county. He is said to have been quarrelsome when under the influence of liquor.— (July 21, 1883.)

The Tragedy in Miller's Canyon

We are able today to add a few additional facts to the tragedy in the Huachuca mountains, Saturday night, and at the same time correct the inaccuracy as to the statement made in our columns yesterday that the murdered man and his assailants were gambling.

The tragedy, as we have ascertained today by telephone occurred in Cam Benningfield's saloon in Miller's canyon, and grew out of the fact that Benningfield remonstrated with a Mexican who had fired off his revolver through the roof, when the Mexican, demon-like, turned his revolver on Benningfield, one ball breaking an arm and the other passing through his lung, inflicting a fatal wound. At this juncture, George Ashton, who had but a few moments before entered the saloon in company with Benningfield, attempted to interfere when a second Mexican drew a revolver and shot Ashton through the head, killing him instantly. The bartender then shot the slayer of Ashton, and beat a hasty retreat for Fort Huachuca, where he made the details of the crime known. The Mexicans then loaded their wounded partners into Ashton's wagon and drove toward the international line.

A posse is now in chase of the fugitives. The Rangers have returned to Naco with three Mexican prisoners, one of whom is wounded.

Filled Full of Lead

Early yesterday morning Fred H. McGowan arrived in this city from Morse Canyon in the Chiricahuas, and gave himself up to Sheriff Slaughter, saying that he had killed Patrick Dawson at that place last Monday morning. McGowan owns a ranch at Morse Canyon and he and Dawson were partners in the proceeds. McGowan says that last Saturday Dawson drove him away from the ranch and threatened to kill him. He remained away that night but returned between four and five o'clock Monday morning accompanied by a double-barreled shotgun. He got close to the house and waited until Dawson came out, when he emptied both barrels of the gun into him, when he went into the house and got a Winchester rifle and put a bullet through the body. A Coroner's inquest was held and the jury returned a verdict of justifiable homicide. McGowan then came to this city and is now in the county jail, awaiting examination which will take place before Justice Johnson next Wednesday at two o'clock p. m. The prisoner seems entirely unconcerned as to the outcome of the examination and is confident that he will be released, as he claims he did the killing in self defense.

A Woman at the Bottom

District Court Clerk Daily yesterday received the testimony, verdict, etc. of the Coroner's inquest on the killing of Jim Barrock, from which it appears that a woman known as Mrs. Miller was at least the indirect cause of the homicide. The woman, it appears from the testimony, was Barrock's mistress, and he, fancying that Moss, or "Deadshot," was trying to supplant him in her affection, called him to account for it at the same time opening fire with a Colt 45 at about ten feet distance, following it up with a second shot before Deadshot made return. Neither of Barrock's shots took effect, while the first shot from Deadshot's Winchester winged his man and the second finished him.— (Jan. 13, 1888.)

Killed by a Skunk Bite

According to a dispatch from El Paso, Tex., Silas Carson a prominent Arizona ranchman, died at the Sisters hospital there Monday, from the results of the bite of a skunk three months before.

When brought to the hospital by a physician the previous night, he was pale and haggard. He talked freely for a while and remarked he was sure to die, and that nothing could save him.

A few minutes later he was seized with a fit which was repeated about every two hours until his death this morning. With each attack he grew less rational, and at times wild, even vicious.

Carson owned a cattle ranch near Willcox. Three months ago he was camping out on a round-up in the mountains. One night he felt something under his blanket, and when he felt to learn what it was, a large skunk seized him by the finger. The wound soon healed up but four days ago it broke out and he began feeling strangely. He went to a physician who pronounced it hydrophobia, and ordered him to El Paso for treatment.— (Nov. 19, 1900.)

A Murder Committed

Another brutal murder has been added to the annals of Cochise county. Andy Griffin was found near the San Pedro yesterday in a ghastly form. He was bloody, covered with dirt, hacked over the body with a knife and shot twice in the head and neck. He was found by a freighter who telegraphed to the coroner at Naco.

The ground bore evidence of a hard fight. The dead man's bedding was doubled up in a pile; the buckboard in which Griffin was riding, had made tracks around and around, and the dead man's carbine was lying in the vehicle. The horse of the dead man is missing and it is supposed the murderer took it and fled.

A Sudden Death

Joe Balley of Bisbee is dead. Fate decreed that his span of life should end with today, and accordingly he is no more.

One of those deplorable accidents for which no one can be held responsible, while it was unavoidable, occurred about 10 o'clock this morning in the Copper Queen smelter.

Man that is born of woman is of but a few days; but he who earns his bread among the roaring blasts and the whirring belts and ponderous machinery is likely to have life's cord torn asunder instanter. While pursuing his daily vocation, unmindful that death lurked high, a pot containing one ton of molten slag became detached from the crane that was conveying it, and fell to the ground below, a distance of twelve or fifteen feet, lighting squarely upon a man. There were no cries of pain, no shrieks of anguish, no pleading for mercy or assistance. The spirit of Joe Balley had taken its flight.

Shooting at Ash Canyon

Sunday afternoon a man named Jack Smith was brought to the county hospital from Ash Canyon in the Huachucas, suffering from two serious wounds, one of which may prove fatal. On account of the suffering of the wounded man it was very difficult to glean any facts about the case, but from other sources we learned that the inhabitants of Ash Canyon were on a general jamboree on the Fourth and that a man named Jack Cade shot Smith. It seems both men were pretty drunk and a dispute arose between them in which Smith was decidedly the aggressor. He abused Cade nearly all afternoon and went so far as to strike him in the face without his "cussedness" being taken up. Finally he drew a knife and made a cut at Cade, when patience ceased to be a virtue, he drew his pistol and fired twice, one bullet entering the abdomen near the navel, and the other taking effect in the right arm.

Cade was immediately arrested by Deputy Sheriff Sperry and taken to Charleston. He had an examination yesterday before

Justice Burnett, and a number of eye-witnesses of the transaction were examined. The testimony was in accord with the facts stated and the prisoner was promptly discharged.—(July 15, 1882.)

Murder Mystery

Another murder mystery developed in Cochise county yesterday and at present there is no clue to the guilty one. The murderer with apparent deliberation set his plans to hide any suspicion against himself by placing his victim on the railroad track and expecting the inanimate form to be mangled beneath the cars.

Last evening the engineer on the N. M. & A. train discovered the form of a man on the track between Fairbank and Benson. There was also the evidence of a fire near the body. When the train came to a standstill and investigation made, a horrible sight met the gaze of the railroad man. The man on the track had been nearly burned to a crisp. All the clothing had been burned from the body. The left hand had been charred so that when the body was moved the hand fell off. The head was the only part of the body that had not been burned, and here was found evidence that the unfortunate man had been foully dealt with. A large gash made by some heavy instrument on the temple told plainly the death blow. Nothing further could be learned and the theory is after being murdered, the victim was placed on the track. A camp fire had been built nearby and it is presumed the clothes of the murdered man caught fire and resulted as above. The body was brought to Fairbank and Coroner Schuster sent for from here. The coroner empaneled a jury to investigate. The verdict is to the effect that the name of the deceased is Francisco Moreno and he "came to his death by being struck on the head with a sharp instrument in the hands of an unknown party." Moreno was a stranger about Fairbank but was known to have money. It is probable the murder was committed for robbery.—(July 12, 1900.)

• We regret to learn of the very sad death of Mrs. May J. Frisk, wife of George Frisk, which occurred at her home six miles from Willcox last Tuesday. It appears that a few days previous she had been bitten in the hand by a coyote which had been chased into her house by the dogs, but no attention was paid to the wound until the hand and arm began to swell and give her great pain. Doctor Porter was sent for and did what he could, but as she experienced but little relief the fear took possession of her that she would die of hydrophobia. This thought evidently unbalanced her mind, and taking her husband's pistol, she placed it to her right temple and fired a ball through her brain. She was buried in the front yard of her home, which she had done so much to adorn and beautify.—(May 27, 1888.)

• A Mexican was killed on the other side of San Simon valley last week. He was found with stolen stock in his possession which was considered sufficient cause for death.

• Carmelita, a woman living in an adobe house adjoining the Elite theater, attempted to shuffle off this mortal coil yesterday afternoon by swallowing two tablespoons of rough on rats. Dr. Willis was called as soon as her condition was discovered and by administering the proper remedies brought her back to her normal condition. The cause of the rash act on the part of the fair lady is said to have been occasioned by jealousy.

• The Elite theater was closed last night out of respect to the memory of Carmelita Jimenez, the woman who committed suicide. She had for a long time been an attache of this place of amusement.

• The following version of a shooting affray near Benson the other day is told by a Bensonite. The Mexican, who was shot by Robinson, was riding a spirited horse. The animal bucked and threw him off and Robinson gave chase after the horse and caught him, bringing him back to where the Mexican was. The latter received the horse without thanking his captor and after mounting began to abuse Robinson. Words followed during which the Mexican pulled and fired at Robinson, who returned the fire, killing the Mexican.—(April 22, 1889.)

• From E. C. Stewart who arrived from San Simon Valley last evening, we learn that a man named Judson White, commonly known as "Comanche" was killed by unknown parties last Monday in Skeleton Canyon, San Simon valley. He had been in the employ of the San Simon Cattle Company about a year and at the time of his death was in charge of their camp in Skeleton valley. He was discovered last Tuesday by Buck Robinson and Joe Taylor, who stopped at the camp on their way to another part of the valley. White had been shot six times and had evidently been dead twenty-four hours. His face was mutilated by wild animals. Everything at the camp had been taken, provisions, clothing, etc., even the spurs, six-shooter and other personal effects of the dead man, leaving only the clothes he had on. San Simon valley lies partly in this county and partly in Mexico.—(Nov. 2, 1889.)

• An unknown dead man was found this morning on the Naco road. Nothing on his person served to identify him and he will be buried at the county's expense.

• Two well known Bisbee ruffians, named Billy Armstrong and Clide Reed, got on a jamboree last Tuesday, and as is customary with such characters, proceeded to run the town. There are no officers of any kind at Bisbee, and the rowdies succeeded in keeping the peaceful population in a state of terror. They drank repeatedly at every saloon, insulted every person they encountered, brandished pistols and discharged them without contemplating or caring what mischief they might do. At this point the ruffians separated and Armstrong entered the saloon kept by Frank Stahley. The latter remonstrated with him for continuing such conduct, but his kind admonition was received with threats and curses and the ruffian's violence seemed to overflow. Stahley ordered him out of the saloon and Armstrong, almost without warning, drew his pistol and fired, the bullet passing through the right lung and coming out near the spine. He fell to the ground senseless and the murderer speedily escaped. At last accounts the murderer had succeeded in evading justice.

• Mrs. Cunningham, wife of a prominent ranchman on the San Pedro river at Dudleyville, lost her life on Sunday through fright on account of the Apache Indians who murdered the Gila county officers Sunday.

• H. H. Holt, better known in Tombstone where he formerly resided as "Shorty" Holt, was killed while mining in the Columbia mine, at Washington camp, last Saturday, by a part of the shaft caving in on him, which caught his left leg, inflicting a wound from which he bled to death. The wound was comparatively slight, but being unable to free himself he was held until he bled to death. He was formerly employed as a pressman on the Epitaph.

• Word was sent to the city last night that a Mexican had been killed at the construction camp on the Bisbee road. All the information that could be gathered was that two of the laborers began quarreling when one of them seized a crowbar and beat the brains out of the head of his antagonist. A dispatch was sent to justice Shearer to come at once and hold an inquest on the remains of the murdered man. As his term of office expired at 12 o'clock last night he could not have reached the locality in time to hold the inquest, and consequently did not go.— (Jan. 1, 1889.)

• A Mexican named Frederick Zamora died suddenly at Fairbank today under circumstances which lead several to believe that he had been foully dealt with. A coroner's jury was also summoned and investigated the case. They learned that Zamora drank some whisky proffered him by a countryman and a few hours later was taken with convulsions and died in great agony.— (June 9, 1901.)

• A dispatch was received at Fort Huachuca about 9 o'clock Wednesday evening, informing the commanding officer that a band of hostiles had raided in the neighborhood of Cedar Springs, attacked a freighting party and killed one of the drivers. The freighters resisted the attack, killed one of the savages and by a vigorous fire succeeded in driving off the red devils. The freighters scalped the dead Indian and possess the top-knot as a trophy of their victory.— (July 22, 1882.)

• Yesterday a report reached Tombstone that the body of a man was found near the road about two miles from the old Broncho mines. Justice Shuster summoned a coroner's jury and left for the scene to make investigation. The jury made a gruesome discovery in finding the bleached bones of a human being which was headless. It developed later that a Benson citizen who happened along the day before, found the body and took the head with him, presumably as an anatomical specimen.— (May 14, 1900.)

• Sheriff Slaughter received a letter today from Col. Kosterlitzky of the Mexican army in which he says, "I have captured the big stud horse branded VX and one branded OT, the other two horses and one man got away, but I am after them. I had to kill one man to get these horses. Nobody knows the man; do you know anything about him?"— (Aug. 7, 1889.)

• Today the startling news was received at the sheriff's office that George Scarborough, the well known brave and fearless detective was killed by outlaws in the Chirichuas in this county on Tuesday and after being brought to San Simon, died there yesterday. The brief news was sent by his son who stated the killing was done by five outlaws who were now heading for Mexico.

• Wealth has resulted to many of the citizens of Tombstone since first the bonanza mines of this district were discovered. Death has resulted to many more of the citizens of Tombstone since first this camp proclaimed its prominence. Death has come upon many, miner and gambler, just and unjust, by crash of blast, by crack of Colt, but never before has the sable plume waved over poor humanity in more ghastly circumstances, more lonely surroundings, or more tardy attention than attended the terrible taking off of Joseph Eisele in the Silver Plume mine on the evening of the 19th of January, 1886. On that evening Thomas Vincent a miner well known in Tombstone, left his employer, the unfortunate Eisele, at off shift and returned to this camp with the Emerald miners. Nothing more was heard of him when Vincent, becoming concerned, went to the mine, descended the shaft and was horrified at the ghastly spectacle of the almost decapitated body of his employer, lying upon its left side and arm with the whole top of the head blown off.

• Yesterday, because of a small rainfall, the San Pedro went on a rampage and during its hilarious frenzy claimed George Kenniston as its prey. Mr. Kenniston, accompanied by his wife, left Tombstone yesterday before noon on horseback for their home. When the river was reached, near Charleston, it was found that the stream was up, but Mr. Kenniston ventured in some distance and, upon request of his wife was about to return, when the animal went into a hole, unseating the rider who was soon lost to view amid the rushing torrent. Mrs. Kenniston was an unwilling witness to the tragedy, being but a few yards behind her husband, mounted on a horse in mid-stream and powerless to render assistance.

5 Guns and Women

When Tombstone holds its annual Helldorado celebration and re-enacts famous killings, one of the actors is always a man in fringed buckskins, who takes the role of Frank Leslie.

His lithe figure draws much attention as he strides through the crowds and this is no more than his due. For the original Frank (Buckskin) Leslie drew plenty of attention in old Tombstone.

Leslie killed two men and one woman in the nine years he spent in the mining camp. A friendly bartender when sober, he was known as a treacherous man when drinking and, drunk or sober, a dead shot. He killed his first man, Mike Killeen, on June 22, 1880, in a gun fight over Killeen's wife, and then married the woman.

The copy of the *Epitaph* of that date is missing but one finds the story in the testimony given at an examination two months later. This was the second examination in the Killeen killing, and Leslie was not the accused.

Buckskin Frank and George Perine, a companion, had been arrested after the gun fight and held until Killeen died. Taken before the court on murder charges, Leslie claimed he fired the fatal shot in self-defense and the court believed him. There was no evidence introduced which implicated Perine so both men were discharged.

But the public heard rumors that the prosecution had failed to present certain facts against Perine, and eventually a citizen swore out a warrant. So they re-arrested Perine and held another examination. This one lasted ten days and the *Epitaph* covered it fully, opening with a story which it captioned, "In the Toils."

George Perine was rearrested for the killing of Mike Killeen. The killing took place at the Cosmopolitan Hotel some weeks since. It is a matter still fresh in the minds of our readers. At the time of the killing W. F. Leslie and George Perine were arrested on the charge of murder, and after due examination discharged. Leslie claimed to have fired the fatal shots, and as he evidently acted in self defense his testimony exonerated both himself and Perine. At the time of Perine's discharge the community was divided on the question of his guilt or innocence, many claiming that if the prosecution had brought out the evidence at hand his commitment would certainly have followed. Perine, since his discharge, has been in and about Tombstone, evidently not fearing further prosecution. Yesterday morning, however, W. T. Lowry swore out a warrant against him on the charge of murder, claiming that he had secured additional evidence against him. The warrant was placed in the hands of Deputy Sheriff Wyatt Earp, who expected no difficulty in its service, from Perine's seeming indifference. By some means, however, word was conveyed to Perine of the threatened arrest and he skipped out. Calling to his aid a posse Earp started on the hunt of the fugitive. It was generally supposed that friends had made arrangements to supply him with a horse and his capture was deemed problematical. The matter was soon set at rest, however, by the return of Morgan Earp with the prisoner, whom he had captured a short distance from Richmond. No difficulty was experienced in making the arrest, Perine being unarmed—in fact he was advancing to meet Earp when arrested, either supposing him to be a friend with the expected horses, or else realizing the impossibility of escape. When captured he asked Earp to go to Contention with him and get his arms, Earp demurred on account of the distance and proffered to lend him one of his if he wanted it. Upon being brought in he was taken before Judge Reilly, who committed him to await his examination on Monday next at 10 p. m.— (Aug. 15, 1880.)

When the second investigation was three days old, the judge thought so little of the prosecution's case that he said in open court he probably would not hold Perine to the grand jury and, therefore, released him under $1,000 bond.

Then the prosecution suddenly introduced new evidence. It produced a death-bed statement from Killeen. This statement described the gun battle in detail, but it also introduced an angle which seems to have been missed by historians of Tombstone. Killeen said definitely that Leslie was not the author of his death, and expressed a regret that he would not live to get even with Perine, who, he said, had shot him without cause.

The defense fought to keep the statement from the record but the judge admitted it and the *Epitaph* reported it in full as follows.

Killeen's Statement

At the ball I wanted to see my wife. I heard that she had gone home with Leslie, and when I was told she had gone home I went down to the hotel with the expectation of finding both of them in Leslie's room, but they were not there; meanwhile, I started towards the porch, having heard voices, and I thought it might be them; I got to the door of the porch and satisfied myself she and Leslie were sitting side by side, his arm around her waist; that settled it; I thought I would go off now; started back again; Perine came along pistol in hand and knowing him to be a particular friend of Leslie I looked for trouble as in the early part of the evening he went into Tasker & Hoke's and bought a box of cartridges and filled all chambers of his pistol and deposited the remainder of the box with me; I started away from the porch when Perine came along and yelled out, "Look out Frank, there is Mike," with that Leslie rose from his chair in a half standing position, pulling his pistol; he fired the pistol at me and I fired one shot at him; I saw I was in for it and I made a jump and caught the pistol and beat him over the head with mine, which I had in my hand at the time; I happened to look and saw Perine standing in the door with his pistol levelled at me; he pulled the trigger, which he repeated twice, firing in all three shots; by this time I had used up Leslie pretty well; then turned and jumped and caught Perine's pistol, and did the same to him; by this time people commenced to congregate and I dropped this man, not thinking of my own wounds; all I knew was I was shot in the nose somewhere. I fired two shots myself intentionally, and every time I would strike the pistol went off accidentally; fired at Perine when he fired at me; one shot was at Perine and one at Leslie; fired at Leslie when he pulled his revolver first and stood in a half stooping position; this was right after he first fired at me.

M. D. Killeen.—(Aug. 24, 1880.)

The *Epitaph* story of the hearing shows that the prosecution substantiated this confession by calling one E. T. Packwood, a nurse who attended Killeen in his last days. This is his testimony:

> I was with Killeen from the time he made his statement until his death, in the capacity of nurse; I frequently had conversation with Killeen concerning the shooting after he had made his statement; on the day that Killeen made his statement he was perfectly rational but on the day following he became at times delerious. He told me that he had no hope of recovery; that he was sorry he could not recover as Perine had shot him without cause and he wished to get even with him; that he knew Leslie had not shot him; that Leslie had fired but one shot and if that shot had hit him he would have felt it.— (Aug. 24, 1880.)

Perine then took the stand in his own defense. By his own statements he was no hero on the night Killeen was killed. One gathers from the testimony that if Leslie didn't kill Killeen it was not because he was unprepared. He was out with Killeen's wife. He had heard that Killeen was making threats. He believed Killeen intended to make a fight that night. He had made it a point to pick up two guns. The *Epitaph* carried this testimony.

> **Perine Statement**
>
> On the night of the 22nd of June last, I was on my way to bed and in going through the Cosmopolitan Saloon I met Mr. Leslie; he asked me if I would loan him my big Colt six-shooter; told him certainly, and went to my room, got it and gave it to him; he, Leslie, then stepped behind the bar to get a small six-shooter which he had there; Gus Williams who was tending bar at the time said, "Frank you are going to leave me without weapons," or words to that effect. I then told Leslie to leave the pistol and I would get him my small six-shooter; Leslie had two or three days previously borrowed my big six-shooter to go with some message for the Government somewhere and it was only that afternoon that I had gotten it behind the bar and taken it to my room; I went to my room and got my small six-shooter . . . then asked him (Leslie) if he was going out again on any service and if he wanted me to go with him; Leslie said no but that he was going up to supper and wanted me to go with him . . . went on up to

the restaurant and had supper; after supper we started to Vizina & Cook's building, where there was a ball going on; . . . he (Leslie) said "Let's go in and take a glass of beer;" we went in and Leslie invited Killeen to take a drink; Killeen said, "No thank you I'm not drinking this evening;" when we went out the door and going across the street where the ball was in progress, I noticed Leslie shaking his head up and down and muttering to himself, "I thought so," I said, "Frank, what is the matter?" He said he would tell me in a few minutes . . . we then went over to the brewery; there were a great many of Frank's friends there and he invited them to take a glass of beer; in a few minutes we walked out; Leslie then said, "George, I fear someone is going to make a break tonight;" I asked him who; he said, "Mike Killeen has sworn he would kill his wife if she went to the ball and has also threatened to kill me." I remarked Frank, I'll stay with you. . . . I then gave him the six-shooter I had in my pocket and we walked to the porch in front of the hall and stood looking in at the dancing; . . . when the dance was over Mrs. Killeen came out and we walked to the Cosmopolitan Hotel; Mrs. Killeen asked Leslie to come up and sit down; . . . I went into the barroom leaving the side door open . . . I had hardly taken my seat when I saw Killeen pass the door and go up the stairs; I thought to myself, here is trouble; I'll try and avert it; I went out the door and passed up the stairs; when I reached the head of the stairs Killeen was standing right in the door, looking first one way and then another; I passed him making some pleasant remark I can't recall at present, going on toward the door of Leslie's room, thinking he was probably there, leaving his big revolver as it was cumbersome. I opened the door and said, "Frank, are you there?" Mr. Robertson who was there in bed said, no; Killeen then came up and looked over my shoulder into the room. . . . I looked toward the porch in the direction that Killeen had gone; saw him go to the parlor and look in; in the meantime I was listening for voices, as I knew Killeen meant business, having noticed his face and eyes when I passed him; I then saw him go to the door of the porch; saw him stand there for an instant, then saw the flash and heard the report of a pistol shot fired by him right in the door; I then heard a scream and at the same instant another shot fired by Killeen, he having stepped out a pace or two on the porch; I then started toward the porch. I had no weapons of any kind on me or in my hands except a pocket knife. Before I got to the front porch there was another shot. Upon the instant of my arrival there was a shot fired at me, then another one that caused me to stop and look for the relative position of the men who were struggling and shooting at the time. I took one step towards them when Leslie went down on his knees, and Killeen came towards the hallway. I grabbed him as he came to the door by the wrist. He had a revolver in each hand; I threw up one of his hands and the weapon went off, down the hallway . . . Killen was trying to point the pistol at me all this time and I was struggling to prevent it. Just at this time I heard voices saying arrest him. In holding to Killeen my hat had got jammed down over my eyes and I could see nothing. When I heard the words, "arrest him" I supposed they were right there, and had Killeen in custody; I threw Killeen's hands up and threw myself towards the floor, not wanting to get shot if his weapons should go off. I had hardly time to raise my hat from my eyes, when Killeen, who had got down near the back porch, fired a shot at me; almost immediately someone whom I believe was Leslie, fired a shot at Killeen and rushed down the hall in the direction of Killeen. I began then to get excited and angry, having prior to this time been perfectly cool, and muttered to myself, "I'll kill the s— of a b—, I'll put six shots in him." I then ran downstairs. I ran through the saloon; ran back upstairs again . . . I ran out to the porch; ran back again. Leslie passed me; he did not seem to be hurt. I then ran again downstairs into the barroom. During all this time I was muttering to myself. . . . I went up the street and after seeing Leslie's arrest came back to the hotel where I was arrested by Fred White.—(Aug. 24, 1880.)

Buckskin Frank Leslie then testified for Perine. He told of a desperate fight in which he was wounded twice and whipped over the head with a pistol, but finally got in a fatal shot while on his knees. This is Leslie's story.

N. F. Leslie Sworn

On the night of the 22nd of June last I was sitting on the front porch of the Cosmopolitan Hotel, in company with Mrs. Killeen, who sat opposite me a few feet away; this was between 12 and 1 o'clock, as near as I can recollect; I had just bid the lady goodnight and was about to rise from the chair, when I heard a voice behind me say, "Take that, you s— of a b—," and a shot was fired at the same time, the bullet from which struck me in the side of head; I stood up immediately and found myself facing Mike Killeen; I was about to speak to him when the lady put her hand on some part of my coat behind, and spoke to me; what she said I could not understand at the moment; Killeen then fired the second shot, the ball striking me in the top of the head; when I saw him raise his hand to fire at me, as I imagined, I dropped on my knees as quickly as I could and catching him around the legs I threw him over my shoulder, but one of the chairs on which Mrs. Killeen and I had been sitting kept him from falling; in getting up I put my hand on a big pistol which I had laid on the porch at my feet when first sitting down, but in trying to cock this pistol it slipped out of my hand. I then stood up and grappled with Killeen. He was trying to get the point of his pistol toward me. I had a firm hold of his right hand with my left hand, and some part of his left side with my right hand. He forced the pistol from me at last and struck me on the top of the cheek with the muzzle of it. I let go of his side and turned the pistol away from me as quickly as possible; the pistol went off just then and I saw Killeen's face distinctly by the flash. He swore and groaned directly when the pistol went off, saying "Oh, my God!" and snuffling as though struck in the face or nose. He staggered back and I sank to the floor of the veranda. While in the act of rising to my feet, I drew a pistol from my right hand hip pocket with my right hand and fired at the upper part of Killeen's body, as he came toward me, I being still on my hands and knees, with my left hand on the veranda floor; I got on my feet and we clenched and struggled a little while; during the struggle I fired again and we both fell; Killeen was the first on his feet, and made for the door and went down the hallway; I then felt along the veranda for this big pistol and found it at once. I then turned into the hallway after Killeen; he, Killeen, stopped some distance down the hallway, and spoke; upon seeing his hand raise as if to fire again I fell on my knees and fired at him. He turned and ran out of the hallway. I struggled along after him, half blind with blood. On getting to the head of the stairs I heard Officer Bennett's voice, asking me for the pistol. I sat down on the head of the stairway insensible—at least I don't recollect anything for a little while. I did not see the defendant Perine from the time I left him at the hall door until sometime after the shooting.— (Aug. 25, 1880.)

Mrs. Mike Killeen, Mrs. Frank (Buckskin) Leslie since August 6, also took the stand for the defense. She told a pretty story in which she spoke of such border epithets as "s– of a b–" as "a bad name." She also reported having been extremely ladylike in her reactions to her enraged husband's attack on her boy friend. Oddly enough she said she did not see Perine.

> **Mrs. May Leslie Sworn**
>
> On the night of June 22nd I was sitting on the front porch of the Cosmopolitan Hotel, between the hours of 12 and 1 o'clock as near as I can remember; I was in company with Mr. Leslie; Mr. Killeen stepped up and called Mr. Leslie a bad name and fired; Leslie rose to his feet facing Killeen; I rose up and put my hand on Leslie, begging him not to go any further; Killeen then fired the second shot; I then ran across the porch to the eastern hall and went to Albert Billcke's room; told him that Killeen had shot Leslie and he was now coming after me and for God's sake to save me; he went to the hall door of the front porch and I went after him; Went out on the porch and saw Killeen and Leslie scuffling. Albert Billcke then went back to his room and I followed him. He got his revolver and then went back to the porch a second time; I followed him. When we reached the porch they were gone. . . . At that time I was the wife of the deceased, M. D. Killeen . . . At the time of the shooting if the defendant, Perine, had been upon the porch while I was there I would have seen him. I did not see him. I am now the wife of Leslie.—(Aug. 25, 1880.)

The prosecution sought to discredit Leslie's testimony by calling Dr. Matthews, who had attended Killeen. Matthews didn't think the wound which killed Killeen was made by Leslie's gun. He said this.

> If Frank Leslie had fired at the upper part of the body of Killeen, he, Leslie, being on his hands and knees, with his left hand resting on the veranda, the deceased being three or four feet from him, I think he could not have made the wound in the left breast of the deceased. Can't say that it would have been impossible. The ball in the left breast struck and passed into the body in a horizontal line.—(Aug. 25, 1880.)

The final arguments lasted five hours, and the *Epitaph* considered the exchange a brilliant forensic debate, for which it praised counsel on both sides impartially.

Here is the scene as the *Epitaph* saw it.

> The argument in the case of George M. Perine, charged with the murder of M. D. Killeen, on the night of June 22nd last, took place before His Honor Judge Reilly this morning. The case has attracted a good deal of attention for the past ten days of its continuance, and as the Epitaph has daily furnished the testimony in full, most everyone was conversant with the salient points in the case and anxious to hear their summing up and presentation. For the prosecution Mr. Anderson wove together the testimony in a net whose meshes seemed so close as to prevent escape to the prisoner, and, per contra, Mr. Barke, for the defense, with equal ingenuity unraveled the web and the discharge of the defendant seemed inevitable. The argument, from a forensic point of view, was a brilliant one and was eagerly watched by the prisoner, his features now lighted up with the assurance of hope and anon clouded with the bitterness of despair. The argument lasted about five hours. At the close Judge Reilly signified his intention of taking the matter under advisement until six o'clock p. m. Speculation during the afternoon was rife as to what action would be taken by the Judge. The matter was set at rest, however, at the hour stated, by the court holding the prisoner to wait the action of the Grand Jury on the charge of manslaughter, with bail fixed at $5,000. Being unable to furnish the amount the prisoner will be taken to Tucson this afternoon by Deputy Sheriff Earp, and thus ends the longest criminal examination ever held in Arizona, and perhaps anywhere.—(Aug. 27, 1880.)

Perine ate free meals at the expense of the county for two months in the Tucson jail. Then the grand jury met. It returned a number of bills against various offenders but not against Mr. Perine. It did not agree with the findings of the Tombstone judge. So Perine was freed and Buckskin Frank's claim was good. He now had one notch in his gun.

A little over two years later Leslie shot and killed a second man. This time he did it in the street before witnesses. The re-enactment is one of the best scenes Tombstone stages during the Helldorado celebration. But, for the full story, one must go back to the old *Epitaph* files.

LESLIE'S LUCK

"Billy the Kid" Takes a Shot at "Buckskin Frank." The Latter Promptly Replied and the Former Quietly Turns His Toes Up to the Daisies

Tuesday morning about seven o'clock another tragedy was added to the already long list that have dotted with crimson the history of our city. The causes which led to the affray, as far as are known, are fully detailed in the testimony elicited at the coroner's inquest. The survivor of the sad affair, Frank Leslie, or "Buckskin Frank," is well known throughout the county. William Claiborne, alias the "Kid," who precipitated the affair which led to his sudden and untimely taking off, has in the past gained considerable notoriety by his connection with desperate characters and participation in deeds of violence. He was arrested something over a year ago for the murder of Hicks at Charleston, but upon being tried was acquitted. Whatever may have been his record in the past, there is no doubt that at the time he met his death he was engaged in an attempt at assassination, which was frustrated by the coolness and determination of his intended victim. Below we give the statement of Mr. Leslie concerning the unfortunate affair, which is fully corroborated by the testimony and verdict of the coroner's jury.

STATEMENT OF FRANK LESLIE

I was talking with some friends in the Oriental Saloon when Claiborne pushed his way in among us and began using very insulting language. I took him to one side and said, "Billy, don't interfere, those people are friends among themselves and are not talking about politics at all, and don't want you about." He appeared quite put out and used rather bad and certainly very nasty language towards me. I told him there was no use of his fighting with me, that there was no occasion for it, and leaving him I joined my friends. He came back again and began using exceedingly abusive language, when I took him by the collar of his coat and led him away, telling him not to get mad, that it was for his own good, that if he acted in that manner he was liable to get in trouble. He pushed away from me, using very hard language, and as he started away from me, shook his finger at me and said, "That's all right Leslie, I'll get even on you," and went out of the saloon. In a short time a man came in and said there was a man waiting outside to shoot me, but I didn't pay much attention to it. A few minutes later another man came in looking quite white and said Claiborne was waiting outside with a rifle

To Shoot Frank Leslie.

I then went out, and as I stepped on the sidewalk saw about a foot of a rifle barrel protruding from the end of the fruit stand. I stepped out in the street and saw it was Claiborne, and said, "Billy, don't shoot, I don't want you to kill me, nor do I want to have to shoot you." Almost before I finished he raised the gun and shot, and I returned the fire from my pistol, aiming at his breast. As soon as I shot I saw him double up and had my pistol cocked and aimed at him again, when I saw, or thought I saw, another man by him, putting his arms around him, and lowered the pistol, and when it was discharged the bullet went in the sidewalk. After I fired, I advanced upon him, but did not shoot, when he said, "Don't shoot again, I am killed," which I didn't, but watched him, with my pistol at full cock, as I didn't know what game he might play to get me off my guard. At that moment Officer Coyle came up and took hold of my pistol hand. I told him to be careful as it was at full cock. I then uncocked it and gave it to him, and said I would go with him. I told him I was sorry; that I might have done more, but I couldn't do less. He then placed me under arrest.—(Nov. 18, 1882.)

Coroner Matthews impaneled a jury, which met at 1 o'clock p. m. at Ritter's undertaking rooms, and the following testimony concerning the killing was elicited:

W. J. Mason,

being duly sworn says, I reside in Tombstone. I recognize the body submitted to the jury as that of William Claiborne; have known him for three years. This morning I came to the Oriental saloon. While I was drinking alone, Mr. Claiborne came into the saloon and had some words with Mr. Leslie, and Claiborne said, "I will see you later." Mr. Leslie replied, "While I am in Tombstone you can see me any time." Mr. Claiborne then left the saloon, and I left the saloon to see Mr. Brophy, and met Mr. Claiborne on the corner near the Oriental, Fifth and Allen. I advised him to wait and I would buy some fish and we would go

McGinnis

to breakfast together. I advised him to do nothing but drop the matter and have no trouble. He said he did not propose to drop the matter, but would go and get his Winchester and would settle the matter at once. This is the last I seen of Mr. Claiborne in good health. I saw him next lying behind the fruit stand beside the Oriental. He complained he was mortally wounded, saying, "My backbone is all shot out." I got on the ground in time to see Mr. Leslie hand his six-shooter to the officer, and being taken off by the officers. The next I saw of Mr. Claiborne was in the undertakers office, dead. I did not see the shooting. I do not know of my own knowledge who killed Mr. Claiborne. Claiborne said that he had some trouble with someone and he was going to get his Winchester and settle the matter, mentioning no names. He passed down Allen street with his gun in his hand, towards the Oriental saloon. I was in Mr. Brophy's saloon when I heard the shots. I did not know of any ill-feelings existing between the parties before this morning. I seen the officers take a rifle from the ground where Claiborne lay.

Dr. G. C. Willis

being first duly sworn, says; I reside in Tombstone, physician and surgeon by occupation. I saw Mr. Claiborne this morning a little before 8 o'clock at my office, being brought there by his friends in a condition of shock, bordering on collapse. I cut open his shirt and found a gunshot wound in the left side, and an opening in the back close to his spinal column, probably the wound of exit. He was not bleeding very much. . . . I gave him stimulants. I dressed the wounds. Then he talked about his opponent and called him a murdering son of a b—. Having no convenience there, I sent him to the hospital. . . . In my opinion it was a fatal wound. He was not dead when he left the office. . . . He was not fully conscious. He said he was a murdering son of a b— to shoot a man in the back. I was examining the back when he made that remark. I think he received the wound in front.

Otto Johnson,

being duly sworn says; I am a saloon keeper at Willcox. This morning as I was about to leave Judge Moses' saloon to go to breakfast at the Can Can chop house, I saw Mr. Claiborne on the corner of Fifth and Allen streets near Mr. Joyce's saloon, with a gun scabbard hung over his left shoulder and a Winchester in his right hand with his thumb on the trigger and gun pointing downward. I said to him, "Hello, Bill, where are you going?" He came up to me and remarked, "I don't allow any man to spit on me, and if he wants to fight to come out here, and if he don't come out I will go in and make him fight." I asked him who he meant by that. He said, "A man in there by the name of Frank Leslie." I tried to talk him out of it and to take a walk down the street with me. He said, no, if I interfered he would turn loose on me. Thinking it better to take a walk I walked into Joyce's saloon. I saw a friend of mine there by the name of Mr. Percy talking to two or three gentlemen there. I shook hands with Mr. Percy and asked him if he knew a man by the name of Frank Leslie. He said yes, and turned around to one of the gentlemen he was talking with, and introduced me to Frank Leslie. I told Mr. Leslie to be careful, that there was a man outside with a Winchester after him. Mr. Leslie asked me whereabouts. Told him outside the saloon. With that he walked to the side door on Fifth street, opened the door, stood there a minute and looked around. He closed the door and walked on the sidewalk. The next thing I heard the shots fired. I went outside, saw Mr. Claiborne lying on the sidewalk and Mr. Leslie about two feet from him with a gentleman holding up his hand that had his pistol in it. I walked away after that.

William Henry Bush,

being duly sworn, says; I reside in Tombstone; occupation bootblack. Billy Claiborne came up the street with a gun on his shoulder and said, "I am going to kill Frank Leslie." He came to me, and I said, "Billy, don't go over there, give me your gun." He said, "No you black son of a b–, I will kill you." I got up by the door and saw Billy across the street with his gun and I hollered to the barkeeper in the Palace saloon that there was going to be a shooting scrape. I saw him raise the gun to shoot Mr. Leslie, and I seen the gun go off, the bullet striking the sidewalk. I heard two shots fired. I seen Mr. Leslie on the sidewalk near the Oriental, with the pistol in his hand. I did not know which was shooting. Claiborne fired first.

Similar testimony followed from citizens John J. Reilly, James Coyle, David Cohn, Leon Jacobs, and E. H. Dean.

THE CORONER'S VERDICT

We the undersigned, a jury of inquest, summoned and impaneled by the coroner of said county to inquire whose the body submitted to our inspection, when, where and under what circumstances he came to his death, after viewing the body and hearing such testimony as has been brought before us, find that his name was William Claiborne, age and nativity unknown, and that he came to his death from the effects of a pistol wound inflicted by Frank Leslie, in the town of Tombstone, Arizona Territory, on the 14th day of November, 1882; and that the shooting was done in self-defense, and, in the opinion of the jury was justifiable.—(Nov. 18, 1882.)

The fact that he had twice been guilty of what Tombstone called "killings" apparently did not hurt Leslie's standing in Allen Street society. He served once as sergeant-at-arms of a state Democratic convention, which met in Tombstone, and he continued to be a member of the sheriff's posses.

Between such details he carried on in his occupation as bartender for seven years. Then he made two mistakes. He committed a "murder." That was mistake number one. His victim was a woman. That was the second mistake. The *Epitaph* had this story of the occurrence.

A SHOOTING

William Reynolds came in from Horseshoe Valley in the Swisshelm mountains this afternoon [July 11, 1889] and reported that last night Frank Leslie, well known in Tombstone as a hard character, had shot a woman supposed to be his wife and a young man by the name of James Neal. The latter is seriously wounded, being shot through the left arm and below the breast.

It is not known how badly the woman is hurt. Leslie was still on the fight and acting like a crazy man when Reynolds left this morning in quest of a surgeon. Leslie was drunk and had been seeking a quarrel in the valley for some time. Dr. Goodfellow left immediately for the scene of the shooting. Deputy Sheriff Shattuck telegraphed Slaughter at Bisbee who has sent officers to arrest Leslie.

Dr. G. E. Goodfellow returned this morning [July 12, 1889] from Leslie's ranch after being in the saddle almost continuously for eighteen hours, and traveling over ninety miles. He arrived at the ranch last night and found the woman dead where she fell and Neal suffering from wounds in the arm and body.

Neal was placed in a spring wagon where a Prospector reporter found him this afternoon resting as easily as could be expected under the circumstances. He welcomed the intruder, with whom he had been acquainted several years and gave an account of the trouble.

Leslie and Mollie Williams had returned from Tombstone and had been home one night previous to the one on which the tragedy had occurred. They both had been drinking heavily at this time and had quarreled incessantly. He slapped her and knocked her down several times during the day and said he was going to Reynolds' place and kill Reynolds but came back about an hour after, saying that Reynolds would not fight.

This was toward evening. Both the woman and Neal were sitting outside the house and Leslie began quarreling with the woman. He took another drink and then started from his seat saying, "I'll put a stop to all this," rushed into the house and came back with a Colt's pistol; took deliberate aim at the woman and fired.

Neal sat dumbfounded for a moment only, for Leslie ran to him, placed the gun close to his chest and fired.

"Don't be afraid, it's nothing," said Leslie, and Neal believed that he was only fooling and that he had not been hurt until he felt the blood running down his body. He then started and ran, glancing around but once to see the unfortunate woman run around the house and fall at the back door.

Before he reached Reynolds place he fell and remained there all night. After he reached Reynolds the next morning, Leslie came there and asked for him, saying he wanted to kill him. Neal saw him coming, picked up a shotgun and waited in the tent for him to come, but Leslie went away believing he was not there.

On the way in this morning, Goodfellow and Neal saw Leslie sitting in front of the house at Abbott's ranch and informed Under Sheriff Shattuck of the fact and Ben James and Deputy Lawrence started after him. A short distance out they met Taylor and Heine, who were on their way in and Frank Leslie riding with them, he was on his way to give himself up, he said, and entered the buggy with the two officers who brought him to the county jail.

To our reporter who visited him at the jail he said he was sick. "Oh, my head is sick, and wants a rest," he said, and then began to cry. He claims to remember nothing of the affair.

Judge Easton left for the ranch this morning to hold an

inquest on the body of the woman, Mollie Williams. A coffin was sent out and the body will be brought in for interment.—(July 11, 1889.)

This time the law did not fool with Leslie. It gave him a life sentence, took his fringed buckskins away from him, and threw him in the stone dungeons high above the muddy Colorado at Yuma.

The wife he had won from Killeen divorced him. His mistress was in her grave, but even in prison this killer had a way with women. The *Epitaph* tells the story of his last amorous adventure in its issue of May 2, 1897, by reprinting an article which first appeared in the San Francisco *Chronicle* under a Stockton date line.

Stockton—On December 1st, last, Nashville F. Leslie, giving his residence as San Carlos, A. T., was married by Justice Parker to Mrs. Belle Stowell whose residence was put down upon the license as Warren County, Ill.

Leslie was an Indian scout, but he came here direct from the Territorial prison in Yuma county, A. T. He exchanged the stripes for wedding clothes. He was released after serving eight years of a life sentence for murder.

Three years ago the Chronicle wrote up Leslie's exploits. In the course of the biography of the prisoner they published a picture of him. Mrs. Belle Stowell, who then lived in San Francisco, and was the ex-wife of a man in the employ of the Southern Pacific company, read the narrative of the scout's adventures and, it is said, fell in love with him.

She had just been divorced from her husband, and she began to correspond with the murderer. Flowers followed the letters, and then fruit was sent. The murderer reciprocated, and the only hindrance to the marriage was the prison bars.

Mrs. Stowell obtained a railroad pass to Yuma, A. T. The prisoner was pardoned and he and his bride to be came to this city and the marriage took place.

During this time Mrs. Stowell has been and still is drawing $40 monthly alimony from her husband. The husband is now tired of paying her and has sent a detective here to investigate.

With this story the *Epitaph* seems to have lowered the curtain on Buckskin Frank. Certainly the stage on which he played the villain so often never saw him again.

6 Frontier Journalism

EDITORIAL

Editor John P. Clum, of the *Epitaph,* was not a man who wasted white paper on long editorial battles with a competitor.

He wrote once, "We hold our space too valuable to be occupied with answering the disjointed brain storms which are as vague in meaning as they are in purport."

Clum did not quite make good on this but he did have a policy of answering attacks in the *Nugget* with a brief paragraph saturated in raw vitriol and then going on about his business.

While the *Epitaph* and the *Nugget* took different sides in the war between the Earps and the Cowboys, and Clum often referred to the "Cow-Boy organ" when he blasted at the doings of this element, under no circumstances did he give a rival editor the satisfaction of seeing his name mentioned.

Two things happened in Tombstone journalism in 1882 which changed this situation: Clum sold the *Epitaph* and the *Nugget* failed. For five years the *Epitaph* had no competition. Then the *Prospector* appeared and from that time on the editors wrote without gloves until the two papers consolidated in March, 1924.

One of the bitterest editorial fights took place when J. O. Dunbar, editor of the *Epitaph,* started a mud-throwing contest with J. J. Nash, of the *Prospector.* The *Epitaph* began it with the following blast.

A BLACKMAILING OUTFIT

For the past few days the Tombstone Prospector has been running "squibs" threatening to publish something "rich, rare and racy." They bore the earmarks of blackmail but not until last evening did the EPITAPH learn the true inwardness of the case. It seems that one of our most prominent business men had been guilty of, or at least had been charged with some indiscretion which might have been laid to the door of nine men out of ten with as much truth. Yesterday he received a note to the effect that the Prospector was about to publish a full account of the affair, and that in order to "square it" he (the business man) had better see James J. Nash. Knowing that Mr. Ritter was a friend of Nash's, he went to see him and induced Mr. R. to have a talk with Nash. It is said that Mr. Ritter offered Nash $25 out of his own pocket to say nothing about it and that Nash's reply was, "No, sir, I've got a family to support, and I think he'll pay more than that." Ritter left the blackmailer in disgust. Soon after, Nash and the business man had an interview, with the result that Nash was given a check, made payable to the order of Benny Hyde, for the sum of $100, and Nash agreed to keep quiet.

The main facts show this to be as plain and unvarnished a case of blackmail as was ever known. The grand jury which meets here in a few days cannot help taking cognizance of the matter and the result will probably be that J. J. Nash will have to stand trial for the crime (if he does not skip in the meantime), and if convicted will land in Yuma where he belongs.

We have some respect for a robber who stops a stage, but for a blackmailer we consider Yuma too good for him.

The *Prospector's* answer was brief and personal. Modern newspaper men will note that fear of libel never held a Tombstone editor back, even though there was a territorial code which provided a jail sentence and a fine, not exceeding $5,000, for such offenses. The *Prospector* ran this three-line reply.

The utterances of the old Drunkard who runs the Epitaph at present do not bother us in the least.

Ignoring the reference to his own capacity, even though spelled with an upper-case "D," Dunbar now got down to the business at hand, using everything but a double-barreled shotgun. His professional pride, he said in his editorial, would not allow him to fail in his clear duty.

The facts as to the blackmailing of a prominent business man of this city by the manager of the Prospector, are substantially as printed in last week's EPITAPH. The attention of the grand jury which assembles in this city one week from Monday, is called to the matter. The crime is one of the most despicable on the calendar and is too frequently practiced in a mining camp, where a sale of property can hardly take place without an attempt on the part of some unprincipled scoundrel to extort money from the buyer or seller. Rarely has there been as plain a case of extortion made as the one in question, and it behooves the court to set the seal of its condemnation upon it. Let one blackmailer be sent to the penitentiary and the practice will become decidedly unpopular in the future. It may be urged that Jimmy Nash is a young man, and did not understand the heinousness of the crime he was committing, but it will hardly do in his case to plead the baby act. As editor of a newspaper in the city for years he occupied a position which gave him great opportunities for good or evil. He chose the latter course and should be willing to abide by the result. It is understood that Judge Swain, counsel for the accused, asserts that Nash was drunk when he made the threats to publish the scandal, in case he was not paid $100 to keep it quiet, but neither will this theory wash for Nash never gets drunk. It is true he is what is called a "soaker," his system being constantly saturated with alcohol, but he keeps on his feet, and has no brain worth mentioning to be affected. This fact may be pleaded in extenuation of the offense, and we cannot gainsay it. But the truth remains that a crime has been committed and it is the grand jury's duty to investigate it. By applying at this office they can get the names of half a dozen reputable witnesses who will substantiate the charge. The position the EPITAPH occupies in the matter is similar to that of a decent attorney when some unprincipled member of the legal profession commits an unworthy act. We desire to see the perpetrator punished to purge the profession of journalism of its disreputable members. We have no personal malice in the matter nor any desire to "down the Prospector" as has been asserted. We care nothing for the Nash opposition and would prefer it to any other that could be mentioned, for no sooner will Nash go to Yuma, than other and more worthy competitors will take his place. As a matter of fact the EPITAPH is acting against its own interests in urging this prosecution. Professional pride alone impels us to do it.

Blackmail was something the *Prospector* apparently did not wish to discuss. It confines its answer to further comments on Dunbar's inability to hold his liquor.

> No, Jim don't get drunk but he is a soaker. He is a confirmed drunkard of the lowest order and time and again has been taken to his home in a beastly state.

Apparently the *Epitaph* decided to admit the sins of its own editor but it asked the *Prospector* to meet the main issue.

> It may be that the editor of the EPITAPH robbed stages in his youth and has been frequently "how come you" in his mature age. We admit, for the sake of closing the argument on that point that it is true. But what has that to do with the *fact* that on Friday evening, Oct. 29, 1887, James J. Nash extorted from A. E. Jacobs a check for the sum of $100 under threats of publishing a certain libelous article in the Daily Prospector which would have placed Mr. Jacobs in a ridiculous light before the community. The law makes such an offense a felony, and subjects the offender to a punishment of five years in the penitentiary. If the grand jury which meets in the city next Monday does not investigate these charges, it will fail in doing its duty.

The grand jury met but, if it considered the *Epitaph's* charges, obviously did not think Mr. Nash was guilty, for it ignored the *Epitaph*. Neither paper mentioned the fact, but a week later the *Prospector* printed the following paragraph.

> It is seldom that the despicable characteristics of Uriah Heep, Oily Gammon and Aminidab Sleek are found united on one person. This trinity of sychopancy, deceit and hypocrisy, however, can be found in Cochise county. Ugh! The snake!

Two months later Nash was quietly dropped from the list of Tombstone newspaper men. What Dunbar thought about that is not recorded.

S. C. Bagg, who liked to refer to himself as "The five foot editor of the six column *Prospector*," replaced Nash and got into a fight with the *Epitaph* which landed him in jail. In August of 1888 Bagg objected violently to an act of the county supervisors, who rejected his printing bid and gave this gravy to the *Epitaph*. He filed suit but the court said the supervisors were within their rights and threw the case out.

Bagg then wrote an angry editorial which the court interpreted as threatening. In one paragraph of his comment the editor said, "We take our medicine with good grace and we hope the Honorable Judge and Honorable board of supervisors will not make any grimaces in taking the pills which have been prescribed for them by our editorial surgeon."

The Judge ordered Bagg to appear in court and gave him a lecture which the *Prospector* faithfully reported as follows.

> "The contempt in this case is a bold, defiant threat to the court. Why, a man may as well stand at the foot of the stairs with a Winchester or a cowhide and threaten court or jury. Still, if Mr. Bagg had appeared before this court and apologized for what he wrote, or said it was done in the heat of passion, it would have been different. But this case is different and the court must protect its dignity at all hazards. If this is not done we may as well tear down the courthouse. . . . Suppose a man stood on each side of the Judge with a Winchester rifle and said, 'You decide for me, or I'll shoot,' what sort of a position would that be for a judge? . . . You must pay a fine of $300 or go to jail."

Bagg went to jail but not until he had written the following editorial.

> The infamy which is about to be consummated under the guise of law, of throwing into prison a citizen of the United States for expressing his opinion of a recent decision of Judge Barnes is, without exception, the most damnable outrage that has ever been perpetrated in this Territory, if not in the United States.
>
> The craven coward who made the order and then adjourned his court and an hour afterwards left town, this man who has not the moral courage to administer the law in opposition to the wishes of a corrupt ring of political adventurers, should receive the denunciations of all good citizens regardless of party affiliations.

The court had ruled that in default of payment of the fine Bagg should "be imprisoned in the county jail of the said county of Cochise until the said fine be satisfied at the rate of one day's imprisonment for each and every dollar of such fine, but not exceeding in all three hundred days."

The editor stayed in jail three days. Then a group of friends raised the cash and paid his fine. He was so angry that he never forgave the Judge and got even with the supervisors by making the *Prospector* a Republican paper.

The editor's enthusiasm, bordering on hysteria, was demonstrated when the railroad, for which the *Epitaph* had been campaigning for twenty-two years, steamed into town on May 5, 1903, and the paper let go a six-column blast of welcome.

It was the longest story the *Epitaph* had printed since President Garfield died and is much too long to reproduce but these paragraphs from the lead and close show its flavor.

A Grand Celebration
And Gala Day for Tombstone

Well say, didn't we celebrate? Well, we guess yes, and we had about 2500 people to help us out. For the past three days the hotels and lodging houses have been filling up with our neighbors from the surrounding country, who came in for the celebration.

Early yesterday morning the incoming train from Tucson brought over a hundred people with whom were the Tucson hose team. Shortly after the hour of twelve the salutes fired from Comstock hill gave notice of the approach of the excursion train from Bisbee, Douglas, Navo and Cananea on which were over one thousand people.

The day was an ideal one, and could not have been better. While there was a slight breeze blowing it was not in the least disagreeable. The sun shone clear and bright and all nature seemed to be in harmony with us.

Now that the celebration is over let every body buckle down and pull together for the advancement of Tombstone.

Hurrah! Hurrah! For the railroad, for Tombstone, Cochise County and the Territory of Arizona.— (May 6, 1903.)

"Slings and Arrows"

Hundreds of thousands of newspaper readers who never saw a copy of the *Epitaph* knew the paper because its editorial paragraphs were reprinted in their home newspapers. Sometimes these were witty, sometimes caustic and very often they were little pictures of what life was like in the town with the unbelievable name.

These are average samples from thirty years of *Epitaph* files.

• Tax Collector Chapman still continues to collect a license tax from the drummers who visit Tombstone, not withstanding the recent decision of the Supreme Court of the United States, declaring the collection of such tax unconstitutional. Chap probably acts upon the theory, if the Supreme Judges make d–d fools of themselves it is no reason why he should.

• When a town can support three or four faro games, a keno game and a first class theater, it is a sure sign that said town is a good one, and there can be no doubt today that Tombstone is the best town on the coast.

• Bad men and bad whisky are said to be too plentiful in Fresno and measures are being taken to stop the mingling of the two. In a climate where the mercury sports around 110 the whisky should be only of the best quality.

• For the benefit of the party who threw a stick of wood through the front window of this office yesterday we will state that cord wood will not be taken for subscriptions during the heated term.

• If Father Lebreton would take mercy upon night shift editors and miners, and not allow the Catholic bell to be rung earlier than 9 a. m., he would add another to his many public benefactions. People who are pious enough to attend early mass ought also to be pious enough to get there in ample season without such noisy admonition.

• A chicken hearted jury were unable to decide yesterday whether or not a chicken ranch located inside the city limits should be declared a public nuisance.

• A yellow dog deliberately committed suicide yesterday by jumping down a shaft. The misguided canine had evidently been reading the "special dispatches" (by stage coach) in the bladder [Note: the *Prospector*] and being seriously affected by the stench arising from them on account of their age, entirely lost control of himself on reading the lucid account of the hanging yesterday in Tucson which commenced "Firmino, who was hung today in Tucson," and wound up with, "but the chances are he will hang tomorrow." This was too much.

• "God tempers the winds to the shorn lamb," but he doesn't increase the temperature any for the fellow who pawns his overcoat and loses the proceeds at faro.

• The present grand jury is composed principally of working men and those in the middle station of life, financially speaking. They are men who, if they have any axes to grind leave them home when they go to the grand jury room. There is more reason, sense and justice locked up in the grand jury room this term of court than has ever been gathered together there in the history of Cochise county, in our opinion. There is a land-grabber or two and a couple or more blackmailers still at large which it might be well to round up while a fearless grand jury is in session. We do not always have them so constituted.

• The largest battleship afloat has been built by Japan, which is doing well for what sixty years ago was a hermit nation. The Mikasa has a displacement of 15,150 tons, a speed of 18 knots and she can steam 9,000 miles without recoaling. Japan evidently intends to have something to say about affairs in the far east.—(Jan. 26, 1902.)

• The cutting off of the drummers' license has reduced the city's revenues from seventy-five to one hundred dollars a month and it behooves the city council to provide for the deficit in some other manner than an increased tax on property holders.

• We respectfully suggest that all persons entering Tombstone on horseback do so at a moderate gait. Those coming down the street at a gallop are sure to be intercepted by a crowd in the belief that they are from the seat of war and our reporter has enough to do without breaking his neck in an effort to meet them. He is a good reporter and we don't want him wind-broken before he reaches the prime of life. Bad whisky will finish him soon enough.

• It seems passing strange that it is the party that thanked God for the rain because rain made the corn grow, corn made whisky and whisky made Democrats that enacted the high liquor license in Arizona.

• King Edward can shake hands with himself. He has met J. Pierpont Morgan and still retains his crown.

• An eastern crank is trying to prove that America was first discovered by a Chinaman, while a Chinaman is always trying to prove that he never discovered anything outside the process of washing a shirt to pieces in three innings.

• Sam Jones, the noted revivalist, is not as big a fool as a casual reader of his sayings would be led to suppose. In a recent sermon he said: "The most beautiful sight in the world is to see a family around a cheerful fire, with the head of the family reading his local paper which he has paid for in advance."

• While the people of the east are chanting "the cold chilly winds of December," we of Arizona can sit gently in our rooms and hum "when the robins nest again." There the frozen elements cause the natives to hover around heated furnaces, while here a palm leaf fan is almost necessary to the comforts of our people. There it is snow and chilling winds, here it is gentle showers and warm sunshine. Then, when the question of locality resolves itself down to climate to say nothing of resources, surely Southern Arizona has no superior and but few equals under the sun.

• It is said that young Hearst, who is running the San Francisco Examiner, employs none but Harvard graduates on its editorial and reportorial staffs. This statement, if true, is rough on Harvard.

• As long as Grover Cleveland occupies the presidential chair, and is used as a figure head by Wall Street Shylocks, just so long will silver keep down to its present price. We need a Western man for president.

• Due to the carbuncles that appeared in the cuticle of the leper up the street Sunday morning we are led to believe that trichina in its worst form must be a curse under which it is laboring. As the case is evidently a very malignant one, and the disease is known to be very deadly, the eminent proprietor of that great and philanthropic journal is probably preparing to take his departure for that bright clime, where Ananias will give him a cordial reception.

SPORT

One must read at least a year or two of *Epitaph* files to get a true conception of what an excellent job this old border paper did in covering the community.

It was not departmentalized. There were no specified columns for society or sport, but the *Epitaph* carried plenty of news of both and was especially interested in Tombstone's favorite sport, which was baseball.

The earliest issues of the *Epitaph* report games between local nines and soldiers from Fort Huachuca. Little interest was taken in the standings of the major leagues but the home team was always sure of support and space.

There were some boxing matches and frequent challenges. The meagre wire reports also carried stories on the bouts of John L. Sullivan, both inside and outside the ring.

Foot races, cockfights, horse races, shooting matches with pistols, rifles, and shotguns were common. Field and stream were not neglected, for there were deer and turkeys in the mountains and ducks on rivers which are now dry gulches.

Perhaps the most famous of all the town's sporting events was the ill-starred trip which the Tombstone nine made to Phoenix—the *Epitaph* insisted on spelling it "Phenix"—in October, 1889, where they had accepted a challenge to play a series of three games at the territorial fair.

Two days passed without news of the results reaching Tombstone, then, on a Sunday morning, the *Epitaph* broke the sad story that the team had been defeated. The editor was so carried away by his writing he forgot to mention the scores. There being no Monday edition, the *Epitaph* remedied this omission on Tuesday morning.

Baseball writers took liberties even beyond those accorded news writers in the mining camps of the eighties. The *Epitaph* reporter went to the Bible for his style. Even the caption came from the Good Book.

YEA, VERILY

And the Morning and the Evening of the Third Day Endeth in Much Trouble

Man who is born of woman, is of few days and full of—baseball. He bandeth together with eight others of like proclivities and after a time they getteth up on their hind legs and croweth an exceedingly large crow that there is none in all the land who can exceed them. And their constituents, having faith like unto that which moveth mountains, sendeth them forth robed in purple and fine linen and girded with vanity and statures like unto the contemplated exposition tower of the great metropolis by the sea. And they hieth themselves to a great inland city and are feasted and made much of at which they are greatly elated. But the inhabitants of that city taketh counsel among themselves and their young men get together and formeth a nine for protection of their fair names and the glory of their fathers. And it cometh to pass that the two nines meet upon the field of battle and the visitors putteth their hands to their faces and winketh their left eyes at one another and say, "How easy will be our victory! Great will be our renown and the glory thereof will be handed down to our children, even unto the fifth generation!" And behold! the visitors were slaughtered until the going down of the sun. And the evening and the morning were the first day. And on the morrow the hostilities were renewed and the visitors were victorious, routing the enemy and pursuing them even unto the walls of the city. And the evening and the morning were the second day. And it came to pass that, on the morning of the third day, both armies gathered all their hosts, even the strangers who had journeyed from afar to witness the mighty struggle. And the two armies fortified themselves after the custom of the country and went forth to do battle in the sight of the people. And the nine that journeyed to a strange land, glorying in their strength and mighty in their boastfulness, were beaten and utterly routed, and were scoffed at by the people and their raiment of purple and fine linen was grievously soiled.

They were despoiled of their treasure and cast forth into outer darkness. And the morning and the evening were the third day. And it came to pass that the vanquished nine returned to the place from whence they came, filled with sorrow and bilge water, and the lamentations of their constituents ascended upward beyond the computation of the wise men and the heavens became overcast with a crimson cloud. And the frightened nine shrank from the wrath that was and gat themselves into a place of safety, beyond the mountains, and girded their loins about with sackcloth and cast ashes upon their heads and wept exceeding sore. And after a time the wrath of their constituents abated somewhat and the nine returned to the land of their fathers with bowed heads and robed in humility. And the fatted calf yet sports joyously upon his native heath and saith unto himself, "Ha, Ha!" And their enemies revile them and say unto them, "Ye who once did crow so valiantly, crow for us now and we will forgive you." And they could not. And the small boy points to them and says, "Behold! They went out after an enemy and found him." And the river of tears was exceeding bitter. Selah!

And the nights are filled with sorrow
And cares infest the day,
Because of the Tombstone tossers
Who didn't know how to play.

Tuesday the *Epitaph* told its readers that Tombstone had lost the first game 10-5, won the second 19-12, and lost the third 9-6. Then it added:

"Every device was resorted to by the Phenicians to win the game and purse money, even going so far as to try to buy the two Prescott boys who assisted the Tombstones, offering them $200 if they would not play with our boys. Such work was not expected in Phenix and everyone denounces it as low and unworthy of an Arizonan."

Tombstone always had a baseball game on national holidays and the *Epitaph* was always there. Its story of the game on July fourth, 1889, tells something about the kind of ball they played.

The Glorious Fourth

The baseball game between the Huachuca and Tombstone nines was not an exciting one up to the fifth inning, the score standing at the end of the fourth ten to three in favor of the home nine. The Huachucas went to bat in the fifth and scored eight runs. Our boys tied the visitors at the end of the fifth, whitewashed them in the sixth and made four runs in the seventh. The visitors scored three and the home team one in the eighth.

The Huachucas went to bat with fourteen runs to their credit while our boys had sixteen. There were two men out and one run to the credit of the visitors when a rank decision caused the visitors to quit the ground in disgust. A large amount of money had been put up on the game which was awarded by the referee to those who had backed the home nine. That the visitors were most shamefully treated was apparent to all present and frequent were the manifestations of disapproval on the part of the spectators, who hissed and cried, "Shame, Outrage," etc. Many persons who had bet on the home nine refused to take the money bet by the soldiers and called their bets down during the game. The excuse given for the action of the home team was that they were treated in the same manner by the Fort Huachuca boys when they visited the post last time. Taken for granted that this was the case, it only causes those who have liberally supported the game for the pleasure of witnessing it once in a while to lose interest in it as a sport which might be enjoyed.

Death seldom took a holiday in Tombstone in the early eighties. But Allen Street was quiet one Sunday afternoon in July, 1882, so he looked into an alley behind the saloons. There was a cockfight there which ended in a killing. This is the *Epitaph* story.

WORK OF A POP

Two Old Men Quarrel Over a Cock Fight, and One Gets Killed

The devotees of the cockpit are willing to swear that it is the most charming sport in the world, and that a chicken fight can produce more excitement and enthusiasm to the square inch than any other known amusement. As is generally known, there is a cockpit on Allen street in the rear of Walsh's saloon and the lovers of the sport are in the habit of assembling there in the afternoon of Sundays to witness the contests. The birds were furnished by two old men named Young and Bobier, who resided on a ranch about two and one half miles northeast of town. These gentlemen brought the original stock from Kentucky and by careful propagation, were the owners of several game birds, which they sold, matched or rented at the cockpit as the necessities of the case demanded. In addition to chicken culture, the old men burned lime, and raised some vegetables for the Tombstone market. A few days ago, they sold a game rooster to a gentleman of this city, and at the main, Sunday, this same bird which they sold a few days previously, was matched against one of theirs. Albert Y. Young, one of the partners, was referee of the contest, while Wm. Bobier, the other partner, handled the bird in the pit. It was generally conceded that the chicken, owned jointly by the old men, was beaten, but a technicality, however, existed, and much chin music was wasted in an endeavor to settle the dispute. Finally, the matter was referred to Young, as referee, and he declared it a draw and all bets off. This angered Bobier more than a little and he denounced the old man in unmeasured terms. He went so far, as was testified at the inquest, as to threaten to kill old man Young, besides hurling at him all the vile names in the calendar of vituperation. Mr. Walsh, the proprietor of the saloon, said that Bobier said he did not fight cocks for his health, and that he did not like the idea of "outsiders" getting away with him. The old men started home together, Young having corn for the chickens, beans and other things in a sack which he carried on his shoulder. According to Young's story as told to an Epitaph reporter early in the day, and testified to before the coroner's jury, as soon as they were out of town Bobier commenced to abuse him violently, threatened to kill him, and finally struck him a blow with his fist on the ear that knocked him down. Young says, notwithstanding that, he preserved his temper and only remonstrated with his angry partner. Bobier's anger still continued to rise; he used foul names in reference to Young's mother, which had the effect of angering the latter and he said his mother was as good as Bobier's; that she had been in her grave a number of years and he would not hear her abused. At this point Bobier commenced hostilities in earnest and picked up a rock weighing about three pounds. When Young saw this he commenced to run, and some twenty feet ahead of Bobier. The latter followed him, and Young drew a toy pistol, carrying a 22-caliber ball and fired as he ran, without taking aim, merely thrusting his hand backward and pulling the trigger. The little bullet entered Bobier's heart; he run a few steps further, and fell forward dead. This occurred near the cabin occupied by Colonel Wiggins, who testified before the jury that he heard quarreling, and came to the door in his night clothes to see what the difficulty was. Just as he got to the door Bobier fell. Young approached him and asked if he wouldn't go and see if he was dead saying he wouldn't have killed him for the world. An examination showed life to be extinct, and the body was put in a passing wagon and brought to the undertakers. Young also came to town and surrendered himself. The deceased had the reputation of being a quarrelsome man and hard to get along with. He was more or less under the influence of liquor at the time of his death. He was about fifty years old and came from Sherman, Texas. His wife is now living about 12 miles from that town. Young is a Kentuckian and is sixty-seven years old. He has a wife in Kentucky and a nephew, a young boy, who resides on the ranch with him. He came to be possessed of the pistol through means of the boy. The lad got the pistol some way and was eternally practicing. He shot a dog a few days ago and the old man, fearing he might do other mischief, took the pop away from him and threw it in the sage brush. While walking around Saturday he came on the pistol and put it in his pocket, and there it remained until taken out on Sunday evening. The killing occurred about half past seven. Coroner Matthews empaneled a jury yesterday and facts in substance as above were elicited.—(July 23, 1882.)

The coroner's jury found that Young fired the shot in self-defense.

When the wires were working the *Epitaph* received a telegraphic report of national news. Occasionally there were references to sports. This is one of them.

Probably Whisky—Special Dispatch

Washington, May 21 (1889)—It is openly stated here that the wretched work of the Washington ball club is caused by the dissipated habits of some of the men. On the morning of the last Boston game, it is said three of the men in company with some of the Boston men were nearly drunk in a well-known saloon in this city and on a number of occasions since the season opened members of the team have been seen in a drunken condition. It is a matter of common talk that in a certain resort here, three or four members of the team can be found nightly drinking and carousing.

The sporting fraternity of Tombstone would bet on anything. The *Epitaph* reports two events which it calls "novel" and "unique."

A novel contest occurred in a saloon on Allen street yesterday between a hawk and a rat. The two were placed in a large mocking bird cage by their respective owners, and bets made upon the results. The hawk made one bolt for the rodent, which action so astonished his ratship that he shot out of the cage in some mysterious manner, and as subsequent events proved, from the frying pan into the fire, for John Bluett's ratter, which was on the outlook for his breakfast, stopped his flight and put an end to the contest. Twenty dollars changed hands on the result.

• The most unique and interesting interurban contest ever pulled off in Arizona was settled between a Tombstone tarantula and a Black Diamond centipede yesterday. It would have been worth a day's travel to any true scientist to have been present. The venomous creatures were placed in a bucket to give them ample room, and to the surprise of all present advanced to the attack, retired and returned to the finish. The big spider finally fastened his fangs into his wriggling adversary and the latter curled over him with his myriad feet and the battle royal was on. So determined was the shaggy spider that his adversary carried him around the ring repeatedly. At last the repulsive things rolled up in an undistinguishable ball and fought to the death. The tarantula, which was captured at the depot yesterday, succumbed first, the centipede, which measured eight inches and was brought from Black Diamond, died later.

Gun battles were more common than ring battles in Tombstone. The *Epitaph,* however, did its best to encourage boxing and gave space willingly to any challenge. Two of these offers follow. Neither found a taker.

Those of our pugilistic fraternity now have a chance to get all the fame they desire and glory enough to cover a good sized ranch. C. C. Perry, of Tucson, signs his name to the following, and if some of our sports want to fight half as bad as they want people to think they do, they will go Mr. Perry a few rounds anyhow, just for luck: I do hereby challenge any man in the Territory of Arizona to box me a given number of rounds in a 12-foot ring for a purse of $100 to $500. Five ounce gloves to be used and winner to take total receipts. No weight barred. This challenge holds good to any man who has been a resident of the Territory for three months.

Acceptance

Having seen the challenge issued by C. C. Perry, of Tucson, to fight any man in the territory, I hereby challenge Mr. Perry to fight with naked hands, any time within two months, London prize ring rules, give or take 5 pounds from 145 pounds; if he is not imported. Frank Broad.

There is no record that the fight was held.

A Challenge

Bob McDonald, of Bisbee, challenges Prof. Costello to a fistic encounter, as follows: Costello being a middle weight champion; I am a light weight. I will bet $500 that he can't knock me out of time in four three-minute rounds. Marquis of Queensbury rules. The fight to come off when or where Mr. Costello may choose.

Bob McD.

No answer appeared from Professor Costello.

The *Epitaph* had no sport column and mixed its sport notes in with society, personals, and local items. When they are picked out of the news columns and grouped together they give a fair picture of the way its male citizens found fun and relaxation in the rough camp. A few of many such notes are reprinted here.

• The Tombstone shooting club will agree to match six of its members against any six men in the territory, in any sum from $50 to $500, to shoot with pistol, rifle and shotgun. In the latter class to shoot at glass balls or pigeons; in the former, snapshooting at glass balls, or wheel and fire at the word. Who wants the game?

• Pete White brought up 21 wild turkeys from Sonora yesterday. He killed them about sixty miles from here and sold ten of them in Bisbee before reaching Tombstone.

• It is estimated by a sporting editor that John L. Sullivan has drank five barrels of ale, four of beer, three of wine and one of whisky in the last seven years and has smoked an average of ten cigars a day.

• The hose race challenge has attracted considerable attention and it is probable all three fire companies will have a team in the field in the effort to win a keg of beer.

• Now that baseball on the Fourth is an assured fact, our boys should provide more shade and additional seats for the benefit and comfort of the spectators. Provide plenty of room for the ladies for they will be there in force. Better have ice water on the grounds, too, for it will be needed.

• The quarter-mile horse race at Solomonville last Monday between Bald Face Calf and Crawford was a genuine race. Crawford won by one foot. Over $3,500 changed hands.

• The ball given last night under the auspices of the baseball club was a very pleasant affair. The members of the nine were arrayed in their playing suits and the ladies outdid themselves to look their prettiest.

• There will be a cockfight in the rear of Stevenson & Walker's saloon this evening at 6:30 o'clock.

• A rather poor game of ball was played last Sunday, the cause being the difficulty of getting sufficient players to form two nines. The score was too large for our columns. Only six innings were played.

• J. L. Waters and Antonio Rodriguez returned from a trip to the Swisshelms Thursday night. They were gone twelve days and killed fifteen deer. They did their hunting above Col. Herring's ranch and are much elated over their success.

• A foot race between two local sports last night attracted much attention and occasioned great gobs of enthusiasm that nearly blocked the street. The clerk was beaten by a length.

• Col. Hafford and Ben Whiston returned from Pantano Sunday evening loaded down with ducks, of which many of their friends received a sample copy. As a hunter the colonel is a brilliant success and he has our thanks for two brace of that savory fowl. It is almost too early in the season for good sport and Mr. Hafford will repeat the trip in a short while.

ADVERTISING

Good as was its sport coverage and its news of churches, clubs, and society, the *Epitaph* had to have advertising and the heavy volume of paid matter which the paper carried probably explains why it outlived many competitors.

There were long periods when the front page carried nothing but advertising. Often there were not more than four or five columns of news, personals, and editorials in the paper.

Much of the advertising copy never changed. The only attention the editor paid to it was to reset the type when it grew too worn to be read.

Saloons, restaurants, and undertakers were heavy advertisers. The Louisiana lottery and some Mexican lotteries appeared regularly.

A firm which manufactured a brand of dynamite it called "Miner's Friend" promised that their product would "outblast any other explosive." Makers of Tennessee White Rye Whiskey illustrated their copy with a drawing of an attractive woman in white.

Patent medicines must have brought in considerable revenue. The list of regulars included Mrs. Winslow's Soothing Syrup, Dr. Pierce's Favorite Prescription and Hostetter's Bitters.

But the cream of the income was furnished by legal notices. Homestead applications, notices of forfeiture and patents of mining claims, county treasurers' and supervisors' reports, sheriff's sales, city ordinances, and official proceedings of the city council were packed into every page of the paper.

Publishers apparently had considerable political influence in those days. For the law said legal notices should be published as many as ten times without change.

There was also a period when ranchers were compelled by law to advertise their cattle brands. These advertisements, consisting of a black silhouette of a cow bearing the brand in white, occupied columns of space in the paper for months at a time.

Nor was this all, for every paper had a job shop and bid on city and county notices and office stationery. This advertising and job printing was the magnet which drew every printer with a hand press and a few cases of type to the mining camps. There might be silver in the hills and blood on the streets but there was gold in the print shops.

No laws in those days said that advertising must be marked as such and the editor took advantage of the fact. He sowed paid liners between his news notes and only the fact that they appeared week after week showed they were not the editor's own comments.

Some of the choice advertisements from the *Epitaph* should interest today's advertising men.

Ask for "Double Stamp Kentucky Bourbon Whisky, $3 a gallon."

Lost—$100 Reward

Pair of Diamond Earrings, wrapped in a piece of linen towel. The finder will be paid $100 for the return of same to Miss Annie Watson, corner of Seventh and Allen streets, and no questions asked.

$500 Reward

The undersigned hereby offers five hundred dollars for the arrest and conviction of person or persons who brutally murdered Nicholas McCormick on August 25th, about three miles from Tombstone.

Copper Queen Cons. Min. Co.

To Let

Furnished house, four rooms, completely furnished, including a piano, $15 per month to a respectable party. Apply bank of Tombstone.

• Game as wild as a tornado, chicken as tender as a maiden's heart, ice cream as delicious as a day in June, dessert that would charm the soul of a South Sea Islander and smiles as bright as the morning sun will be found at the Can Can today.

• Exchange. A square grand piano in good order for a span of horses.

Stop!

At the Pony Saloon and try some of that fine Old Berry Bourbon Whisky, eight years old, and do not fail to call for some of that elegant Ripy Rye, six years old, the finest Rye Whisky in the world. I also make a specialty of hot drinks, consisting of Beef Tea, Hot Scotch, Hot New England, Hot Jamaica and Hot Santa Croix Rums. Also a fine line of imported wines and brandies and nothing but the best brands of Key West Cigars kept constantly on hand. I can assure the patrons of the Pony Saloon that these are the finest goods ever brought to Tombstone. Come and try them and you will be convinced.

Henry Campbell
Proprietor

• Scarlet flannel ladies vests and hosiery at the Bonanza Cash Store. Come early as they are going very fast.

$200 Reward

I will pay the above reward for the return of

Thomas Forget

Who escaped from the Cochise County jail on the evening of May 7th. Description: He is a man about 5 feet 6 inches high, a French Canadian 42 years of age; talks broken English, wears moustache and sideburns, dark complection, had on a pair of shoes.

John Slaughter
Sheriff Cochise County

Do you want a good meal,
And if so do you feel
That if such you could get you'd be smiling—
If you only could go
To a place where you know
That good food would round you be piling?

We can tell you a place
To which people all race—
That of all houses in town leads the van;
You can eat to your fill
And with hearty good will,
And the place is well known as the Can Can

Take Notice, Liar

Whoever started the rumor that we intended closing our shop, and going into partnership with Mr. Miano, is a liar, and he had better mind his own business.

Marks & Whittig

• 44 Winchester cartridges 75 cents per box at New York Store.

• Notice to Parents: Parents or the guardians of children must keep them from jumping on and off our ore teams, or we will not be responsible. J. E. Durkee & Co.

• For sale—Premises 918 Fremont Street, 65 foot front, containing one house of five rooms and two cabins. The five rooms furnished. Will sell the entire place for $200, or without furniture for $150. A big bargain. Call at once.

Reward

I am authorized by the City Council to offer a reward of $25 for information that will lead to the arrest of the parties who have been in the habit of hauling dead animals and leaving them inside of the city limits, or $50 for the conviction of anyone who may hereafter do the same.

C. N. Thomas, Mayor

• Notice: The Tombstone Wholesale Butcher Association will pay five cents a pound for good fat beef cattle.

•A man may want a Poker game, Billiards, Pool, or say! if he should want to play Seven Up to the Fashion he'll wend his way.

• If you want to purchase Louisiana Lottery tickets call on Stevenson & Walker, the accredited agents in this city.

• "Congratulate me dear, I am engaged to my soul's idol," said a well known society girl to her bosom friend yesterday; "and just look at this superb solitaire which he gave me as a token." "Oh, isn't it lovely" said her companion, "where was it purchased?" "Why at Seamans & Son's, the Allen street jewelers who keep such an elegant assortment of jewels, etc. Of course."

• For fifty cents in silver one can get enough chicken and ice cream at the Can Can to give he or she the stomach ache for a week.

• A nice line of gents' white vests at Sydow & Kieke's.

• Artistic barbers at the Occidential Tonsorial Parlors.

TO NEWSPAPER MEN

We have, lying at Benson, Arizona, a complete outfit for a 7 column newspaper, including a fine Washington Hand Press. The outfit cost new, a few months ago, $900; will be sold for $600 cash. It is all packed, ready for shipment. Apply to

Miller & Richard
Scotch Type Foundry,
San Francisco, Cal.

1889—THE WEEKLY HERALD—1889
One Dollar a Year
to keep posted on
News of the Entire World
Subscribe for The
NEW YORK WEEKLY HERALD
It is and Will Continue to be the
Greatest and Cheapest Family Journal
In the United States
The coming year promises to be crowded with stirring events.

In the United States the entrance of new issues into the political arena has been followed by a change of administration. But the great economic question on which the campaign turned is still unsettled, and its solution is now committed to Congress, almost equally divided between the two great parties.

Europe is a vast camp. Army corps patrol the frontiers, and millions of men await the signal for the most titanic war the world has seen.

The Herald's news gathering machinery is unequalled. Its correspondents dot the habitable globe. Nothing can escape their vigilance, and no expense is spared in spreading the results of their efforts before Herald readers.

THE NEWS OF AMERICA
Will be found each week in the Herald, while its

FOREIGN DEPARTMENT
Will contain a panorama of the Old World, flashed under the sea over the

COMMERCIAL CABLES
Special Features
Practical Farming, Progress in Science, Woman's Work, Notable Pulpit Utterances, Literature and Art, Stories by Some of Our Best Authors

COMPLETE INFORMATION ON ALL SUBJECTS
Address James Gordon Bennett
New York Herald
New York.

7 Fire and Storm

Two things were feared far more by Tombstone than gunfights, killings, and graves on Boot Hill. One of them was fire and the other was what the *Epitaph* called "a severe agitation of nature."

Fire wiped the business section of the camp out twice in less than a year. An earthquake shook it, a cyclone swept it, and lightning played fatal tricks around it. So Tombstone made heroes of its volunteer firemen, and kept its eyes on the skies for signs of trouble.

The first great fire came when the *Epitaph* was little more than a year old and was caused, strangely enough, by the town's favorite beverage. A barrel of whiskey exploded on a bright June afternoon and before suppertime four square blocks of buildings were smoking ruins.

The *Epitaph's* story is retold here.

BAPTISM OF FIRE

An Era in the History of Tombstone
That Will Never Be Forgotten

Yesterday after noon Tombstone received her first baptism of fire and one that will be long remembered. The day was one of those exceptionally fine ones that come occasionally to make the heart glad. There was just a faint zephyr blowing from a few points north of west that tempered the otherwise heated atmosphere. People were all engaged in their usual avocations and as unsuspecting of the calamity that was to overwhelm the utterly helpless city as the babe unborn. It came like a clap of thunder and spread with a celerity unparalleled.

How It Occurred

Messrs. Alexander & Thompson, proprietors of the Arcade saloon on Allen street, three doors above the Oriental saloon, on the corner of Allen and Fifth had a barrel of liquor that had been condemned by them for a long time which they intended to re-ship and as fate would have it they had a team ready to take it away at this time. They rolled it out in front of the bar and knocked out the bung for the purpose of measuring the quantity in the package. Mr. Alexander, in putting the gauge rod into the barrel accidentally let it slip from his fingers into the same. His bartender got a wire to fish it out and came to the front with a lighted cigar in his mouth, one report says, and another that he lighted a match for some purpose, when the escaping gas caught fire and communicated with the liquor which caused an instantaneous explosion, scattering the burning contents in all directions. There were two men in the saloon at the time besides Mr. Hazelton the bartender. Their names L. L. Sales and David Cotter. Mr. Sales says the concussion was terrific. The three escaped through the backdoor exit through the front being effectually blocked by the flames. Almost by a miracle they escaped unhurt. In less than three minutes the flames had communicated with the adjoining buildings and spread with a velocity equalled only by a burning prairie in a gale. The heated condition of the woodwork assisted the devouring element in its rapid spread. This, as also the Vizina & Cook block on the corner was an adobe building. It was ceiled with cloth which acted as tinder for communicating the flame.

The Alarm Given

Seemingly, instantaneously with the bursting of the flames through the door into Allen street the alarm spread and people rushed to the scene, but lack of facilities for extinguishing the fire gave it time to spread to adjoining buildings. Before anything could be done to check it the store of Meyers Brothers, Glover & Co., and the Occidental were all ablaze. The firemen were promptly on hand but they were almost as powerless as the citizens, with only this difference, they had a head which they implicitly obeyed. The first thing was to save books, money and valuables by those whose premises were on fire, which was only partially done. It is said a demand was made on Meyers Brothers and Tucker & Pridham for blankets wet and put over the adjoining buildings which was peremptorily refused and this resource for fighting the fire was thus summarily cut off. The moment the alarm was given Mr. M. B. Clapp, manager of Safford, Hudson & Co.'s bank rushed all money and valuables into the inner safe—the books being taken outside to a safe place—and proceeded to lock everything up. While locking the outer door the plastering began to fall around his head and he escaped, after having performed his last duty, by the back door the front being inaccessable from the flames. Joyce, of the Oriental saloon, rushed to his safe, the outer door of which was unlocked and made an effort to unlock the inner to get the cash box out but the flames came sweeping through with such fury that he had to flee for his life, leaving over $1200 in greenbacks, no gold or silver—of his own money besides a large amount of deposits. He did not save a farthing's worth of anything.

The Burned District

Thus far we have only touched upon the first incidents of the origin of the fire which all told did not occupy more than five minutes in transpiring so rapid was the progress of the work of destruction. The firemen, assisted by the people, all of whom gave freely, fully and voluntarily of their energies in herculean efforts to check the flames. At once the demolishing of awnings, porches, et cetera began, as they were found to be the great elements for spreading the flames. The heat of the fire—added to that of the sun—the thermometer standing 100 degrees in the shade at 4 o'clock, made it impossible to get within reasonable distance of the points most available for checking the flames. All was hurry and confusion among those in the line of destruction. One of the first acts of self-abnegation was that of Wells Spicer, whose office was on Fifth street. After saving his official and private papers he gave orders to demolish the building which was a frame—as were the majority in the burned district. The work immediately began but the fire came sweeping down upon them so rapidly but little more than tearing down the porch was accomplished before they had to abandon the work and go to another outpost. In spite of the herculean efforts the fire swept onward to Fremont street on the north and crossed over Allen on the south burning in its eastward course across to Toughnut street reaching as far as Seventh where, owing to the number of vacant lots it was stopped. On the north side of Fremont street the fire was prevented from spreading by the use of wet blankets and water constantly dashed upon the fronts of the buildings. Schaffer & Lord ordered the broad porch around two sides of their store to be demolished at an early stage, and by playing a stream of water from the hose attached to the water pipes connected with the store the fire was kept at bay,

By 6 p. m. the fury of the flames had spent itself and nothing remained but the charred and ghastly skeletons of the adobe buildings while here and there thirsty tongues of flame would break forth as if the greedy element, not satisfied with having consumed everything in its course, still craved for more.—(June 23, 1881.)

The *Epitaph* carried a list of sixty-six stores, saloons, restaurants, and business houses and an estimate of the damage. The total loss was set at $175,000, of which only $25,000 was covered by insurance.

For some reason the *Epitaph* gave little attention to the swift rebuilding of the business district although it must have been a considerable achievement.

There was timber in the mountains and adobe blocks could be made on the spot, but all other building materials and furnishings had to be brought in from Tucson.

The probability is that the editor was merely pursuing his policy of ignoring news which might discourage the investment of new capital and an increase in population.

If this was the reason, then the *Epitaph* found it less than sufficient for playing down the next disaster which came a year later, when a second and greater fire practically wiped out the town.

This time the editor told the full story and though his account was flamboyant as the flames themselves it makes the scene vivid even today.

THE FIRE

Tombstone's Devastation

THE FIRE KING REAPS A HARVEST

The Heart of the City Destroyed
Scenes and Incidents of the Great Conflagration
The Losses—Individual Sufferers
Building Will Commence Today

FULL PARTICULARS OF THE FIRE

Once again has the fiery demon of destruction spread his baleful wings over the fateful town of Tombstone, and once again within a year has the bonanza camp been visited by the fiery scourge. Yesterday morning the bright sun rose over as happy and prosperous a camp as any on the Pacific coast. Ere the God of day sank behind the western hills a scene of desolation and destruction met the eye in every direction. The blackened walls and smoking ruins of what were once handsome and beautiful buildings is all that remains of what was the very heart of Tombstone. The business portion of the town has been destroyed and many a man and woman too, who yesterday was in affluent circumstances, find themselves today reduced to poverty. The baleful fates which seem to hover over us, have once more thrown a deadly blight on our progress and prosperity. But despite the frowns of Fortune the bonanza city will rise Phoenix-like from its ashes and in a few short weeks what are now smouldering ruins will be built up and ready for business. Below we give a succinct account of the origin and progress of the great fire. No pen can describe the scenes and incidents of the fearful conflagration. The fiery flames rose high in the heavens while dense volumes of smoke obscured the light of day, and made Tombstone look like a hell on earth. The shrieks of women, and the imprecations of men, the mad rushing of vehicles, and the indescribable confusion, was a scene long to be remembered. The Epitaph office had a close call but thanks to the indomitable exertions of our gallant fire department, and the untiring exertions of our gallant printer boys, we are enabled to present to our readers this morning a full account of

The Fire

which started in a water closet in the rear of the Tivoli saloon on Allen street. It soon communicated with the framework of the "garden" in rear of the saloon. The wood being dry it ignited and burned with the rapidity of cotton. Numerous shanties surrounded the burning pile. Closets, kitchens, storerooms, on the rear, with the wood trimmings on the adobe walls in front, the flames were easily fed. The sumptuous apartments of the Tombstone club in the Grand Hotel building were among the first to kiss the flames; the general building of the Grand Hotel was next embraced in the fiery arm; the wooden staircase on the outside of the building in the rear fell

An Easy Victim.

Next the window frames were taken in and the flames communicated to the interior, and carpets, floors, furniture, etc., fed the fiery elements. An Epitaph reporter, immediately after the alarm of fire, and before the department was yet on the ground, climbed to the top of the adobe building in rear of the Grand Hotel. A glance was sufficient to convince that the fire would be of enormous extent. All the surroundings were particularly adapted to flame food. In less than fifteen minutes the entire space between Fourth and Fifth streets and Allen and Toughnut was one steaming, smoking, blazing mass of desolation and ruin. The firemen, than whom no braver body of men or more worthy of thanks exist, turned their attention to the herculean task of saving the north side of the street. But it was impossible.

The Firemen

fronted the flames until most of them were scorched, and finally doggedly retreated to keep up their contest in another quarter. The flames spread rapidly. Soon the Occidental saloon was enveloped, the Alhambra soon followed, and the mad sea of vicious fire spread on each side to the Cosmopolitan Hotel on the West, and the Eagle Brewery on the east. Hafford's saloon was soon a seething mass of flames. Brown's hotel followed suit, and the fire ere many minutes had the Fourth street gun store safely in its arms. Here a scene was presented magnificent in its

Lurid Fierce Grandeur.

A large quantity of powder was stored in the cellars, and a number of cartridges and other explosive material were in the store. Here, as soon as the flames were communicated to the combustibles, a wild scene presented itself. The loud bursting of cartridges, the bursting of powder, added to the shouting of men and timid screams of women made the air horrible with their resounding echoes. But

The Heart of Tombstone

was doomed. None but visionary enthusiasts hoped that anything but the straggling suburbs could be saved. But hope beats high in the human breast, and the gallant firemen, aided by the police, under Chief Neagle, and a number of deputies under Sheriff Behan, struggled manfully to stem the storm. The wind was not blowing an extraordinary gale, and only the fiery elements had to be fought. The flames reached Fremont and rapidly spread across the entire distance between 4th and 5th streets. At the corner of 5th and Allen a noble struggle took place. The fiery elements with gaunt, hungry arms thirsted to cross the street and

Capture the Oriental.

Here the firemen got in their best work. It was a pitched battle. The weak water and the impetuous onset of the flames made it almost certain that the latter would conquer. But Blackburn rallied his gallant little fire company, a steady stream was poured on and the gaudy destroyer was beaten. Joyce, who suffered so heavily in the former fire came off in this instance with moderate damage. His loss will be about a couple of thousand dollars. All the liquors he had on hand he distributed to the gallant defenders of the city, and his house is much gutted up with the water strewn, the porch torn down and most of his glassware either broken, lost or destroyed. But the

Flames Swept Onward.

Fourth street was crossed, the clothing house of Levinthall on the corner of Fourth and Allen was enveloped. The Nugget office was reached and quickly swept from the face of the earth. The other buildings on the same block were quickly swept away. It reached Fremont on that side, but thanks to the combined efforts of firemen, deputy sheriffs, police and citizens, the fire was conquered. The backbone of the fell destroyer was broken and the west end of the block bounded by Third street was saved. The postoffice went. Schieffelin Hall, the Gird building and the Epitaph were in momentary danger. The Epitaph staff rallied like gallant sailors on a well-beloved ship, removed the material promptly, and rallied valiantly with buckets to save the building. Their efforts were successful and the Epitaph still holds forth to disseminate the daily news of the world, defend the right and condemn the wrong.

The Losses

are considerable, and will foot up perhaps five hundred thousand dollars, with a probable insurance of half that amount. There are several severely wounded by falling timbers, walls or scorches, but only one death. The unfortunate victim is unknown. His charred remains were found in the rear of the Cosmopolitan hotel after the flames had subsided.—(May 27, 1882.)

The *Epitaph* carried five and one-half columns of solid, handset type on the fire, including a complete list of the individual losses, and the insurance carried on the property.

But it had space for one of its best editorials, with which it closed the news account of the disaster. It follows.

> Such has been the effects of the most destructive conflagration that has yet visited Tombstone. Its depressing effect on the camp cannot be denied, but we feel sure that the depression will be only temporary and that the burnt district will be rebuilt and in a more solid and substantial manner than ever before. Already preparations are being made for the erection of fireproof structures. So long as the marvelous mines of this camp continue to send forth their treasure, so long will the town of Tombstone exist and flourish. Although it may experience many a setback, the wealth which lies hidden in the treasure vaults which surround it will give life, vim and vigor to its people. Their buoyant spirits and unconquerable energies will rise above the accidents of fortune, and their manhood and untiring energy are bound to command success. Although there is today many an aching heart in our city, let them remember that the darkest hour is just before the dawn, and that while we have experienced a temporary disaster, the sun of our future prosperity shines as bright as ever, so let us be of good cheer. Let us rely upon and lend a helping hand to each other. The resources which have built up the most flourishing camp in the territory are still here, and will yet make this town of Tombstone the Virginia City of the southwest.* Let us not repine about the past which cannot be recalled; but let us resolutely turn our faces to the future which makes all things even.

A week later the *Epitaph* acknowledged the receipt of $180 "to provide medicines and necessaries for the firemen wounded in the late flames." But it accompanied this with a polite note from the chief of the department, who refused the contribution, "being not in need of pecuniary assistance and believing as firemen, it was our duty to accept the consequences of the fire, however serious."

* A territorial census taken at this time gave Tombstone a population of 5,300.

In the same spirit the *Epitaph,* in its issue of June 3, said an editorial word to Arizona citizens.

"While the people of Tombstone sincerely thank those citizens of the territory who have proffered assistance, they wish it to be understood that they are in no need of aid. No one is suffering on account of the fire, and if there was, our citizens are both able and willing to take care of them."

There spoke the spirit of Tombstone and the *Epitaph.* The spirit which has met a hundred reverses and fights back "with strokes of controversy."

This time the *Epitaph* waited a month and then it reported that the work of rebuilding was proceeding rapidly.

THE WORK OF REBUILDING

Progress Made in One Month After the Great Fire

One month ago yesterday the fire fiend desolated Tombstone. The heart of the city was burned out, business prostrated and enterprise blocked. We can now even, imagine the flames speeding across Allen street, and the firemen making their gallant stand at Joyce's corner. It was impossible to witness the awful scene without being impressed with the savage grandeur. Who that heard the screaming of women, that witnessed the trembling of men, and saw the lurid flames spreading havoc and destruction on that dreadful day could believe that Tombstone was possessed of such Roman firmness as to again be rebuilt one month after? Who that witnessed the wholesale destruction of property, that saw valuable goods piled on the street at the mercy of the vagabond, that saw the aimless almost desperate look on men's faces, and the silent tear laving the cheeks of women, could suppose than one month from the date thereof a more substantial city [Note: Here a tear in the page destroys this sentence] determination of our people that such a monster calamity could not discourage them? Is it not a convincing proof that they who know Tombstone best have unlimited confidence in its resources and perpetuity? With the exception of Fourth street that portion of our city ravaged by flames is now rebuilt, or on the end of being so, and in no instance is there a less substantial structure than formerly.—(July 1, 1882.)

Tombstone's trouble in fighting fires was lack of pressure in its water mains. When they finally overcame this, it was too late to halt the second disaster, but it did stop a third fire which might have easily wiped out all the work of rebuilding. The *Epitaph* account features the strong streams thrown through the nozzles of the fire companies.

WEDNESDAY'S BLAZE

A Fierce Battle With the Flames—A Young Man Seriously Burned—Hurrah for Huachuca Water.

At ten minues past eleven Wednesday night the whistle of the Vizina hoisting works puffed for the alarm of fire. Instantly an excited crowd of people assembled at the scene of the conflagration at the corner of Fourth and Toughnut streets. Already the desolating flames were waving hither and thither, engulphing everything that touched them in their fierce embrace. The fire started in a bedroom attached to the New Orleans restaurant, kept by Mrs. Jones. The building, being constructed of light lumber and parched with drought, accepted the flames with the same readiness as loose cotton. The adjoining building, the truck house of the Rescue hook and ladder company was soon enveloped by the desolating element and for a while it seemed as if the dreadful scenes of destruction and ruin that were witnessed less than two months ago were about to be repeated. On Fourth street a scene of wild confusion prevailed. Women with bare feet and scanty clothing were darting from the burning building; excited men jostled each other hither and thither; furniture was strewn on the streets, law books went flying through the air, costly tableware was trampled underfoot and everything chaos and hopelessness. The headway made by the flames was the assurance that destruction must ensue. The fierce, proud, destructive monster of flame, under the impulse of a slight breeze, jumped fifty feet high, bending sideways in the descent and lashing the adjoining buildings. Seven minutes after the first alarm of fire the Engine Company had a stream on the flames. The excited crowd awaited in silent agitation the effect of a stream from the new water works. A glance taught them that the water was boss, and a shout of joy and thanks and praise rent the air. The Engine Company never performed better service. With good water power they showed what mettle they were made of.

Two streams were turned on, one from Toughnut and the other from Fourth. A few dashes of water extinguished the flames and heeding not the torturing smoke, the gallant fire boys entered the building, extinguishing the flames as they went, until they reached the rear of the building, the point from which the flames were being fed. They were now in the center of the partially demolished structure. A few gushes of the powerful water against the ceiling, bored a hole through the roof, thus allowing the stream to pass through and fall in graceful ease on the igniting top of the building. Twenty minutes after the first alarm the fire was extinguished, and it was as well performed a piece of work as could be done by the crack fire department of the United States. Dr. McSwegan gave the alarm and he is loud in praise of the engineer of the Vizini on account of his promptness in sounding the general alarm. The origin of the fire is unknown but is supposed to be either accident or carelessness.

The most serious matter connected with it, is the serious, perhaps fatal burning of Billy Fee. This young man had his trunk and clothes in a room in the burning building, and recklessly rushed in to try and save his property. Before he could do so he was completely enveloped in the flames, and all avenues of escape cut off. A friend of his who accompanied him, deserted him in his peril and escaped unhurt, and Fee, with tenacity and pluck, that cannot be too highly commended, struggled and fought and pushed and climbed, surrounded by the burning flames that were eating into his flesh, and the suffocating smoke scarcely worse, until he regained the highway. He was borne to the Sunnyside lodging house and Dr. Blackwood summoned to render medical assistance. He was fearfully burned, the flesh being blistered and the skin almost burned off and his face scorched horribly.

The doctor attended to his wants as well as possible, but at midnight could not say whether the patient could recover.

The principal losers are Mrs. Jones, the restaurant keeper, who was not insured, and Webster Smith, the well known lawyer, whose furniture and library were much damaged by the hasty removal. The building is owned by Jordan Peters, who was fully insured. The loss at this time is almost impossible to determine, but it will certainly be not less than $5,000. The truck house of the Hook and Ladder Company, was also demolished, and clothes and other articles belonging to some of the members destroyed. There were also a number of individual losses of clothing and valuables, almost impossible to compute at the present time.—(July 22, 1882.)

Still clear in the minds of the older residents of southern Arizona is the memory of the day when the mountains trembled.

There is no *Epitaph* issue for this day but its contemporary, the *Prospector,* with which it later consolidated, reports the earthquake lasted thirty-five seconds.

Outside of cracks in the walls of some buildings, Tombstone for once escaped damage. Walls wavered, clocks stopped, and the citizens were frightened but that was all.

Probably from sheer relief at their escape, the *Prospector* took this "severe agitation of nature," lightly. The story was brief.

EARTHQUAKE

Everyone Runs Out in the Street.
The Movement Up and Down.

At six minutes past three this afternoon a severe shock of earthquake was felt in this city. At first as a reporter of the PROSPECTOR was sitting at his desk, he thought it was a heavy ore team or freight wagon running away, and stepped to the door to see if he could catch an item, when some one hollered earthquake which was good news for the poor reporter, who immediately pulled out his watch and counted the seconds while it lasted and by his timepiece it lasted about 35 seconds. After the first shock was over he began rummaging around for particulars. The first man he met was Palmer Seamans, who said it was a dandy—it stopped all the clocks in his store.

Proceeding on further everyone that the reporter met, in one voice said, there's an item.

The second shock occurred about eight minutes later, but was very slight, just causing the people to step out in the street, and lasted about two seconds. The third shock was hardly felt, it occurred about fifteen minutes of four o'clock.

Notes

A lady walking up Fremont street feeling the shock fainted, but soon recovered.

Several of the girl school children fainted but the reporter did not ascertain their names.

The walls of the Occidental hotel waved a little but they proved to be solid.

The plaster on the outside of the San Jose House was cracked, and some of it peeled off.

Several bottles in Peto's drug store were shaken from the shelves.

Mr. W. D. Monmonier at the time of the shock was in the lodge room at Schieffelin hall, and was struck in the head by a hook that was shaken from the wall, but was not injured.

Shortly after the shock in this city, Supt. Clark of the Huachuca Water Company, received through the company's telephone word from Mr. Kimball, who is stationed at the company's reservoirs at the Huachuca mountains, that the shock lasted fully three minutes, and that if the reservoirs had been full they would have been badly damaged; but as it was they were all right.

The north wall of Schieffelin hall is badly cracked.

Up to the hour of going to press it was not learned how the shock was felt in the mines.

Our citizens were very badly scared.

Most every clock in town was stopped.— (May 3, 1887.)

The *Prospector's* correspondent at Bisbee, twenty-six miles away, told of a very different experience in his town. The camp lay, as it does today, at the bottom of a canyon, and boulders rolled down the steep walls for ten minutes with reports like cannon shots. Miraculously, the town escaped death and disaster, but the nerves of the inhabitants must have been frayed. Here is the story.

BISBEE, May 3, 1887—There were some heavy shocks of earthquake here this afternoon. They commenced at 3 o'clock and 12 minutes and lasted something like ten minutes. From the first sound they seemed as if heavy artillery had turned loose. The mountains shook to their very center and the stones came tumbling down their sides as if they were likely to split from base to crown. It was a most sublime scene. The rocks falling from the mountains raised clouds of dust and the rumbling was as of distant cannon, and followed by three light shocks at different intervals. The shocks seemed to come from the northwest. There were about six of us here who saw the grand phenomenon as it passed. At Carr's stable the shock was so hard as to break the lantern chimney and the houses rocked as a cradle and the glass rattled in the windows at a fearful rate. There have been heavy reports since and what is going to come next is hard to tell.

Yours truly,
W. F. BANNING

Two days later ranchers rode into Tombstone from a valley twenty miles away and reported what was, for Arizona, nothing less than a miracle. An enormous geyser had spouted forth in the desert. This is their story.

Messrs. Storms and Abbot came in from the latter's ranch today upon inquiry of a reporter in regard to the rush of water in the Sulphur Springs valley that was caused by the earthquake, stated that it was immense, and that just after the shock on the plain about one and a half miles from C. S. Abbott's house the water shot up into the air to a considerable height, about 4 or 5 feet in width, and extended fully 100 feet in distance. Messrs. Storms and Abbott left the ranch today and stated that the flow of water was decreasing very fast, but for miles the plains were covered with water, so much so as to wade their horses through. —(May 5, 1887.)

Having lived through two disastrous fires, an earthquake, and underground floods in the mines, the *Epitaph* was inured to anything.

So when Tombstone was unroofed by a cyclone it took this visitation in its stride. It even smiled a little over the fact that the carrier boy's papers blew away. The subscribers had to wait a day for this story.

A CYCLONE

Strikes Tombstone on the Bias Doing Considerable Damage

An Arizona cyclone, which though a harsh name for it is a just one, visited Tombstone last night about sundown. It approached in the direction of South Pass from the Dragoon mountains, and could be seen ten miles distant. It resembled a huge ball of earth propelled by some unseen force, which would roll over the ground, gathering fresh force and substance with each revolution. It was a most peculiar and awful sight. As it neared the town it grew dark and ominous, and when it struck the upper portion of the city there was no doubt as to its identity. It was a real live cyclone. The dirt and gravel which it had carried for miles was distributed in all directions. The center of its force struck the neighborhood of Sixth and Allen streets. The large building on the south side formerly used as a carpenter shop was leveled to the ground. The awning on the Allen street side of Atchinson's former tin shop was thrown into the street. The big sign in front of Kohler's was blown away. The roof of the old Silver City Stables was blown off and scattered throughout the block, smashing in roofs and causing people to run from their buildings in wonder and fright. The kitchen in the rear of Hattich's tailoring establishment was entirely demolished. In other parts of the city the storm, although not quite so severe, was bad enough. The last of the beautiful cottonwood trees in Frank Moore's yard on Third street was uprooted and leveled to the ground. The porch in front of Dr. Goodfellow's office was almost razed; the heavy posts that support it were lifted out into the street where they barely supported the heavy weight above. Tribolet's corral below town was leveled to the earth and one hundred head of steers, which had just been purchased, were scattered in all directions this morning.

The paper was out a little late last night, and the burro on which the carrier delivers the outside route was nearly lifted from his feet; the papers which were carried in pockets for that purpose were blown off the saddle and two hundred Prospectors went flying down the street toward Pick Em Up, much to the consternation of the carrier, who had just started out and the loss of valuable information to subscribers who did not get their paper.—(July 29, 1889.)

One year after the cyclone passed, Tombstone was washed by a flood of rain such as no living resident had seen before.

Even a light rain can cause fearsome floods on an Arizona desert in a matter of minutes and though the camp was spread out on a shelf of hills, foothills too may be swept by flash floods, which roar down their slopes with tremendous force.

The *Epitaph* was particularly jocular about this affliction although the damage done to the district was considerable, and the caption it carried over the story seems, at least, inadequate.

TUESDAY NIGHT'S STORM

The storm Tuesday night proved to be the most severe ever known in this part of Arizona. Reports from outside districts show the rainfall to have been enormous, and in many places the hail was terrific, destroying fruits, melons, vines and plants wherever it fell. Nearly every gulch of any size shows a watermark of from eight to twenty-five feet, and in many places bedrock that has not been exposed since the year one is now uncovered. Adobe walls and buildings melted down like sand and left only a mass of mud and debris. So far no loss of human life is reported, but much stock was drowned, in one place on the San Pedro river several horses and cattle that were corraled being swept entirely away.

The San Pedro has ceased to be a river and is a moving sea of raging and foaming waters, carrying everything within its reach—fences, corrals, trees, orchards, gardens, and in many cases stables and farming implements. No such flood was ever known before and many people who prayed for rain during the dry season are beginning to think their prayers are being answered to a greater extent than is necessary.

The Brady house at Pick-em-up, a short distance from the city, had about eighteen inches of mud on the floor and there is no danger of falling down the well.

The roof of Mr. Bracken's house was lifted and he got a plunge bath.

Fred Castle incautiously left his transom open, and early yesterday morning was observed in negligee costume, with the bottoms rolled up, using a bailing bucket and naughty words.

Col. Hafford lost an adobe wall twelve by sixty feet but saved his temper.

It is estimated that it will be three weeks before the trains are running from Benson to Fairbank.—(Aug. 7, 1890.)

Lightning was one of nature's manifestations which was always sure of attention in the *Epitaph*. If a house was struck but the occupants escaped injury it was featured as a miraculous intervention. No bolt fell in the town without being noted by the editor.

Oddly enough there were many narrow escapes; and some deaths, and lightning did play strange tricks around the Tombstone hills. So the *Epitaph* editors were probably displaying good news judgment. In fact, all of the five stories which follow would be used by an alert editor today.

Strange Weather Phenomena Visits Tombstone New Year's Eve

A strange weather phenomena occurred in Tombstone with the dying of the old year and the birth of the new. Tombstone was enveloped in a mantle of snow—in itself an unusual visitation—but the strangest caprice of the weather clerk was to follow. Precisely at the hour of 12 o'clock, during the fiercest of the storm a single terrific flash of lightning illuminated the entire heavens, while within a few seconds a heavy peal of thunder followed. The peculiar combination of snow, lightning and thunder, with no sign of rain and the added coincidence of occurring at just 12 o'clock, caused much comment, and by the more timid and superstitiously inclined was regarded as a portending omen of some kind. The new year revelers, however, accepted it as a celestial signal for the ushering in of the new year and following the annual custom a regular fusillade of pistol shots, ringing of fire bells and blowing of steam whistles, announced the dawn of the new year.

Narrow Escape From Lightning

During a rain storm at Dos Cabezas the other day Judge and Mrs. T. B. Stark had a narrow escape from death by lightning while driving to their ranch from Dos Cabezas. A heavy thunderstorm accompanied the rain and suddenly a bolt of lightning struck the Stark conveyance, both horses dropping dead on the spot. Judge Stark was not injured but for a time it was feared that his wife was shocked beyond recovery. Her clothing caught fire, but the flames were quickly extinguished. She was carried unconscious to the home ranch of the Riggs Cattle company where she quickly recovered.

• A telephone message was received this morning from St. David announcing the fact that during the rain storm which visited that section last evening, a cowboy named Webb, was struck by a bolt of lightning and instantly killed as was his horse. From what can be learned of the accident, Webb was engaged in rounding up a bunch of cattle between the Stone House and St. David, and when the storm broke he was making for the ranch when he was struck by a bolt of lightning that took his life as well as that of his horse.

The only marks on the body of Webb was a black streak down his spinal column which indicated the course of the lightning. On the horse a big scar was burned on the top of its head and another mark along its back.

• There have been several deaths caused by lightning in this territory during the recent storms. Another death, which occurred several days ago, has been reported in which the curious pranks which may be practiced by the fluid are well illustrated.

A cowboy by the name of Lacey was riding on the range in Tonto Basin, when a storm came up. A bolt of lightning struck him on the back between the shoulders. The current traveled down his body and escaped through his feet. The skin was burned where the current had struck the man. The heels of both shoes had been burned off, but the socks the man wore were uninjured. His heavy spurs had been melted enough by the electricity to twist them all out of shape. But perhaps the strangest thing of all was that the horse he was riding escaped without injury, and was found wandering around with the saddle on.

• The heavy storm last night did not confine its damage to Tombstone, but in the Dragoon mountains it was terrific. Lightning struck on the high peak just to the right of middle pass, tearing a passage way through the massive rocks and rolling an immense boulder down the mountain side which in its descent tore trees and smaller rocks from their anchorage and traveled at least a mile and a half before losing its force. Our informant was an eye witness to the scene, and is a Mexican woodchopper who was on his way to town. He declares that the boulder was as large as the City Hall when it started on its course, but in striking against the solid foundation which crops from the mountain side, it was broken into several pieces, the largest of which when it stopped would weigh at least a hundred tons.—(Aug. 9, 1889.)

Although most modern editors are weather conscious, very few of them work in offices which command breathtaking views of mountains and deserts. Approaching changes in the weather may, therefore, escape them or it may be they have no time to dwell upon the probable significance of the appearance of the sky. They can have the cub reporter call the weather bureau.

But the editor of the *Epitaph* needed only to glance out a window to see if there was a possible news story brewing thirty miles away. And he was his own weatherman. The result was that there were few weeks in which such comments as these failed to appear in the old journal.

> • The atmosphere yesterday was hazy and dull looking all day and continued throughout the night. The temperature has been the same for several days. A few clouds were visible at intervals yesterday, but soon disappeared. The air is heavily laden with electricity and gives a sense of stillness next preceding a severe agitation of nature. The opinion is prevalent of an approaching calamity—either a disastrous storm or a severe shock of earthquake. The setting sun last evening appeared of a deep red color and was observed by many people until he disappeared behind the mountains. All nature seemed in a state of suspense.
>
> • The western sky presented an unusual sight last evening. The atmosphere was extremely hazy and the sun appeared like a dark red ball against a leaden colored background. Oldtimers predict an earthquake or a severe storm.

8 The "Cow-Boy" Curse

We call them gangsters today, but in 1880, 1881, and 1882 the country spoke of the lawless frontiersmen in southeastern Arizona as the "cow-boys."

For two years this element ran wild in a series of daring and ruthless murders, killings, stage robberies, and wholesale cattle rustling that centered the attention of the nation on Tombstone.

Most of these desperadoes were members of organized gangs. Charleston and Galeyville, two small settlements, were their favorite hangouts, but they rode the trails to the bright lights of Tombstone so often that they kept the dust rising over the mesquite and greasewood.

The *Epitaph* and the *Nugget* disagreed over the Cowboys. While the *Epitaph* called such men a curse to the county and business, the *Nugget* belittled all attempts to control them. The San Francisco *Chronicle* finally called the *Nugget* "the cowboy organ."

County law enforcement officers were either unable or unwilling to break up the rings, and finally the acting governor of the territory called on Washington for aid.

The famous battle of the OK Corral, in which the legendary Earps killed three Cowboys in a gunfight, was the outgrowth and the culmination of this situation.

Many books have been written around Tombstone and this lawless period, but none of the authors had access to the early *Epitaph* stories which are reprinted here. All accounts, except *Helldorado,* written by Wm. M. Breakenridge, agree that the Cowboys were vicious, unprincipled thieves and murderers. Breakenridge, however, was a member of the sheriff's force, which the *Epitaph* charged was too friendly to the rustlers.

The files of the *Epitaph* give the best perspective, and only the *Epitaph* tells the final chapter—a proclamation in which President Arthur denounced the reign of terror and warned the territory that unless organized resistance to law ceased it might expect the Army to move in and take over Arizona.

The *Epitaph* first called attention to conditions on Oct. 20, 1880, in the following editorial.

> We understand that the Grand Jury brought in indictments the other day against two Mexicans, and when the cases were called in court the witnesses who had appeared before the jury were nowhere to be found, having probably packed up and started for the Magdalena feast. It appears to us that about enough of this kind of business has been going on in Pima County. [Note: Tombstone did not become the county seat of Cochise County until 1881.] Men are shot in the streets and the killers are turned loose because no evidence is brought before the Grand Jury to indict them; men are found dead in various places and a newspaper item is all that is known of the matter; indictments are found and no witnesses are at hand to convict.

In the same issue, the *Epitaph,* which was Republican in its politics, printed a communication from the Republican County Committee indicting the Democratic district attorney for failure to bring accused Cowboys to trial. The figures charge twenty-five homicides in a year, fifteen arrests, and but one trial. The committee's statement follows.

> DISTRICT ATTORNEY
>
> Hugh Farley, the Democratic candidate for District Attorney, is the present incumbent in that office and has held the position since the first of January, 1879. During his term of office there have been more than thirty homicides committed and crimes of all classes have been of frequent occurrence in Pima County. The use of the six-shooter has become so common as to be scarcely remarked and soon forgotten except by the unfortunate person against whom the argument was directed.
>
> From the first of October, 1879, to the opening of the present term of court, not less than twenty-five homicides have been committed in this county and fifteen persons have been confined in the Tucson jail awaiting investigation on a charge of murder. [Note: Tucson was then and is now the county seat of Pima

County.] Of this number not one has been convicted and but one has been tried. . . .

Quite a number of cattle thieves have been bound over to appear before the Grand Jury, and they have not appeared, and the Grand Jury left in ignorance of the evidence against them. There are cases where indictments have been made against cattle thieves and receivers of stolen cattle, and the indicted persons have not even been assigned and the indictments left to slumber in the pigeon holes of the clerk's office until time and dust have hidden them from view.

These facts are all of record. The records are open to the public, and any person who doubts or denies them may be convinced of their truth by examination.

Signed
Republican County Committee
Oct. 20, 1880

Late the next spring a cattle dealer got up enough courage to dare the vengeance of the Cowboys, and complained about them in a signed letter to the *Epitaph.*

Wholesome Truth

Editor Epitaph: I am not a growler or chronic grumbler, but I own stock, am a butcher and supply my immediate neighborhood beef, and to do so must keep cattle on hand, and do try to and could do so always if I had not to divide with unknown and irresponsible partners, viz: "Cow Boys," or some other cattle thieves. Since my advent into the territory and more particularly on the San Pedro River, I have lost 50 head of cattle by cattle thieves. I am not the only sufferer from these marauders and cattle robbers on the San Pedro, within the last six months. Aside from 50 head of good beef cattle that I have been robbed of, Judge Blair has lost his entire herd. P. McMinnimen has lost all of his finest fat steers (oxen). Dunbar at Tres Alamos, has lost a number of head. Burton of Huachuca, lost almost his entire herd, and others—and in fact all engaged in the stock business—have lost heavily from cattle thieves. And not always do these thieves confine themselves to cattle; horses and mules are gobbled up by these robbers, as well as cattle. Is there no way to stop this wholesale stealing of stock in this vicinity or in the county?

T. W. Ayles, Cattle Dealer.
March 18, 1881

Walter Noble Burns, author of the popular, romantic, and highly fictional book, *Tombstone,* devoted nine pages to a thrilling Cowboy tale which he called, "The Affair of Skeleton Canyon."

In this gory account of the ambushing of a Mexican pack train Burns say the Cowboys slaughtered nineteen Mexicans in cold blood and captured $75,000 in Mexican silver, which they later spent across the bars of Charleston and Galeyville.

The *Epitaph* says the ambush took place but puts the death list at four and the booty at $4,000.

An Interrupted Breakfast

Report comes to us of a fresh outrage perpetrated by the cow-boys in Sonora. Early last Monday morning a party of sixteen Mexicans from the interior of Sonora on their way to this Territory to purchase goods and carrying $4,000 for that purpose, stopped in a curve in the road at Los Animas, near Fronteras, to prepare their frugal breakfast. While busily engaged preparing their tortillas they were saluted with music of twenty rifles fired by cow-boys who lay in ambush awaiting them. The Mexicans took this as an invitation to leave and did not stand upon the order of their going but left all their mules and pack saddles in which they carried their money for the purchase of goods. When they stopped running they were at Fronteras and their party was four short. The missing men are supposed to have been killed. The citizens of Babispe and troops are after the cowboys and are disposed to take summary vengeance if they overtake them. —(Aug. 5, 1881.)

Two weeks later the *Epitaph* reported new depredations, including the story of a second attack on a Mexican pack train. Here the *Epitaph* gave the background of the gangs and described their field of operations.

The Murdering Cowboys
More Depredations by the "Rustlers"
An Attempt to Steal Cattle Frustrated—
Three Mexicans Attacked and Robbed.

News was brought to town yesterday of further depredations by a party of five men who are supposed to belong to the gang of outlaws infesting this country, calling themselves "Rustlers." They are principally from Western Texas and Lincoln County, New Mexico, from whence they have been driven by an outraged community and now seem to have found the place they long have sought where they can commit their depredations without fear of arrest. For a long time this gang have confined themselves and their operations to the east of Tombstone and along the line of Sonora, but seeing that no steps were taken for their arrest they have become emboldened to take up their haunts and perpetrate their depredations nearer the center of business and population. About half past three on Friday morning the son of Mr. Henning, who runs a milk ranch about three miles above Charleston, on the San Pedro, suspecting something wrong among the cows, which run on the bottom below the house, aroused the two Mexican herders and a party of campers—ten in number also Mexicans—and started down, when they found a couple of cow-boys gathering up the herd. Henning and his party being in the majority frightened them off and saved the stock. About 10:30 that same day a party of four gentlemen, who were coming to Tombstone, saw a couple of suspicious characters, who left the road when they saw the carriage and rode about forty rods towards the river, heading upstream until they were a safe distance past the carriage, when they rode back to the traveled road again. Both were armed with rifles in leather cases and were well mounted. One, a large man on a powerful bay horse, and the other a medium sized man on a dark sorrel horse with a white face. Shortly after passing these men the party in the carriage met three Mexicans who had a quantity of packages tied upon their saddles going up the San Pedro also. This party proved to be three of General Pesqueira's men from the Cananae, who had been to Tombstone and were taking out some supplies with them, as also $1,000 in gold and Mexican silver for the General. When the latter party got above Hereford and about half way to Ochonville, they were set upon by a party of five cow-boys, who fired, mortally wounding one of the Mexicans and killing one of the horses. They took a rifle and one package of goods and it is supposed killed the one who had the money as he had not, up to last evening, been seen or heard from since the encounter. It is said the Mexicans who escaped recognized one of the bandits having seen him in Tombstone the day before.

Grown bold with the deeds of crime they have committed between here and Deming and their merciless murders at Fronteras these outlaws, having no fears of the civil authorities, have taken up the San Pedro Valley as their headquarters, knowing that there is a large travel between Benson, Contention, Tombstone, Charleston and Bisbee, besides the Mexican travel from Sonora to these points. It will be seen from the foregoing that they have made a good beginning and unless immediate steps are taken by the citizens to rid the county of these outlaws, there will be no more protection to life and property between Benson and the Sonora line than there has been in the San Simon and eastward for the last year. When the civil authorities are insufficient or unwilling to protect a community the people are justified in taking the law into their own hands and ridding themselves of the dangerous characters who make murder and robbery their business. It remains to be seen how much longer such damnable acts as the Fronteras massacre and the San Pedro murders shall go unpunished.—(Aug. 13, 1881.)

The following day the *Epitaph* reported the theft of stock pastured inside the city limits. It added an editorial snapper to the story.

More Stock Stolen

Friday night Mr. Leopold Graff, who runs a freight team between this city and Benson, turned his stock out to graze in the east end of town, believing that the gang of horse thieves infesting this region would not dare to come so near to commit their depredations. He was mistaken, however, for in the night the stock was rounded up by two cow-boys and five mules and a horse run off. Some men engaged in hauling lumber from the Chirichua mountains encamped four miles out of town, saw the men and stock pass their camp at 2 o'clock yesterday morning. Now isn't it about time the people organized?—(Aug. 14, 1881.)

The financial welfare and expansion of Tombstone always came first with the *Epitaph*. In this serious editorial the *Epitaph* makes the point that unless the city can promise and deliver law and order it cannot expect venture capital from outside.

There are many things and causes which militate seriously against the internal improvement of our territory, even in the face of the potent fact that we possess in a large measure everything calculated to attract attention and win capital. The cause to which we especially allude is the fact that our people as a class have not that reverence for the law necessary to induce men of money to cast their lot with us in an earnest endeavor to develop our wonderful mining and stock raising resources. We may cry as we please about lawyers—those eaters of oysters and dividers of shells—but until we come to a just comprehension of the fact that civilized communities cannot exist without law and executed law at that, we cannot reasonably expect an influx of capital, which is always wary and circumspect. We do not mean to intimate that our people are less law-abiding than other frontiersmen, but we do mean to say that until a man's property is free from invasion, his person free from causeless attack, his character free from gratuitous slander we cannot hope for a change that will result in lasting prosperity to our county, our territory, our town. When capital learns that our county offers a promiseful interest on every investment in legitimate business; when the East and the West shall know that the arm of the law is as strong in Arizona as it is in Massachusetts or California; when the world shall know that our people, with one accord, demand a fair and just administration of the law, and individually endeavor to carry out its decrees, the rush of capital and capitalists will surprise our lethargy and wake us up to activity and fortunes.—(April 16, 1881.)

This warning to the citizens was followed by an editorial shot at the sheriff.

There is altogether too much good feeling between the Sheriff's office and the outlaws infesting this county.—(Aug. 19, 1881.)

On October 26, 1881, the Earps clashed with the Cowboys and killed one Clanton and two McLowrys. There was a sharp division of opinion over whether the Earps were justified, with the *Nugget* leading the Cowboy pack and its adherents in violent criticism.

Acting Governor John J. Gosper had meanwhile made a personal investigation of the breakdown of civil law in Tombstone. He also gathered statements from residents in the county and sent a report to the Secretary of State in Washington.

The *Epitaph* was slow in getting on the ball but when it did get the news it ran this story.

The Cow-Boy Scourge

Following is a portion of correspondence that has passed between acting Governor Gosper and the U. S. State Department, with letters appendant written by residents of Galeyville to the Governor. We apprehend this matter will give our law-abiding and peaceably disposed population food for serious reflection. If the officers of the law cannot, or will not protect the industrial portion of the community against the depredations of the great band of organized thieves and murderers classed under the generic name of cow-boys, the people will most assuredly protect themselves in the end.

Extract from a letter bearing date Sept. 30, 1881, from the governor of Arizona to the secretary of state:

. . . At Galeyville, San Simon and other points isolated from large places the cow-boy element at times very fully predominates, and the officers of the law at times either unable or unwilling to control this class of outlaws, sometimes being governed by fear, at other times by a hope of reward. At Tombstone, the County seat of Cochise county, I conferred with the sheriff of said county upon the subject of breaking up three bands of outlaws, and I am sorry to say he gave but little hope of being able in his department to cope with the power of the cow-boys. He represented to me that the deputy United States Marshal, resident of Tombstone, and the city marshal of the same, and those who aided him (the deputy marshal) seemed unwilling to heartily co-operate with him (the sheriff) in capturing and bringing to justice these outlaws. In conversing with deputy United States Marshal, Mr. Earp, I found precisely the same spirit of complaint existing against Mr. Behan (the sheriff) and his deputies. And back of this unfortunate fact, rivalry between the civil authorities, or an unwillingness to work together in full accord in keeping the peace, I found two daily newspapers published in the city taking sides with the deputy marshal and sheriff, respectively, each paper backing its civil clique and berating the other; and back of all this unfortunate fact that many of the very best law-abiding and peace-loving citizens have no confidence in the willingness of the civil officers to pursue and bring to justice that element of outlawry so largely disturbing the sense of security, and so often committing highway robbery and smaller thefts. . . .

Respectfully, your obedient servant,

John J. Gosper.

Galeyville, A. T. Sept. 1881

To His Excellency the Hon. John J. Gosper, Acting Governor Arizona Territory:—Dear Sir: In reply to your inquiry concerning the "cowboys" who are reported to have been and are still raiding the line of Sonora and Arizona, I will say: The gang who are known as "cowboys" are engaged in stock raising in the valley of San Simon and Cloverdale in the southeastern portion of Arizona, and from good authority I learn that the cattle, horses and sheep now controlled by said cowboys have been stolen from the citizens of Sonora and Arizona and New Mexico; they are reported to have about 300 head of cattle at or near Granite Gap in New Mexico and close to the line in Arizona. It is a well known fact that they are in the habit of making raids along the border. Until recently it has been the custom to steal cattle and horses in Arizona and drive them into Sonora for sale, and on the return trip steal stock in Sonora and drive them into Arizona and New Mexico for sale; Consequently quite a traffic was kept up. This practice has abated somewhat lately, on account of the killing of four cowboys at Fronteras in, I think, June last. The circumstances as near as can be obtained are these: Last spring, George Turner and M. McAllister, two well known cowboys, obtained the contract at Fort Bowie for furnishing beef for the command; they and two assistants went to Sonora to either buy or steal beef; they succeeded in driving a large herd as far as Fronteras, where they were attacked by the Mexican citizens. They [the cowboys] were all killed and one Mexican citizen was killed. Upon the bodies of Turner and McAllister was found the money which they ostensibly took to purchase cattle, which amount compared with what they are known here to have started out with proved that the cattle they were driving had not been paid for. This affair has caused bad blood between the cowboys and the citizens of Sonora, each party taking revenge upon the other whenever opportunity occurs; consequently it is unsafe for any person to travel across the border. About a month ago the cowboys went across the border into Sonora, and seeing a good-sized pack train in charge of Mexicans, laid in ambush and at the word of command, made a dash and succeeding in capturing the whole outfit, consisting of about $4,000 in Mexican silver bullion, mescal, horses and cattle. One of the cowboys in relating to me the circumstances said it was the d——st lot of truck he ever saw. He showed me a piece of the bullion; I should judge it to be one-half gold. Upon my telling him that trouble would likely arise from this, he replied that it was a smuggling train and they would not dare say much. There were three Mexicans killed in the affray. A notorious cowboy known as John R. [Note: obviously Johnny Ringo] offers to sell all the mutton the town can consume at $1 per head. No secrecy is observed in this kind of transaction.

The writer quotes an editorial from the *Star* of Tucson, and then continues his personal report.

I will also state another case: "Billy the Kid,"* a stripling belonging to the profession, was arrested for stealing horses. Upon his examination the court ruled that the affidavit upon which he was arrested charged him with the crime of theft, while the statutes showed no such crime, but should have been larceny. Also the person from whom the horses had been stolen voluntarily stated to the court that he did not want the boy prosecuted, as he agreed to return the horses. The same person told me afterward that if he prosecuted the boy the other cowboys would steal every head of stock he had, which he, being a poor man, could not afford to stand. The cow-boys frequently visit our town and often salute us with an indiscriminate use of fire-arms, and after indulging in a few drinks at the saloons, practice shooting at lamps, bottles, glasses, etc., sometimes going to the length of shooting the cigar out of one's mouth. This, of course, produces a nervous feeling.

The situation at this writing is not materially changed from the above. The cow boys, as a class, are not over brave, although there are some among them who have gone through so much difficulty that they have become desperate and will take desperate chances.

Your obedient servant
(unsigned)

Dec. 9, 1881

The *Epitaph's* attacks on banditry and its support of the Earps were not overlooked by the Cowboys. They might not be able to get Governor Gosper, but they apparently intended to kill John P. Clum, editor and mayor. At least that was the view the *Epitaph* and Clum took of the attempted holdup of a stage on which Clum was riding.

It must have been a stirring December night in the *Epitaph's* little office, when this story was written and set in type.

* This was not the "Billy the Kid" of Lincoln County, N. M., fame.

Holdup

As we go to press this morning we learn through the kindness of Mr. Samdom, one of Sandy Bob's drivers that an attempt was made to stop the stage last night about three and one-half miles out of town. Simultaneously with the command to stop the coach came a volley of shots evidently aimed at the horses for the purpose of disabling them and thus stopping the coach.

It could not be discovered in the darkness from whence the shots came or how many men were engaged in the assault. The horses were frightened at the firing and started off at a dead run, continuing their flight for about half a mile, when one of the lead horses fell dead, having been wounded by the highwaymen, and the coach proceeded on without him. The robbers did not overtake the coach and nothing more was heard of them. The only casualties to the passengers was a slight wound on the leg received by "Whistling Dick," and the disappearance of Mayor Clum, who was on his way to Tucson.

As near as could be ascertained, Mr. Clum was on the outside and either fell or jumped off during the shooting. As nothing has been heard of him at the present writing—2:30 a. m.—the gravest apprehensions are felt concerning his safety as unless he had been killed or wounded by the fusillade, it would seem that he must have reported himself by this time. . . . This information was obtained by Sandy Bob's driver when he met Kinnear's coach on his way in last night.

Arrangements are now being made to send out a party in quest of the missing Mayor.— (Dec. 15, 1881.)

The next day the *Epitaph* reported Clum was safe and gave further details of the attack on the stage.

Mayor Clum Safe

The announcement in yesterday's Epitaph of the attack upon the coach, night before last, threw the city into the wildest excitement and the gravest apprehensions for Mayor Clum. As before stated, upon receipt of the news, a party started out about 3 a. m. to obtain some tidings of the missing mayor, among whom were Sheriff Behan and C. D. Reppy. [Note: Reppy was Clum's business partner.] The sheriff and Mr. Reppy started first and arrived at Contention between 4 and 5 o'clock where they learned from Mr. Dunham, of Philadelphia, who was on the stage, the first particulars of the affair. The six-horse coach driven by Jimmy Harrington and the bullion wagon driven by "Whistling Dick" had just left Malcolm's water station, which is the last house on the road to Contention, and only about four miles from Tombstone and were bowling along at a rapid gait when the order to "Halt" was given from the roadside and almost simultaneously a volley was fired into them. The off leader of the coach was struck in the neck and all the horses became unmanageable. Dick was hit in the calf of the leg and received a painful flesh wound but kept his seat and his wagon right side up. The horses ran about half a mile when the wounded one weakened and fell from loss of blood. Mr. Clum, with the assistance of other passengers, cut the leaders loose and on they went, it being the general impression that all the passengers were aboard. Mr. Clum had been riding on the inside and he was missed but it was supposed by his fellow passengers that he had taken a seat on the outside, consequently his absence was not detected until the arrival of the coach at Contention.

Upon learning this Messrs. Behan and Reppy started from Tombstone and upon arriving at the place where the attack was made examined the locality carefully but no trace of the missing man could be found. In the meantime the second party which had left Tombstone about 4 a. m., upon arriving at Malcolm's station, learned that two teamsters in the camp with their wagons at that point, had not only heard the noise of the shooting but could distinctly see the flash, the attack having been made at about the apex of the first rise beyond. . . . The party proceeded on to Contention where from Mr. Dunham it was learned that, after assisting in releasing the wounded leader, it was supposed by the passengers that Mr. Clum had either taken a seat with the driver or on the bullion wagon, while it was rationally presumed by the driver than he was inside and his absence was not ascertained until arrival at Contention. Just after leaving Mr. Dunham it was stated that Mr. Clum had been heard of at the Grand Central mill whither the party proceeded, and learned that the mayor had taken the ore road to the mill, from whence, after resting, he had gone by saddle to Benson, arriving between 7 and 8 o'clock.—(Dec. 16, 1881.)

In the issue publishing this story the *Epitaph* printed an editorial in which it revealed, for the first time, that the Cowboy group was believed to be preparing to assassinate its enemies. Rumors named the Earps, Doc Holliday, and four other citizens, including Clum. The editorial closed by recommending the government move in and declare military law in Cochise County.

The Last Outrage

The assault upon the Benson stage by would-be assassins, Wednesday night, within four miles of town is the greatest outrage ever perpetrated upon the traveling public of Arizona, and is an event calculated to do more harm to the business interests of Tombstone than all other causes operating against us put together. It is a well known fact that the night stages do not carry either treasure or the mails; therefore the ordinary excuse for plunder cannot be alleged as an incentive to the deed. Since the late unfortunate affair [Note: the famous fight at the OK Corral between the Earps and Cowboys] rumors have been rife of the intended assassination of not only the Earp brothers and Holliday, but of Marshal Williams, Mayor Clum, Judge Spicer and Thomas Fitch. Why the feeling of deadly hatred should exist in relation to the Earps and Holliday everyone here can understand; but as against the others it is one of those inscrutable mysteries that none but the most depraved can possibly assign a reason for. That the affair of Wednesday night was intended for the murder of John P. Clum, we are fully satisfied. The threats of the last few days have been too well authenticated to leave any doubt on that point. That the damnable deed miscarried, does not rob the event of one jot or tittle of its enormity. The killings and attempted killings heretofore recorded as occurring in Tombstone and the surrounding country have been the outgrowth of drunkenness, wrongs or fancied wrongs, suffered at the hands of one or the other parties to the difficulties. This last has neither the one nor the other to plead in extenuation of the crime. As affairs now stand there seems to be no remedy for our evils other than for the general government to step in and declare military law and keep a sufficient force here to maintain law and order. It is evident that the civil authorities are unable to put down the lawless element. This remedy is one that we exceedingly dislike to see applied, but where all other remedies fail we must accept the only remaining one, for life and property must be made as safe in Tombstone as elsewhere in the Union or else all good men will abandon the place.—(Dec. 16, 1881.)

Judge Spicer, who presided at the examination of the Earps and Holliday, was next on the Cowboy list. He got a letter threatening him with death if he did not leave Tombstone. The *Epitaph* ran this copy.

> **A Cheerful Letter**
>
> Editor Epitaph:—On Saturday morning I received the following spirited letter from the postoffice at this place, viz:
>
> Tombstone, A. T. Dec. 13, 1881.
>
> To Wells Spicer—Sir, if you will take my advice you will take your Departure for a more genial Clime as I don't think this One Healthy for you much longer. As you are liable to get a hole through your coat at any moment. If such sons of Bitches as you Are allowed to dispense justice in this Territory, the Sooner you depart from us the better for yourself And the community at large you may make light of this but it is only a matter of time you will get it sooner or later So with those few gentle hints I Will Conclude for the first and Last time.
>
> A. Miner.

In a long public answer to this threat the Judge paid his respect to the Cowboy element in the following paragraph.

> There is a rabble in our city who would like to be thugs, if they had courage; would be proud to be called cow-boys, if people would give them that distinction; but as they can be neither, they do the best they can to show how vile they are, and slander, abuse and threaten everybody they dare to. Of all such I say, that whenever they are denouncing me they are lying from a low, wicked and villainous heart; and that when they threaten me they are low-bred, arrant cowards, and know that "fight is not my racket"—if it was they would not dare to do it.— (Dec. 18, 1881.)

Before the month ended the Cowboys struck again. They shot Chief of Police Virgil Earp from ambush at Allen and Fifth streets on a dark night. He lived, but all Tombstone wondered who would be next.

Governor Gosper had made a second appeal to Washington after the attempt on Clum's stage and the President sent his letter to Congress early in February, together with a special message asking Congress to amend the posse comitatus act so that he might send the military into the warring city.

The *Epitaph* reported events in this special wire story from Washington.

The Cow-boy Curse

The Attention of Congress Called to It.

Special to the Epitaph

Washington, Feb. 9, (1882) —The President, in a special message to Congress, transmitted a communication from Secretary Kirkwood, enclosing a letter from Acting Governor Gosper of Arizona in relation to the prevalence of lawlessness in that territory. The president calls attention to the recommendations in his annual message that the posse comitatus act be amended to permit the use of the military in assisting the civil authorities to maintain order, and suggests again such legislation as seems required. In his communication Secretary Kirkwood states that the New Mexico and Arizona difficulty in the way arises from the fact that the sheriffs are intimidated; that from personal motives they desire to curry favor with the disorderly element of society. It is therefore suggested whether it would not be expedient and proper that authority should be conferred by law upon the governor of any territory to remove or suspend the sheriff for neglect of duty and appoint a person in his place.

The Posse Comitatus Act

In a letter dated December 18, 1881 Acting Governor Gosper, of Arizona, urged the repeal of the posse comitatus act as the best means of giving that territory relief from the reckless rule now cursing the peace and liberty of otherwise favored portions of the territory.

Cow-boys and their Sympathizers

In another letter, relating to the cause of lawlessness, Governor Gosper says: "The people of Tombstone and Cochise county, in their mad career after money, have grossly neglected local self-government until the lazy and lawless element of society have undertaken to prey upon the more industrious and honorable classes for their subsistence and gains. The cowboys are not always white; some are Mexicans; but Americans direct and control the lawless element." The acting governor estimates the whole number of cowboys, which term, he says, includes skilled cattle thieves and highway robbers, in the county of Cochise, where most of the trouble has occurred, from twenty-five to fifty. Other bands are scattered over the territory. Besides the cowboys there is a class, much larger in numbers, of the "good-Lord and good devil" kind, who keep up a secret partnership with the robbers and profit by their lawlessness.

Congress to Act Promptly

The committee on territories of the senate has decided to act promptly. They will probably within a few days report a bill to modify the posse comitatus act, so as to allow the military to be employed to assist the civil officers in the territories and border states in enforcing law and maintaining order. The indications are that the democrats will oppose any modification of the posse comitatus act and take the position that civil officers should be increased where lawlessness prevails to a sufficient number to put it down.

If the Federal Government thought it could quiet the turmoil in Tombstone with harsh threats it was wrong. There is no bloodier period in the history of the camp than that of the next few weeks.

Morgan Earp was shot in the back and killed. Three men paid for that act with their lives before the flaming gun of Wyatt Earp and while he was on the vengeance trail a notorious character known as Zwing Hunt stepped out on the temporarily deserted Tombstone stage.

Hunt was born in Texas and moved to Tombstone early in the eighties. For a time he was an industrious freighter and bore a good reputation. But cattle rustling was more exciting and frequently paid better than driving six plodding oxen, and Hunt gave up freighting and joined company with Billy Grounds, sometimes known as "Billy the Kid."*

The two men were believed to have been members of a band of rustlers who ambushed and murdered a party of Mexican smugglers in Skeleton Canyon. The Mexicans were shot down, and their loads of silver dollars and bullion were spent in the bar rooms and gambling houses of Tombstone and Charleston.

* Still another "Billy the Kid." Not the New Mexico desperado.

Nothing was done about this, but in the fall of 1881, Hunt was indicted on a charge of rustling thirty head of cattle. He beat the law across the line into Mexico and dropped from sight.

Then on a dark spring night in March, 1882, a mining man who is referred to as "Mr. Peel," was murdered in his office a few miles from Tombstone.

Under the heading, "Murder Most Foul," the *Epitaph* told the story of the killing.

About twenty minutes after eight on Saturday evening, Messrs Austin, Cheyney, Hunt and Peel, were sitting in the office of the Tombstone Mill and Mining company, at Milville, all being connected with the company in various capacities. Mr. Peel was outside of a counter that runs through the center of the office and he sat close to the door. All others were behind the counter, Mr. Austin being directly in front of the door. A fumbling at the doorknob was first noticed, and then a heavy rap, probably given with the butt of a gun. Instantly the door was flung wide open and a man entered with a rifle presented, and was immediately followed by another who brought his rifle down as he entered.

TWO SHOTS FIRED

Almost in the same moment both rifles were discharged, one at Mr. Peel, who was shot through the body near or through the heart, and at such close range that his clothes were set on fire. He died without uttering a sound or making a motion, except to rise from his chair and fall. The position of the wound makes it appear that he had not fully risen at the time the bullet entered. Mr. Peel was shot by the rifle that was ready for use at the time the door opened. The second rifle was aimed at Mr. Austin, but the slight difference in time of firing, caused by the delay of the second assailant, who probably had flung the door open, gave the three gentlemen behind the counter time to drop, and the shot missed, burying itself in the wall. Instantly both assailants fled.

The Murderers Flee

They had a confederate hold their horses a few hundred yards from the office and succeeded in getting away before the alarm could be given. No order to "hold up" was given and no word spoken; the whole affair passing without a sound except a cry that is variously attributed to the unfortunate Mr. Peel and to the assassins. The latter were masked with handkerchiefs and the only one who was well seen wore a white hat that he lost on the way to the horses.

No Attempt at Robbery

No attempt at robbery was made and the motive for the assault is a mystery. Many ridiculous stories are afloat, but those best informed of all the facts do not hesitate to pronounce them untrue.– (March 27, 1882.)

What these ridiculous stories were and whom they involved is not revealed in subsequent issues. But Zwing Hunt and Billy the Kid were suspected of the crime and warrants were quietly issued for them.

Word came to the sheriff's office in a few days that the rustlers were spending the night on a nearby ranch, so Deputy Billy Breakenridge and a posse went after them and the bloody morning battle which developed got the *Epitaph's* largest one-column head.

DESPERATE FIGHT

Two Cow-Boy Rustlers Come to Grief And a Good Man Killed in Enforcing the Law.

About seven o'clock last evening, Mr. E. A. Harley, deputy sheriff in charge of the office in the absence of Sheriff Behan received word that two notorious characters for whom warrants were lying in the sheriff's office, named Billy Grounds, alias "Billy the Kid" and Zwing Hunt, would be within eight or ten miles of town during the night or early this morning. Upon receipt of this information Mr. Harley ordered Deputy Sheriff Breakenridge to organize a posse and start about one or two o'clock so as to be on the ground at an early hour in the morning in order to make the arrests, which Mr. Harley thought might be done by four men without resistance. By nine o'clock Deputy Sheriff Breakenridge had his posse, consisting of Jack Young, E. H. Allen and John A. Gillespie, ready for action, and at the appointed hour they started on their mission.

The First News

Early in the morning, probably about 6:30, a messenger arrived in town and reported to Chief of Police Nagle that a fight had taken place at Chandler's ranch, and that one man was dead and several wounded. Mr. Nagle immediately got an ambulance and took Dr. J. Goodfellow with him and started for the scene of action. About 7 o'clock another messenger arrived with a note for Mr. Harley which read as follows: "Harley, send coroner out to Jack Chandler's ranch; one of our men dead. Billy Grounds dying and Hunt also; Jack Young shot through the thigh. I got creased in the neck. (Signed) E. H. Allen."

Immediately the news spread through the town that Deputy Sheriff Breakenridge had been

Killed by the Cowboys

whom he was sent out to arrest, and there was a great deal of excitement, which was naturally intensified by the absence of definite news of the encounter and the further fact that Mr. Breakenridge is a general favorite with all classes of the people. He is genial and social in private life and prompt but courteous in the discharge of his official duty. The parties whom he was sent out to arrest were notoriously hard cases—the worst of the type of cowboy rustlers. . . .

About half past eleven Chief of Police D. Nagle returned to town bringing Mr. Young, whose wound admitted of his being brought in without serious inconvenience, and also bringing the first authentic details of the lamentable affair. Mr. Nagle arrived at the ranch about 8 o'clock in the morning and found Gillespie, (one of the special officers who accompanied Mr. Breakenridge) dead on the ground, and Hunt shot through the breast, the ball coming out through the back, the wound supposed to be mortal. Grounds was placed hors du combat by a charge of buckshot received full in the face and upper part of the head, and life was slowly but surely ebbing away. Mr. Young was wounded through the front of the thigh, the ball having entered the right side of his pant about six inches below the waistband, ranging downward across the groin, cutting into the muscles of the thigh just below that point, doing no injury to the groin whatever. Mr. Allen had a slight flesh wound on the right side of the neck and Mr. Breakenridge, fortunately, escaping with no serious damage whatever.

The Fight

The party arrived at Chandler's milk ranch just as the rosy streaks of the morning were heralding the near approach of the glorious orb of day, but before there was sufficient light to see objects at any considerable distance away. It was the intention of the party to get as near the house as possible without giving any alarm, and then to wait until broad day light before making the attempt to arrest the parties. They were frustrated in this by the barking of a pack of dogs kept at the house, therefore after their approach was thus heralded they determined to proceed to business at once, so they rode boldly up to near the house, where they dismounted and one of the party

Rapped at the Door

which summons was followed by asking who was in the house. The answer came, "Those who belong here," or something to that effect. They asked the man to get up and get them some breakfast, when they were told to go to the other house (a small house about one hundred yards below). Thinking that possibly the parties they wanted might be at the other house, Mr. Young and another one started down and when part of the way there, they found by looking around that the whole party were on the way. It was decided that the upper house ought to be watched so Mr. Breakenridge and Gillespie returned. About this time the door was opened and a man by the name of Lewis, a teamster who was staying overnight there, stepped out, immediately followed by Hunt who commenced firing. Mr. Young is of opinion that as many as two or three shots were fired before

Gillespie Was Killed,

but this is not certain, for as soon as the battle opened the entire attention of all concerned was too closely turned to self defense to note consecutively how matters did happen. Of one thing they are sure however, and that is that Hunt shot Gillespie through the left temple, when he fell dead in his tracks. He then fired at Mr. Allen, the ball passing through his coat on top of the right shoulder, causing a slight crease in the side of his neck. Allen then blazed away and shot Hunt through the breast the ball coming out of his back. Hunt must have fired several shots at Breakenridge who had taken refuge behind a large oak tree almost directly opposite the door, for several bullets were found in the tree after the battle was over. In the meantime and a few seconds after Hunt opened the battle,*

Grounds Came Out,

and Breakenridge blazed away at him with his shot-gun and was so fortunate as to put a full charge of buckshot into his head which laid him out. When Mr. Young returned from going toward the lower house he started to go around the house, thinking there might be a door or window through which the cowboys might escape. The firing commenced and one of the shots, it is supposed from Allen's gun, passed through the house going through two board partitions and the side of the house, striking him as above described.

These are the facts as nearly as can be arrived at up to the time of going to press. John Gillespie who was acting as a special deputy, was a miner and highly spoken of by all who knew him, and his taking off in this manner is a deplorable event. That the whole posse did their duty unflinchingly and bravely is evidenced by the narrative of the events that occurred, and they are deserving of the commendation of all law-abiding citizens. Coroner Matthews was out to the scene of battle, arriving a short time after Mr. Nagle's departure.—(April 1, 1882.)

Hunt now had two murder charges against him and a bullet in his breast, but neither fact kept him in the county hospital long. In two weeks the *Epitaph* printed what seems, under the circumstances, to have been a rather modest report of his escape, which it headed, "Abducted."

The *Epitaph's* story follows.

Abducted.

The noted cowboy, Zwing Hunt, whose capture cost the life of one good man, and who has been lying in the county hospital suffering from a wound through the lungs received in the fight at the time of his capture, was quietly taken out last night between the hours of eight and nine o'clock and put into some kind of conveyance and driven away, when or where no one knows.

* This account differs in minor details from the story which Breakenridge wrote forty-eight years later in his book, *Helldorado*. The *Epitaph* might have been wrong on some of the facts or a half-century of time may have dimmed Breakenridge's memory of the event.

No One to Blame

The above statement covers the whole facts as far as can be learned. At the time of the occurrence there was no one in the front room with the patient, but there were two patients in bed in the adjoining back room and three or four convalescents sitting out under the awning in the rear of the building. They say they heard nothing and did not hear of the occurrence until a few minutes before nine o'clock when the janitor went to the front room and found him gone.– (April 28, 1882.)

Posses could not even pick up Hunt's trail. They were certain he could not have gone far in his condition, and that he must be hiding in nearby mountains. The problem was, which range of mountains.

It was all settled in a month. Zwing's brother Hugh, who had helped him escape, came in and reported Zwing had been killed by Apaches on May 31st.

For some reason the dead killer suddenly became a hero to the *Epitaph*. Clum was gone and the new editor, or perhaps a sentimental reporter, wrote the story this way.

Death of Zwing Hunt

The restless character who so often has faced death unflinchingly, has at last "crossed the divide" into the great unknown valley of the future. Whatever else may be laid to his charge, the fact of his bravery all will admit. It is hardly necessary to state that he was not a saint, but whether he was a mortal or venial sinner, those who know him best must determine. From all accounts Zwing was a child of circumstances and a creature of excitement. Generous to a fault, rash to the extremity of foolishness, and as brave as an Arabian fire-worshipper, Zwing would do to go tiger hunting with. But he is dead. The same deadly aim impelled by the same insatiable thirst for the blood of white men, that has caused many a brave man, tender woman and innocent babe to seek the presence of the Creator unushered, sent Zwing Hunt to "the bosom of his father and his God."

Yesterday afternoon Hugh Hunt, brother of the deceased, reached here, and states that after escaping from the hospital they struck out for the Dragoons on horseback, and reached there well nigh into the night. Zwing was very weak and sick, vomited several times during the journey and when they got into the Dragoons declined to go any further in consequence of his disability. The original plan was to keep on until they reached the fastnesses of the Chiricahuas mountains, where they could dodge the officers of the law with more celerity than in the exposed plains of the timberless foothills. They lay all the following day in the Dragoons, and when night again enshrouded their movements from the prying gaze of their fellow men, they sped on towards the mountains. They were heading for Morse's sawmill, but thought it best to linger through the different canyons for some time, until the excitement consequent on the escape would have abated to a considerable extent. During the entire month of May the brothers wandered through the strongholds of the Chiricahuas. Zwing, who was very sick on the first night out, recovered with remarkable rapidity, when brought under the healthy mountain breezes. On the 30th of May they removed from the Sweetwater, near the end of the Swisshelms, and from there he went to what he calls Russels canyon in the Chiricahuas, their objective being Morse's mill in Pinery canyon. They camped about eight miles up the canyon and on the morning of the thirty-first of May arose about the usual hour and proceeded to cook breakfast. Zwing baked the bread and Hugh made the coffee and broiled the meat. They had just sat down to breakfast and commenced to eat when a volley was fired at them. Hugh thought when he heard the report that it was the sheriff's posse, but looking hastily around beheld several Indians in close proximity. Steadying their rifles to take aim. Zwing pulled his gun and exclaimed, "damn it; go to shooting." It was the last sentence he ever spoke. He was shot four times. The first shot fired took effect in his left hip and was inconsequential, the next was in the abdomen a short distance under the navel, and was serious, the next two he received in the head. He died almost instantly. The Indians, about five of them in number, crept up within ten steps of them and hid behind the rocks, plenty of which were in the vicinity. Zwing fired two shots. Hugh fired five times, emptying his revolver. He stood his ground until his brother expired, then he retreated, darting into the heavy timber and heading in the direction of the horses which were hobbled in the vicinity. The Indians ran after him keeping up a continual fire. He escaped almost miraculously and reached his horse. He jumped on bareback, not having time to remove the hobbles and rode the fettered animal for about half a mile. He kept in the thick timber and when he was a sufficient distance from the redskins removed the hobbles from his horse and sped on to Camp Price. The hostiles were on foot and followed him for three miles. Arriving at the post he reported the affair to the commanding officer, and the scouts were sent out in pursuit under command of Jim Cook, chief of scouts. . . . Lieutenant Clark of the cavalry with ten mounted men accompanied Hugh Hunt to the scene of the murder and helped him inter his brother's remains. The cutting off of the middle finger of the right hand was the only mutilation the body was subjected to. At the scene of the outrage are three large Juniper trees and under the middle one of these a "hollow grave" was scooped for the remains of him, who, even in dying, distinguished himself for cool bravery. The words, "Z. Hunt, May 31, 1882," were carved on the tree and there let the weary spirit rest. He was twenty-four years old the day he was shot at Chandler's and stated to his brother several times that he mistook the Sheriff's posse for the Earps and that was the reason he gave battle.—(June 10, 1882.)

Had Hunt been captured and returned to Tombstone he would scarcely have known the old town. The Earps were gone and so were some of his old friends. John P. Clum had left and the *Epitaph* had been sold to Samuel Purdy, who made it a Democratic organ.

The new publisher had scarcely warmed his chair when he found this red hot copy on his desk.

"His Accidency" is a sarcastic reminder that Arthur was President of the United States because of the death of James A. Garfield.

TELEGRAPHIC
ARTHUR ON ARIZONA

His Accidency Declares This Territory to be in Turmoil Attention Cowboys

Washington, May 3, by the President of the United States of America:

A PROCLAMATION

Whereas, it is provided in the laws of the United States, that wherever by reason of unlawful obstructions, combinations or assemblages of persons, or rebellion against the authority of the

United States, it should become impracticable in the judgment of the President to enforce by ordinary course of judicial proceedings the laws of the United States within any state or territory, it shall be lawful for the President to call for the militia of any state or territory, and employ such part of land or naval forces of the United States as he may deem necessary to enforce the faithful execution of the laws of the United States, to suppress such rebellion in whatever state or territory the laws of the United States may be forcibly opposed or execution thereof forcibly obstructed and

Whereas it has been made to appear satisfactory to me by information received from the Governor of the Territory of Arizona, and from the General of the army of the United States, and other reliable sources, that in consequence of the unlawful combinations of evil disposed persons, who are banded together to oppose and obstruct the execution of the laws it has become impracticable to enforce by ordinary course of judicial proceedings the laws of the United States within that Territory and that the laws of the United States have been therein forcibly opposed and execution thereof forcibly resisted; and whereas, the laws of the United States require, whenever it may be necessary in the judgment of the President to use the military forces for the purpose of enforcing a faithful execution of the laws of the United States, he shall forthwith by proclamation, command such insurgents to disperse and retire peaceably to their respective abodes within a limited time. Now, therefore I, Chester A. Arthur, president of the United States, do hereby admonish all good citizens of the United States, and especially of the Territory of Arizona, against aiding, countenancing, abetting or taking part in any such unlawful proceeding; and I do hereby warn all persons engaged in or connected with such obstructions of the laws to disperse and retire peaceably to their respective abodes on or before noon of the 15th day of May.

In witness whereof I have hereunto set my hand and caused the Great Seal of the United States to be affixed. Done at the City of Washington this third day of May, in the year of our Lord, one thousand eight hundred and eighty-two, and of the independence of the United States one hundred and sixth.

Signed Chester A. Arthur
By the President
Signed Fred Frelinghuysen
Secretary of State.

The *Epitaph's* first reply was an editorial in which the new publisher declared Arizona was one of the most peaceful sections of the nation and all it wanted was to be left alone.

So hastily did Purdy rush to the support of his community he forgot that in the last three months the *Epitaph's* pages had reported four holdups and robberies, five shootings, and eight killings.

But at least he ran true to *Epitaph* policy when he defended Tombstone in this editorial.

An Advertisement

In today's Epitaph will be found a proclamation of the President of the United States declaring in effect that the Territory of Arizona is abandoned to lawlessness. The proclamation states that "in consequence of the unlawful combination of evil disposed persons who are banded together to oppose and obstruct the execution of the laws, it has become impracticable to enforce by ordinary course of judicial proceedings the laws of the United States within the territory." Only this and nothing more. For all this gratuitous advertising we may thank Governors Gosper and Tritle, and we have much to be grateful for. Over the official signature of the president it is announced there is no law in Arizona, that good people must keep away, capital be turned into channels leading in another direction, industries become paralyzed, mines grow valueless and labor be wasted. With the exception of the late Indian trouble, there is not a state or territory in the Union more peaceable than Arizona nor one in which the law is more promptly obeyed or thoroughly respected. This proclamation is based upon nothing but the fact that the governor had the folly to listen to a few selfishly interested persons who happened to be of the same political faith as himself. Of course the action of the President is directed primarily against Cochise county, and yet perfect peace and quietude reigns all over this section of the county. We were never in a more peaceable community than Tombstone and law and order is absolute. The police regulations are perfect and the slightest disturbance of the peace is instantly quelled. In view of the actual state of facts the president's proclamation would be as ludicrous as a chapter from Don Quixote were it not that it is prone to injure this territory most seriously. It is nothing more or less than a vicious advertisement operating against the value of our resources and the interests of our people. The latter should join in an indignant protest addressed to the President and Governor, denying the premises alleged in the proclamation, and stating that all we ask is to be let alone. Why Governor Tritle, who, it is alleged, is speculating in Arizona mines, should so act as to deter the investment of capital in the territory, is difficult to determine. Very likely he did not stop to consider the probable effects of his action.—(May 3, 1882.)

Tombstone called a mass meeting. The *Epitaph* growled once or twice. But peace of a kind came to Cochise County for a while and the Army did not move in. Whether it was due to the President's threat or to the Earps, who had riddled the ranks of the Cowboy leaders one cannot say.

All the record shows is that the next territorial legislature wrote a neat period to the whole affair by passing a joint resolution thanking the President for his interest in Arizona.

The OK Corral, scene of the Earp-Clanton Battle

9 The Lion of Tombstone

There is no way of telling the story of the *Epitaph* and Tombstone without including at length and in detail the deeds and daring of Wyatt Earp. He lived in Tombstone only from December, 1879, to March, 1882, yet in that span he wrote his name boldly on almost every page of the early history of the town.

If you measure with a printer's ruler the space the *Epitaph* gave Wyatt Earp and his brothers you get a total of seventeen thousand words; and this in a six-page, seven-column paper which often published no more than three or four columns of local news.

Even more significant is the fact that, with the exception of the testimony he gave on the witness stand, there are only three direct quotations of anything Wyatt Earp may have said. All the rest of the thousands of words concern what he did.

The *Epitaph* never published personality features and it left us no description of Marshal Earp. But pioneers remember him as a handsome six-footer, lean and hard, in his early thirties. He moved gracefully and his demeanor was dignified. His eyes were cold blue, his hair brown, and his moustache swept luxuriantly above a firm mouth. They remember too, that he dressed quietly and usually wore the long, black coat so common among the lawmen of the West.

Unlike many men who were attracted to the rich silver camp, Earp's reputation was made before he reached Tombstone. He served on the police force of Wichita and was city marshal in Dodge City until he went to Arizona. Those were hard, tough, quick-shooting towns and they schooled Earp well in the ways of Western bad men.

It would be too much to expect that a man of Earp's character would have no enemies in Tombstone. They were ready made and waiting for him before he arrived. Nor can one expect he would escape being a figure around which the storms of controversy would beat. In his trade even men who respect life must sometimes shoot first or die.

The fact that men still debate him may or may not be a tribute to Wyatt Earp. But it is certainly an acknowledgment that, good or bad, he was a man of action, who shook the deserts and the mountains of the border when he walked.

There is no doubt that Earp both backed and bucked games of chance. He was a partner in the lush Oriental gaming rooms and sometimes sat in as a faro dealer. The *Epitaph,* however, spoke of him only as a law officer, and it is in the latter capacity that he is remembered in Tombstone.

Many articles and books have been written around Earp; some by those who think he was the outstanding law officer of the West and others by writers who believe that he was merely a killer with a badge. Some authors have relied on their own memories, some have employed the facts gathered through personal association. Still more have heard the heated and sometimes bitter arguments which still flame when the name of Earp is mentioned in Arizona and New Mexico; arguments based on old family loyalties during early days on the border.

This account is free from such influences. Here, with only such factual interpretation as is necessary to connect them, are the *Epitaph's* old stories on Wyatt Earp and his brothers. They are reprinted in the chronological order in which they were published.

To understand the events which follow in this chapter it must be realized that there were three law enforcement agencies in the Tombstone district. The state was heavily Democratic, and John Behan, the sheriff, was a Democrat. The national administration was Republican, and Wyatt Earp, deputy United States marshal, was a member of that party. The office of city marshal was elective or, in case of a vacancy, could be filled by the mayor. When Mayor Clum had to fill the office he selected Virgil Earp, who appointed his brother, Morgan Earp, a deputy.

The sheriff had jurisdiction over crimes in the district. The city marshal was responsible for Tombstone and the United States marshal moved in when there was interference with the mails. Since stagecoach holdups usually included the robbery of a strongbox containing bullion and mail, Wyatt Earp's duties sometimes conflicted with those of the sheriff. The same situation prevailed inside the town's limits, with both the sheriff and the city marshal enforcing such ordinances as the one forbidding the carrying of weapons.

Finally when one highway robber was allowed to walk out of Behan's jail before he saw the inside of a cell and another proved to be one of Behan's deputies, the Law and Order League of citizens set up a vigilante group, with Wyatt Earp at its head.

This fourth law enforcement agency is said to have been authorized by the governor, and served warrants issued by the judge of the district court. Here Wyatt Earp and Johnny Behan clashed again.

Obviously such conflicts in authority were certain to breed trouble, and they do much to explain why Wyatt Earp became so controversial a figure in the history of Tombstone.

With these facts in mind and with the record from the *Epitaph* as evidence, one may reach a true estimate of Wyatt Earp; may decide finally whether he was another murdering marshal, or a brave and efficient law officer who was forced to kill in line of duty.

Earp appeared first in Tombstone as a shotgun messenger for Wells, Fargo & Co., but the *Epitaph* did not mention him for eight months and then it spoke of him as a deputy sheriff who formed a posse and went in search of George Perine, who was wanted on a murder charge in connection with the killing of Mike Killeen. A month later the paper formally congratulated him on his appointment.

Good Appointment

The appointment of Wyatt Earp as Deputy Sheriff by Sheriff Shibell, is an eminently proper one, and we, in common with the citizens generally, congratulate the latter on his selection. Wyatt has filled various positions in which bravery and determination were requisites, and in every instance proved himself the right man in the right place. He is at present filling the position of shotgun messenger for Wells, Fargo & Co., which he will resign to accept the latter appointment.

Morgan Earp succeeds his brother as shotgun messenger for Wells, Fargo & Co.—(Oct. 20, 1880.)

One week after his appointment as deputy sheriff, Wyatt Earp clashed with the lawless and powerful Cowboy group for the first time. A wild bunch of these rustlers were shooting at the moon one night and Fred White, city marshal, went out to pick them up. He found William "Curly Bill" Brocius first and, in attempting to take the Cowboy's gun, was fatally wounded.

Historians differ from here on. Wm. Breakenridge, later an anti-Earp deputy sheriff in Tombstone, says in his *Helldorado* that Virgil Earp threw his arms around Curly Bill and as White reached for the outlaw's gun it went off. Stewart Lake, in *Wyatt Earp—Frontier Marshal,* declares that White seized the weapon by the muzzle and the gun was discharged, after which Wyatt Earp knocked Curly Bill out with a blow from a pistol.

Like Lake, the *Epitaph* says nothing of any Earp throwing his arms around Curly Bill and definitely settles the point that it was Wyatt and not Virgil who went to the assistance of White.

This is the *Epitaph* news story of the first killing in the feud that was to rage between Wyatt Earp and the Cowboys.

THE MURDEROUS PISTOL

City Marshal Fred White Dangerously and Perhaps Fatally Wounded—Arrest of the Shooter and His Companions

About 12:30 last night a series of pistol shots startled the late goers on the streets, and visions of funerals, etc. flitted through the brain of the EPITAPH local, and the result proved that his surmises were correct. The result in a few words is as follows: A lot of Texan cowboys, as they are called, began firing at the moon and stars on Allen street, near Sixth. City Marshal White, who happened to be in the immediate neighborhood, interfered to prevent violation of city ordinance, and was ruthlessly shot by one of the number. Deputy Sheriff Earp, who is ever to the front when duty calls, arrived just in the nick of time. Seeing the Marshal fall, he promptly knocked his assailant down with a six-shooter, and as promptly locked him up, and with the assistance of his brothers, Virgil and Morgan, went in pursuit of the others. That he found them, an inventory of the roster of the City Prison this morning will testify. Marshal White was shot in the left groin, the ball passing nearly through, and being cut from the buttock by Dr. Matthews. The wound is a serious though not a fatal one. Too much praise cannot be given to the Marshal for his gallant attempt to arrest the violators of the ordinance, nor to Deputy Sheriff Earp and his brothers for the energy displayed in bringing the murderers to arrest. At last accounts, 8 A. M., Marshal White was sleeping, and strong hopes of his ultimate recovery were expected.—(Oct. 28, 1880.)

The *Epitaph* apparently did not know the name of the marshal's assailant when it went to press on the night White was shot. When it did identify him in its second-day story it misspelled his name which probably went unnoticed, since he was known only as "Curly Bill." The second-day story, however, is important because, like the first, it shows how quickly the Earps chose sides and which side they took.

Assault to Murder

The party who shot Marshal White on Tuesday night was brought before Judge Gray yesterday morning on a warrant charging him with assault to murder. The complaint was made by Deputy Sheriff Earp. The prisoner asked until 10 o'clock to enable him to secure counsel. At 10 o'clock the prisoner reappeared in company with his counsel, Judges Haynes, of Tucson, and waiving examination, was committed to jail to await the next meeting of the Grand Jury. He gave the name of William Rosciotis, and claimed to hail from San Simon county. Rumor at the time being rife that Marshal White would not live until sundown, and that a Vigilance committee was organizing to hang the prisoner, it was deemed best to take him at once to Tucson. A buggy was at hand and Deputy Sheriff Earp, accompanied by George Collins, started. They were guarded for several miles out of town by Messrs. Virgil and Morgan Earp, and others.—(Oct. 29, 1880.)

White died of his wound and in reporting the funeral the *Epitaph* commented caustically on the sermon which it did not like. For some reason it did not report an important fact on which all historians agree. This was a deathbed statement by Marshal White in which he absolved Curly Bill of intent to kill him. White said he attempted to jerk the outlaw's gun out of his hand and the weapon was discharged accidentally.

As a result Curly Bill was freed but his unexpected deliverance did not make him a better citizen. He came back to Tombstone to resume his leadership of the Cowboy group and to plot against Wyatt Earp until the day the marshal's gun finally snuffed out his life.

Marshal White's Funeral

The circumstances attending the death of Fred White, Marshal of Tombstone, who was murdered in the discharge of his duty, called out the largest assemblage which has ever followed to the tomb any deceased person in Tombstone. The funeral services were held in Gird's Hall and long ere the hour for the funeral services the spacious building was crowded to its utmost capacity. Rev. Mr. McIntyre preached the funeral sermon, and took occasion to indulge in a speculative philosophy of the great unknown, of which he is as ignorant as the babe unborn. To say that the reverend gentleman trenched upon the bounds of common sense is but to echo the sentiments of the vast congregation which had assembled to listen to a funeral sermon and not to hear a dissertation on speculation, would be but stating the exact truth. The reverend knows just as much about the Great Unknown as any living creature who has never been there, and his captious flings at the firemen's resolutions were as injudicious as they were ill-timed. The cortege following the murdered Marshal to the grave was the largest ever seen in our embryo city. It embraced all classes and conditions of society from the millionaire to the mudsill and numbered fully 1,000 persons.—(Nov. 1, 1880.)

If the killing of Marshal White is considered the opening incident in the war between the Earps and organized gangs, then the next development was the attempted holdup of the Benson stage and the killing of the driver and a passenger.

From this event, which took place early in 1881, there grew bitter hatreds, charges and counter charges, and at least nine killings.

The *Epitaph's* story of the attempted holdup closes with a sentimental tribute to "Budd" Philpot, the driver.

HOLD!

Eight Road Agents Attempt to Stop Kinnear's Stage

At about 11 o'clock last night, Marshal Williams [Note: Wells, Fargo agent] received a telegram from Benson stating that Kinnear & Company's coach, carrying Wells Fargo & Co.'s treasure, had been stopped near Contention and "Budd" Philpot, the driver, killed and one passenger mortally wounded. Almost immediately afterwards A. C. Cowan, Wells Fargo & Co.'s agent at Contention City, rode into this city bringing a portion of the details of the affair. In a few minutes after his arrival, Williams, the Earp brothers, and several other brave, determined men were in the saddle, well armed, enroute to the scene of the murderous affray. From telegrams received from Benson at the Epitaph office, the following particulars of the affair were gathered:

As the stage was going up a small incline about two hundred yards this side of Drew's Station and about a mile the other side of Contention City, a man stepped into the road from the east side and called out "Hold." At the same moment a number of men—believed to have been eight—made their appearance and a shot was fired from the same side of the road instantly followed by another. One of these shots struck "Budd" Philpot, the driver, who fell heavily forward between the wheelers carrying the reins with him. The horses immediately sprang into a dead run. Meanwhile Bob Paul, Wells Fargo & Co.'s messenger, one of the bravest and coolest men who ever sat on a box-seat, was ready with his gun and answered back shot for shot before the frightened horses had whirled the coach out of range. It was fully a mile before the team could be brought to a stand, where it was discovered that one of the shots had mortally wounded a passenger on the coach named Peter Roering. As soon as the coach could be stopped, Paul secured the reins and drove rapidly to Benson, and immediately started back for the scene of the murder. At Benson a telegram was sent to the Epitaph office stating that Roering could not possibly live. There were eight passengers on the coach and they all unite in praise of Mr. Paul's bravery and presence of mind.

At Drew's Station the firing and rapid whirling by of the coach sent men to the scene of the tragedy, where they found poor "Budd" lying dead in the road, and by the bright moonlight saw the murderers fleeing rapidly from the place. A messenger was at once dispatched to inform agent Cowan of the circumstances, and within 20 minutes after the news arrived Mr. Cowan had dispatched nearly thirty well-armed volunteers after the scoundrels. He then rode rapidly into Tombstone, when the party mentioned above started out to aid in the pursuit. This, with Mr. Paul's party, makes three bodies of determined men who are in hot chase and Mr. Cowan stated to an Epitaph reporter that it is almost impossible for the murderous gang to escape, as the pursuers are close at their heels and have the moonlight in their favor. Should the road agents be caught they will meet with the short shift which they deserve.

"Budd," the murdered driver, whose real name is Eli Philpot, was one of the most widely known stage drivers on the coast. For years he had borne a high reputation as a skillful handler of the "ribbons," won on the principal stage lines in California, and during a year's residence in Arizona, most of the time in the employ of Kinnear's (formerly Walker & Co.'s) line. He will be sincerely mourned, not only by hosts of personal friends, but by thousands of passengers who have ridden on the box seat with him and been captivated by his simple manners and frank, manly ways. It was a rare treat "to make the trip" with him, for his memory was rich in reminiscences of the "old stage days" in California, and when he so willed he could keep a companion's attention riveted by his quaint, droll conversation. He has a wife and young family at Halistoga, California, who had the tenderest place in his big heart. And now there is another little home in the world which has been desolated and despoiled by the ruthless bullet. There is something inexpressibly sad in the sudden death of such outwardly rough, and inwardly brave, true hearted men and no better representation of this class could be found than the man whom the murderers last night sent unwarned to his last home. He was as proud and fond of his team and the big new coach on which he met his death as if they were human, and the horses always seemed to know when "Budd" was at the other end of the lines.— (March 16, 1881.)

While the posses were trailing the holdup men, Morgan Earp captured Luther King, who confessed that he had held the highwaymen's horses. Sheriff Behan who, with his own posse, had done little more than trail the Earps, now stepped in and insisted that King was his prisoner. He made the point that, since the mails had not been molested, no federal crime had been committed and Wyatt Earp, as United States Marshal, had no jurisdiction.

The Earps complied unwillingly and Behan started for Tombstone with King. Once inside the jail, King walked through an open door and escaped. Behan's excuse was that King disappeared while a bill of sale was being drawn up for a horse which he had sold the sheriff during the ride to Tombstone.

Three other suspects, who were still at large, picked up fresh horses from Cowboy friends and escaped into Mexico.

The Cowboys waited until September before they tried another holdup. This time they got the Wells, Fargo box and the mails. The Earps and Wells, Fargo men took up the chase again and so did the sheriff. They came back with two prisoners. One of them was T. C. Stilwell, who was one of Behan's deputies, and the other a Cowboy whom the *Epitaph* identified as P. Spencer, although the name appears later as P. Spence.

Here are the *Epitaph's* accounts of what happened.

Stage Robbery

Thursday night, about 10 o'clock, as the stage was nearing Bisbee, being some four or five miles this side in the broken ground, it was stopped by three, some say four, masked men, who, with pistols leveled at the driver and passengers, demanded Wells, Fargo & Co.'s treasure box. The box was thrown out, when they went through the passengers, getting eight dollars and a gold watch from one and about six hundred dollars from another. From the treasure box they got a fat haul, there was $2,500 in it. The report is that they also went through the baggage and mail sacks but this is rather doubtful.

About 9:30 yesterday morning two messengers rode into Tombstone, with their horses upon a lope, halting in front of Wells, Fargo & Co.'s office, dismounted and went in. Those seeing the men come in such hot haste, at once surmised something wrong and in a short time the robbery was the talk of the street. Marshal Williams, agent for W. F. & Co., immediately notified the sheriff's office and in a few hours himself, Deputy Sheriff Breakenridge, Wyatt and Morgan Earp were in the saddle on the way to the place of the robbery from whence they will take up the trail and do their best to overtake the robbers. This, we fear, is a hopeless task, as so much time was lost by the messengers, riding from Charleston into Tombstone when they might better have telegraphed and had the whole thing managed in secrecy.—(Sept. 10, 1881.)

Important Capture

Wyatt and Morgan Earp, Marshal Williams and Deputy Sheriff Breakenridge, who went to Bisbee to arrest the stage robbers on Sunday evening, brought in Deputy Sheriff T. C. Stilwell and P. Spencer, whom the evidence strongly points out as the robbers. They were examined before Will Spicer, Esq., yesterday and were admitted to bail in the sum of $7,000 each—$5,000 for robbing the mail and $2,000 for robbing D. B. Rea. The evidence against Deputy Sheriff Stilwell is circumstantial, and rests principally upon the tracks made by his bootheels in the mud, which corresponded with those he had removed by a shoemaker upon his return to Bisbee. The Epitaph has no desire to prejudge the case, but if it turns out as now anticipated, that the officers of the law are implicated in this nefarious business, it would seem to be in order for Sheriff Behan to appoint another deputy.—(Sept. 13, 1881.)

The storm which had been gathering since Wyatt Earp pistol-whipped Curly Bill and threw him in jail, after the shooting of Marshal White, was about to break. Cowboys were out of control in the district, terrorizing ranchers, driving off cattle and murdering the drivers of Mexican pack trains coming up from the border.

It was different in Tombstone. Here they had to deal with Virgil Earp and his brothers, Wyatt and Morgan. The Cowboys hated all three but their chief hatred centered on Wyatt. He had captured two of their gang and chased three others into Mexico. He had made stagecoach holdups a bad risk.

Ike Clanton, a minor chief of the outlaws, called down the thunder. He got drunk one day in October, quarreled with Wyatt Earp's friend, Doc Holliday, and threatened Wyatt with death.

The immediate result was the famous gun battle at the OK Corral, which opened with the three Earps and Doc Holliday marching down Fremont Street four abreast and ended one minute later with three dead Cowboys and two wounded Earps.

The town knew the showdown was coming. The Cowboys had been bragging for twenty-four hours that they were after the Earps. Virgil Earp had pistol-whipped Ike Clanton early that afternoon when he caught him with a Winchester and a six-gun. Wyatt had done the same to Tom McLowry, who had threatened him on the street. With a courage which should have shaken the nerve of the group he backed up the play by following three of his enemies to a gunshop, where they were filling their cartridge belts, and, finding Frank McLowry's horse standing on the sidewalk with its head in the gunshop door, seized the animal by the bridle and backed it into the street. As a deputy city marshal he was acting within his authority but it must have taken cold chilled nerve to perform the significant act in the face of three armed foes.

The last act came within a few minutes. The point at issue was whether the McLowrys and Clantons were to be disarmed. Behan, scuttling back and forth between the two groups, promised to get the Cowboys' guns but failed to do so. As city marshal, Virgil called his brothers and Holliday and started for the corral to do the job. For all they knew they were striding to their death and they would probably have been surprised to learn they were going to immortality.

Here is the complete *Epitaph* story, in which Clum first gives the background of the battle and then proceeds to report it chronologically.

YESTERDAY'S TRAGEDY

Three Men Hurled Into Eternity in the Duration of a Moment

The Causes That Led to the Sad Affair

Stormy as were the early days of Tombstone nothing ever occurred equal to the event of yesterday. Since the retirement of Ben Sippy as marshal and the appointment of V. W. Earp to fill the vacancy the town has been noted for its quietness and good order. The fractious and much dreaded cow-boys when they came to town were upon their good behaviour and no unseemly brawls were indulged in, and it was hoped by our citizens that no more such deeds would occur as led to the killing of Marshal White one year ago. It seems that this quiet state of affairs was but the calm that precedes the storm that burst in all its fury yesterday, with this difference in results, that the lightning bolt struck in a different quarter from the one that fell a year ago. This time it struck with its full and awful force upon those who, heretofore, have made the good name of this county a byword and a reproach, instead of upon some officer in the discharge of his duty or a peaceable and unoffending citizen.

The Proximate Cause

Since the arrest of Stilwell and Spence for the robbery of the Bisbee stage, there have been oft repeated threats conveyed to the Earp brothers—Virgil, Morgan and Wyatt—that the friends of the accused, or in other words the cow-boys, would get even with them for the part they had taken in the pursuit and arrest of Stilwell and Spence. The active part of the Earps in going after stage robbers, beginning with the one last spring where Budd Philpot lost his life, and the more recent one near Contention, has made them exceedingly obnoxious to the bad element of this county and put their lives in jeopardy every month.

Sometime Tuesday Ike Clanton came into town and during

the evening had some little talk with Doc Holliday and Marshal Earp but nothing to cause either to suspect, further than their general knowledge of the man and the threats that had previously been conveyed to the Marshal, that the gang intended to clean out the Earps, that he was thirsting for blood at this time with one exception and that was that Clanton told the Marshal, in answer to a question, that the McLowrys were in Sonora. Shortly after this occurrence someone came to the Marshal and told him that the McLowrys had been seen a short time before just below town. Marshal Earp, now knowing what might happen and feeling his responsibility for the peace and order of the city, stayed on duty all night and added to the police force his brother Morgan and Holliday. The night passed without any disturbance whatever and at sunrise he went home and retired to rest and sleep. A short time afterwards one of his brothers came to his house and told him that Clanton was hunting him with threats of shooting him on sight. He discredited the report and did not get out of bed. It was not long before another of his brothers came down, and told him the same thing, whereupon he got up, dressed and went with his brother Morgan uptown. They walked up Allen Street to Fifth, crossed over to Fremont and down to Fourth, where, upon turning up Fourth toward Allen, they came upon Clanton with a Winchester rifle in his hand and a revolver on his hip. The Marshal walked up to him, grabbed the rifle and hit him a blow on the head at the same time, stunning him so that he was able to disarm him without further trouble. He marched Clanton off to the police court where he entered a complaint against him for carrying deadly weapons, and the court fined Clanton $25 and costs, making $27.50 altogether. This occurrence must have been about 1 o'clock in the afternoon.

The After-Occurrence

Close upon the heels of this came the finale, which is best told in the words of R. F. Coleman who was an eye-witness from the beginning to the end. Mr. Coleman says: I was in the O. K. Corral at 2:30 p. m., when I saw the two Clantons (Ike and Bill) and the two McLowrys (Frank and Tom) in an earnest conversation across the street in Dunbar's corral. I went up the street and notified Sheriff Behan and told him it was my opinion they meant trouble, and it was his duty, as sheriff, to go and disarm them. I told him they had gone to the West End Corral. I then went and saw Marshal Virgil Earp and notified him to the same effect.

I then met Billy Allen and we walked through the O. K. Corral, about fifty yards behind the sheriff. On reaching Fremont street I saw Virgil Earp, Wyatt Earp, Morgan Earp and Doc Holliday, in the center of the street, all armed. I had reached Bauer's meat market. Johnny Behan had just left the cowboys, after having a conversation with them. I went along to Fly's photograph gallery, when I heard Virg Earp say, "Give up your arms or throw up your arms." There was some reply made by Frank McLowry, when firing became general, over thirty shots being fired. Tom McLowry fell first, but raised and fired again before he died. Bill Clanton fell next, and raised to fire again when Mr. Fly took his revolver from him. Frank McLowry ran a few rods and fell. Morgan Earp was shot through and fell. Doc Holliday was hit in the left hip but kept on firing. Virgil Earp was hit in the third or fourth fire, in the leg which staggered him but he kept up his effective work. Wyatt Earp stood up and fired in rapid succession, as cool as a cucumber, and was not hit. Doc Holliday was as calm as though at target practice and fired rapidly. After the firing was over, Sheriff Behan went up to Wyatt Earp and said, "I'll have to arrest you." Wyatt replied, "I won't be arrested today. I am right here and am not going away. You have deceived me. You told me these men were disarmed; I went to disarm them."

This ends Mr. Coleman's story which in the most essential particulars has been confirmed by others. Marshal Earp says that he and his party met the Clantons and the McLowrys in the alleyway by the McDonald place; he called to them to throw up their hands, that he had come to disarm them. Instantaneously Bill Clanton and one of the McLowrys fired, and then it became general. Mr. Earp says it was the first shot from Frank McLowry that hit him. In other particulars his statement does not materially differ from the statement above given. Ike Clanton was not armed and ran across to Allen street and took refuge in the dance hall there. The two McLowrys and Bill Clanton all died within a few minutes after being shot. The Marshal was shot through the calf of the right leg, the ball going clear through. His brother, Morgan, was shot through the shoulders, the ball entering the point of the right shoulder blade, following across the back, shattering off a piece of one vertebrae and passing out the left shoulder in about the same position that it entered the right. This wound is dangerous but not necessarily fatal, and Virgil's is far more painful than dangerous. Doc Holliday was hit upon the scabbard of his pistol, the leather breaking the force of the ball so that no material damage was done other than to make him limp a little in his walk.

Dr. Matthews impaneled a coroner's jury, who went and viewed the bodies as they lay in the cabin in the rear of Dunbar's stables on Fifth street, and then adjourned until 10 o'clock this morning.

The Alarm Given

The moment the word of the shooting reached the Vizina and Tough Nut mines the whistles blew a shrill signal, and the miners came to the surface, armed themselves, and poured into the town like an invading army. A few moments served to bring out all the better portions of the citizens, thoroughly armed and ready for any emergency. Precautions were immediately taken to preserve law and order, even if they had to fight for it. A guard of ten men were stationed around the county jail, and extra policemen put on for the night.

The Earp Brothers Justified

The feeling among the best class of our citizens is that The Marshal was entirely justified in his efforts to disarm these men, and that being fired upon they had to defend themselves, which they did most bravely. So long as our peace officers make effort to preserve the peace and put down highway robbery—which the Earp brothers have done, having engaged in the pursuit and capture, where captures have been made of every gang of stage robbers in the county—they will have the support of all good citizens. If the present lesson is not sufficient to teach the cow-boy element that they cannot come into the streets of Tombstone, in broad daylight, armed with six-shooters and Henry rifles to hunt down their victims, then the citizens will most assuredly take such steps to preserve the peace as will be forever a bar to further raids.

Two black hearses took the dusty road to Boot Hill the next afternoon. Young Billy Clanton was in one and the McLowry brothers in the other. Scores of Cowboys came in from their ranches and their hangouts at Contention and Galeyville, to watch the procession and curse the Earps, but there was apparently no disorder. The *Epitaph,* which had taken pains to warn the lawless that the citizens of Tombstone would undoubtedly take matters into their own hands if there were further disorders, dismissed the funeral with this short story.

The Funeral

The funeral of the McLowry brothers and Clanton yesterday was numerically one of the largest ever witnessed in Tombstone. It took place at 3:30 from the undertaking rooms of Messrs. Ritter and Eyan. The procession headed by the Tombstone brass band, moved down Allen street and thence to the cemetery. The sidewalks were densely packed for three or four blocks. The body of Clanton was in the first hearse and those of the two McLowry brothers in the second, side by side, and were interred in the same grave. It was a most impressive and saddening sight and such a one as it is to be hoped may never occur again in this community.— (Oct. 28, 1881.)

The coroner's jury discussed the gun battle for two hours and returned an inconclusive verdict which the *Epitaph* reported, "did not seem to meet with general approval."

This proved of no importance, however, for Wyatt Earp and Holliday were immediately arrested on warrants sworn out by the sheriff and Ike Clanton, and a hearing began before Justice Spicer. The *Epitaph* said.

Coroner's Verdict

The coroner's jury after deliberating for two hours in regard to the late killing of William Clanton, Frank and Thomas McLowry, brought in a verdict that the men named came to their deaths in the town of Tombstone on October 26, 1881, from the effects of pistol and gunshot wounds inflicted by Virgil Earp, Morgan Earp, Wyatt Earp and one Holliday commonly called "Doc" Holliday. The verdict does not seem to meet with general approval, as it does not state whether the cowboys were killed by the marshal and his party in the discharge of their duty, or whether the killing was justifiable.

On Saturday warrants for the arrest of Wyatt, Virgil and Morgan Earp and J. H. (Doc) Holliday were placed in the hands of the sheriff but as Morgan and Virgil Earp were confined to their beds through wounds received in the late street fight, the warrants were not in their cases served and only Wyatt Earp and

Holliday were placed under arrest. When these persons were taken before Justice Spicer he at first denied bail, but upon showing of the facts by affidavits bail was granted and fixed in the sum of $10,000 each, being justified in the sum of $20,000 each for each of the defendants, which amount was furnished.

Today Holliday and Wyatt Earp were before Justice Spicer to answer to the charge. The investigation was conducted with closed doors. No one, except the officers of the court, and the witness whose testimony was being taken up, were allowed inside. The investigation is not yet concluded and will probably occupy the court for several days.— (Oct. 31, 1881.)

If Judge Spicer thought he could quiet the town by holding the investigation behind closed doors, he soon found he was wrong. So many garbled accounts of the proceedings were circulated that he decided to open the doors to the press and the public.

The *Epitaph* immediately began to carry the testimony in full. Stenographers were not used in Tombstone courts, which accounts for the ragged narrative, but the testimony of witnesses and the participants, which was taken down in longhand, as well as the final opinion of the court, fill columns of hand-set type.

Sheriff Behan appeared for the prosecution and, as expected, was extremely hostile to the Earps and Holliday. This was his testimony.

John H. Behan

was sworn and testified as follows: About 2:30 I was in the barber's shop and heard of trouble between the Clantons and Earps. I went over to Hafford's corner. I asked Virgil Earp, the marshal, what was the excitement. He said there was a lot of — in town looking for a fight. He mentioned no names. I said to Earp, "You had better disarm the crowd." He said he would not, but would give them a chance to make a fight. I said, "It is your duty as a peace officer to disarm the parties." I meant any parties connected with the cowboys who had arms. Morgan Earp and Holliday were the ones I was talking to at the intersection of Allen and Fourth. Virgil Earp had a shotgun. I saw no arms on the others. I then went down Fourth street to the corner of Fremont and crossed to the opposite side of Fourth street and saw Frank McLowry holding a horse and in conversation with somebody. I told McLowry I would have to disarm him; that there was likely to be some trouble in town and I proposed to disarm everybody that had an arm. He said that he would not give up his gun that he didn't intend to have any trouble. I insisted. About that time I saw Ike Clanton and Tom McLowry down the street below Fly's building. I said to Frank, "Come with me." We went down to where Ike Clanton and Tom McLowry were standing. I said to them, "Boys, you must give up you arms." Billy Clanton and William Claiborne, alias Billy the Kid,* were also there. Frank McLowry demurred. Ike Clanton told us he was unarmed. I put my arm around his waist and found that he was not armed. Tom McLowry pulled his coat open and showed that he was not armed. I saw five standing there and asked how many there were in their party. They said four. Claiborne said he was not one of them; that he was there wanting them to leave town. I said, "Boys, you must go up to the sheriff's office, lay aside your guns and stay until I get back." I told them I was going to disarm the other party. At that I saw the Earps and Holliday coming down the south side of Fremont street. They came by the post office and Bauer's shop. I mean Morg Earp and Doc Holliday. I said to the Clanton party, "I see them coming down; wait here; I will go up and stop them." I walked twenty-two or twenty-three steps up the street and met them as they were coming out from under the awning at Bauer's shop, and told them not to go any further, that I was there for the purpose of disarming the Clanton party. They did not heed me. I said, "Go back! I am not going to allow any trouble if I can help it." They brushed past me and I turned and went with them or followed them, expostulating. When they arrived within a few feet of the Clantons and McLowrys, I heard one of them say, I think it was Wyatt Earp, "You s— of b—s, you have been looking for a fight and now you can have it." About this time a voice said, "Throw up your hands." During this time pistols were pointed. I saw a nickel-plated pistol in particular. It was in the hands of the Earp party. I think Doc Holliday. It was pointed, I think, at Billy Clanton. I am not certain that Holliday had it. When the order was given to "throw up your hands," I heard Billy Clanton say, "Don't shoot me. I don't want to fight." At the same time Tom McLowry threw open his coat and said: "I have nothing," or "I am not armed," or words to that effect, making the same remark and gesture he had previously made to

* Not the New Mexico "Billy."

me. I don't remember the position of Billy Clanton's hands. My attention was directed on the nickel-plated pistol for a couple of seconds. The nickel-plated pistol was the first fired and almost instantaneously came two shots right together. The first two shots could not have been fired from the same pistol. They were too close together. The nickel-plated pistol was fired by the second man from the right. After the first two or three shots were fired very rapidly the firing was general. The first two shots were fired by the Earp party. I thought the next three shots came from the same side, but was not certain. It was only my impression. After the words, "throw up your hands," immediately the nickel-plated pistol went off. I saw Frank McLowry with one hand to his belly and with his right hand shooting toward Morgan Earp. As he started across the street I heard a couple of shots from the direction in which Frank McLowry went. I looked and saw him running and a shot was fired and he went over on his head. I heard Morg Earp say, "I got him." There may have been a couple of shots afterwards but that was the end of the fight. I did not see the effect of the first two shots that were fired; the only parties I saw fall were Frank McLowry and Morgan Earp. I saw no effects from the next three shots. The first man I thought was hit was Frank McLowry. I saw him staggering and bewildered after the first five shots. I never saw any arms in the hands of anybody of the McLowry party except Frank McLowry and Billy Clanton. I saw Frank McLowry on the sidewalk a few feet from the line of the front of the lot. I think eight or ten shots had been fired before I saw arms in the hands of any of the McLowry or Clanton party. Frank McLowry was the first man in whose hands I saw a pistol. After the first few shots Ike Clanton broke and ran. I saw him at the corner of Fly's house running into the back building.

When Ike Clanton broke and ran I did not know where he went. I found him afterwards in Emmanuel's building on Tough Nut street. I saw a shotgun with Holliday before the fight commenced, as they were coming down the street. He had it under his coat. I did not see the gun go off and if I heard it, I did not distinguish it from a pistol. I afterwards examined Billy Clanton, before he died, as he was lying in the street. After he was taken in the house all I heard him say was to go away and let him die. I saw him lying on the sidewalk and saw him when he shot Morg Earp. A number were in the room when Billy was carried in. Dr. Giberson said it was no use to give him anything. I left before Billy Clanton died. Tom McLowry's body was in the same room.

One Wesley Fuller then took the stand and testified that he had intended to warn Billy Clanton the Earps were coming but could not reach him in time. He said he saw the Earps pass from his position in an alley. He could not see the Clantons or McLowrys but said he heard Billy Clanton cry out, "Don't shoot me, I don't want to fight," and that he saw Doc Holliday fire the first shot.

On cross-examination Fuller said he did not know whether Holliday had a shotgun or a six-shooter. Defense also drew out an admission that the witness had been drinking heavily on the day and night preceding the battle, going to bed at three o'clock. The witness, however, volunteered that he did not "have a fit of delirium tremens."

Wm. F. (Billy) Claiborne, one of the Cowboy group, took the stand next. His testimony was to the effect that the Clantons and McLowrys threw up their hands when Virgil Earp gave the order and that Doc Holliday and Morgan Earp fired on them immediately.

Claiborne refused to answer when the defense, in cross examination, asked whether it was not true that he had been arrested by the Earps on a charge of taking part in a killing at Charleston and was now out on bond. The court upheld him.

The prosecution then called its chief witness, Ike Clanton, who promoted the fight and then ran away from it. He told this story of the battle at the OK Corral.

> I, the McLowry brothers, and William Clanton and Billy Claiborne were standing talking in a vacant lot, west of the photograph gallery on Fremont street, between that and the building next to it. The sheriff, Behan, came down and told us he had come to arrest and disarm us. I asked the sheriff what for. He told me to preserve the peace. I told him I had no arms. Then Wm. Clanton told him he was just leaving town. The sheriff then said if he was leaving town all right. He then told Tom and Frank McLowry he would have to take their arms. Tom McLowry told him he had none. Frank McLowry said he would go out of town, but did not want to give his arms up until the parties that had hit his brother were disarmed. The sheriff told him he should do it

and to take his arms up to his—the sheriff's—office and lay them off. Then Frank McLowry said he had business in town he would like to attend to, but he would not lay aside his arms and attend to his business unless the Earps were disarmed. The Sheriff then put his arms around me and felt if I was armed. Tom McLowry said, "I'm not armed either," and opened his coat this way. (Witness throws back the lapels of his coat.) The sheriff then looked up Fremont street and ordered us to stay there until he came back.

The Earp party and Holliday just then appeared. Clanton and I remained because the sheriff ordered us to. Behan met the Earps, held up his hands and told them to stop, that he had our party in charge. They never stopped but passed by and came on where we were. It was about twenty paces from where we were to the point where Behan met the Earps and Holliday. As they got where we were they pulled their pistols and Wyatt and Virgil Earp said, "You s—s of b—s, you have been looking for a fight," and at the same time ordered us to throw up our hands. We threw up our hands and they commenced shooting. The first two shots were fired by Holliday and Morgan Earp. Wyatt and Virgil Earp fired next in quick succession. Morg shot before Wyatt did. The first two shots were fired so close together I could not tell who fired first. Almost immediately after, perhaps a couple of seconds, Virgil Earp fired. Morgan Earp shot William Clanton. I don't know which of the McLowry boys Holliday shot at but at one of them. I know Morgan Earp shot Billy Clanton because I saw his pistol pointed within two or three feet of his bosom and saw Billy stagger and fall against the house and put his hand on his breast where he was shot. When Billy Clanton staggered and fell against the house he was holding his hands up level with the top of his head with the palms of his hands out. When those first shots were fired Frank McLowry was holding his hands up level with the top of his head. I was holding my hands the same way. Tom McLowry threw open his coat by the lapels and said he had no arms. I was never armed at any time during the shooting. Morg Earp had taken my arms a short time before that and left them behind the Grand hotel bar. He took a Colt 45 pistol and a Winchester carbine.

When the Earp party came up where Billy Clanton and I were standing, Wyatt Earp shoved his pistol up against my belly and told me throw up my hands and said, "You s— of a b—, you can have a fight." I turned on my heel, taking hold of Wyatt and his pistol with my left hand and grabbing him around the shoulders with my right hand and held him for a few seconds. While I was holding him he shot. I pushed him around the corner of the photograph gallery and I jumped into the door of the photograph gallery. I went right on through the hall and out the back way. I went on across to Allen street and into the dance hall. As I jumped into the door of the photograph gallery I heard one or two bullets pass by my head. I ran across Allen street and seen no more of the fight.

Before completing his direct testimony, Ike Clanton testified to a fact which has often been denied. He said that there were Winchester rifles on the saddles of the two Clanton-McLowry horses. This meant that even though Ike Clanton and Tom McLowry had no guns on their persons there were enough arms for all four men.

Clanton then gave his version of his clash with Doc Holliday the night preceding the fight in the corral. He said Holliday abused him in foul language, meanwhile keeping his hand in his bosom near what Clanton suspected was a gun.

He denied that he had threatened the Earps and said that he refused an invitation to shoot it out even though Holliday dared him to fight, since he had no weapon.

Clanton, who was on the stand four days, then told a long story of an offer of $6,000 made him by Wyatt Earp for the killing or capture of Billy Leonard, Harry Head, and Jim Crane. These were the men wanted for the holdup of the Benson stage and the murder of Budd Philpot, the driver.

As Clanton told of the plot, Wyatt Earp took him into the center of Allen Street, where they could not be overheard, and confessed that he and Morgan had piped off (robbed) the strong box before the stage left Tombstone and that Leonard, Head, and Crane knew it. He wanted them out of the way before they betrayed him, and was willing to pay a huge reward for their deaths. Clanton said he ignored the offer.

He said also that Head had told him Doc Holliday was a member of the holdup gang and that it was Holliday who shot and killed the driver.

Questioned by the defense as to why he had not revealed this before, Clanton said he had promised Wyatt Earp, "as a gentleman" that he would never reveal the conversation and that he had done so now only because he was under oath.

The prosecution closed its case with Clanton's testimony, and Wyatt Earp took the stand in his own defense.

Here is his story in full, for the first time since he told it in 1881.

The Statement of Wyatt Earp

The difficulty between deceased and myself originated first when I followed Tom McLowry and Frank McLowry with Virgil and Morgan Earp and Captain Hearst and four soldiers, to look for six government mules which had been stolen. A man named Eustice, told us at Charleston, that we would find the mules at McLowry's ranch, that the McLowrys were branding "D. S." over "U. S." We tracked the mules to McLowry's ranch, where we also found the brand. Afterwards some of those mules were found with the same brand. After we arrived at McLowry's ranch there was a man named Frank Patterson made some kind of a compromise with Captain Hearst. Captain Hearst came to us boys and told us he had made this compromise and by so doing he would get his mules back. We insisted on following them up. Hearst prevailed upon us to go back to Tombstone and we came back. Hearst told us two or three weeks afterwards that they would not give up the mules to him after we left, saying they only wanted to get us away; that they could stand the soldiers off. Captain Hearst cautioned me and Virgil and Morgan to look out for those men; that they had made some hard threats against our lives. About one month after that, after those mules had been taken, I met Frank and Tom McLowry in Charleston. They tried to pick a fuss out of me, and told me if I ever followed them up again as close as I did before they would kill me.

Shortly after the time Budd Philpot was killed by those men who tried to rob the Benson stage, as a detective I helped trace the matter up, and I was satisfied that three men named Billy Leonard, Harry Head and Jim Crane were in that robbery. I knew that Leonard, Head and Crane were friends and associates of the Clantons and McLowrys and often stopped at their ranches. It was generally understood among officers and those who have information about criminals, that Ike Clanton was a sort of chief among the cow-boys; that the Clanton and McLowry ranches were the meeting places, and places of shelter for the gang.

I had an ambition to be sheriff of this county next election, and I thought it would be a great help to me with the people and business men if I could capture the man who killed Philpot. There were rewards offered of about $1,200 each for the robbers. Altogether there was about $3,000 offered for their capture. I thought that this amount might tempt Ike Clanton and Frank McLowry to give away Leonard, Head and Crane; so I went to Ike Clanton and Frank McLowry when they came in town. I had an interview with them in the back yard of the Oriental Saloon. I told them what I wanted. I told them I wanted the glory of capturing Leonard, Head and Crane—tell me where these men were hid—I would give them all the reward and would never let anybody know where I got the information. Ike Clanton said he would be glad to have Leonard captured, that Leonard claimed a ranch that he claimed, and if he could get him out of the way he would have no opposition about the ranch. Ike Clanton said that Leonard, Head and Crane would make a fight, that they would never be taken alive, and that I must first find out if the reward would be paid for the capture of the robbers dead or alive. I then went to Marshal Williams, the agent of Wells, Fargo & Co., in this town and at my request he telegraphed to the agent of Wells, Fargo & Co., at San Francisco to find out if the reward would be paid for the robbers dead or alive. He received in June 1881, a telegram which he gave me, promising that the reward would be paid dead or alive. I showed the telegram soon after I got it to Ike Clanton in front of the Alhambra and afterwards told—[Note: The next 26 lines of the testimony have been cut out of this page of the *Epitaph*]—After that Ike Clanton and Frank McLowry said I had given them away to Marshal Williams and Doc Holliday and when they came in town they shunned us, and Morgan and Virgil Earp and Doc Holliday and myself began to hear of their threats against us. I am a friend of Doc Holliday because, when I was City Marshal of Dodge City, Kansas, he came to my rescue and saved my life when I was surrounded by desperadoes. A month or so ago Morgan and I assisted to arrest Stilwell and Spence on the charge of robbing the Bisbee stage. The McLowrys and Clantons have always been friendly with Spence and Stilwell and they laid the whole blame of their arrest on us, although the fact is we only went as a sheriff's posse. After we got in town with Spence and

Stilwell, Ike Clanton and Frank McLowry came in. Frank McLowry took Morgan into the middle of the street where John Ringgold, [Johnny Ringo] Ike Clanton and the Hicks boys were standing, and commenced to abuse Morgan Earp for going after Spence and Stilwell. Frank McLowry said he would never speak to Spence again for being arrested by us. He said to Morgan, "If you ever come after me you will never take me." Morgan replied that if he ever had occasion to go after him he would arrest him. Frank McLowry then said to him, "I have threatened your boys lives, and a few days ago I had taken it back, but since this arrest it now goes." Morgan made no reply and walked off.

Before this and after this Marshal Williams and Farmer Daly, and Ed Barnes and three or four others told us at different times of threats made to kill us by Ike Clanton, Frank McLowry, Tom McLowry, Joe Hill and John Ringgold. I knew that all these men were desperate and dangerous cattle thieves, robbers and murderers. I knew of the Clantons and McLowrys stealing six government mules. I heard of Ringgold shooting a man down in cold blood near Camp Thomas. I was satisfied that Frank and Tom McLowry killed and robbed Mexicans in the Skeleton Canyon two or three months ago, and I naturally kept my eyes open and I did not intend that any of the band should get the drop on me if I could help it.

Three or four weeks ago Ike Clanton met me at the Alhambra and told me that I had told Holliday about this transaction, concerning the capture of Head and Leonard. I told him I never told Holliday. I told him when Holliday came up from Tucson I could prove it. Ike Clanton said that Holliday had told him so. When Holliday came back I asked him if he said so. I told him that Ike Clanton had said so.

On the 25th of October, Holliday met Ike Clanton in the Alhambra saloon and asked him about it. Clanton denied it and they quarreled for three or four minutes. Holliday told Ike Clanton that he was a d—n liar, if he said so. I was sitting eating lunch at the time. They got up and walked out on the street. I got through and walked out and they were still talking about it. I then went to Holliday who was pretty tight and took him away. Then I came back alone and met Ike Clanton. He called me out to one side and said his gun was on the other side of the street at the hotel. I told him to leave it there. He said he would make a fight with Holliday any time he wanted to. I told him Holliday did not want to fight, but only to satisfy him that this talk had not been made. I then walked away and went to the Oriental, and in a few minutes Ike Clanton came over with his six-shooter on. He said he was not fixed right; that in the morning he would have man for man; that this fighting talk had been going on for a long time, and it was about time to fetch it to a close. I told him I wouldn't fight no one if I could get away from it. He walked off and left me, saying, "I'll be ready for all of you in the morning." He followed me into the Oriental, having his six-shooter in plain sight. He said, "You mustn't think I won't be after you in the morning." Myself and Holliday walked away, and we went to our rooms.

I got up next day, Oct. 26, about noon. Before I got up Ned Boyle came to me and told me that he met Ike Clanton on Allen street near the telegraph office that morning; that Ike was armed; that he said, "As soon as those d–d Earps make their appearance on the street today the ball will open." That Ike said, "We are here to make a fight; we are looking for the sons of b–s." Jones came to me after I got up and went to the saloon and said, "What does all this mean?" I asked him what he meant. He says, "Ike Clanton is hunting you Earp boys with a Winchester and a six-shooter." I said, "I will go down and find him and see what he wants." I went out and on the corner of Fourth and Allen streets I met Virgil Earp, the Marshal. He told me how he had heard that Ike Clanton was hunting us. I went up Allen street and Virgil went down Fifth street and then Fremont street. Virgil found Ike Clanton on Fourth street in an alley. He walked up to him and said, "I hear you are hunting for some of us." Ike Clanton then threw his Winchester rifle around towards Virgil. Virgil grabbed it and hit Clanton with his six-shooter and knocked him down. Clanton had his rifle and his six-shooter was exposed in his pants. By this time I came up and Virgil and Morgan took his rifle and six-shooter away (and took them to the Grand Hotel after examination), and took Ike Clanton before Justice Wallace. Before the investigation Morgan Earp had Ike Clanton in charge; as Virgil Earp was out. A short time after I went into Wallace's court and sat down on a bench. Ike Clanton looked over to me and says, "I will get even with all of you for this. If I had a six-shooter I would make a fight with all of you." Morgan then said to him, "If you want to make a fight right bad I will give you one," at the same time offering Ike Clanton his own six-shooter. Ike Clanton started to get up and take it, when Campbell, the deputy sheriff, pushed him back on his seat, saying he wouldn't allow any trouble. I never had Ike Clanton's arms at any time as he has stated.

I would like to describe the positions we occupied in the court room at that time. Ike Clanton sat down on a bench with his face fronting to the north wall of the building. I myself sat down on a bench that was up against the north wall right in front of his. Morgan Earp stood up against the north wall with his back against the north wall, two or three feet to my right. Morgan Earp had Ike Clanton's Winchester in his left hand and his six-shooter in his right hand; one end of the rifle was on the floor. Virgil Earp was not in the court room any of this time and Virgil Earp came there after I walked out.

I was tired of being threatened by Ike Clanton and his gang. I believed from what they had said to others and to me, and from their movements, that they intended to assassinate me the first chance they had, and I thought if I had to fight for my life against them I had better make them face me in an open fight. So I said to Ike Clanton, who was then sitting about eight feet away from me, "you d—d dirty cur thief, you have been threatening our lives and I know it. I think I should be justified in shooting you down any place I should meet you, but if you are anxious to make a fight, I will go anywhere on earth to make a fight with you, even over to the San Simon among your own crowd." He replied, "All right, I'll see you after I get through here. I only want four feet of ground to fight on." I walked out just then and outside the court room, near the Justice's office, I met Tom McLowry. He came up to me and said to me, "If you want to make a fight I will make a fight with you anywhere." I supposed at that time that he had heard what had transpired between Ike Clanton and me. I knew of his having theatened me, and I felt just as I did about Ike Clanton, that if the fight had to come I had better have it come when I had an even show to defend myself, so I said to him, "all right, make a fight right here," and at the same time I slapped him in the face with my left hand, and drew my pistol with my right. He had a pistol in plain sight on his hip, but made no move to draw it. I said to him, "jerk your gun and use it." He made no reply, and I hit him on the head with my six-shooter, and walked away, down to Hafford's corner. I went into Hafford's and got a cigar, and came out and stood by the door. Pretty soon I saw Tom McLowry, Frank McLowry and Wm. Clanton. They passed me and went down Fourth street to the gunsmith shop. I followed them to see what they were going to do. When I got there Frank McLowry's horse was standing on the sidewalk with his head in the door of the gunshop. I took the horse by the bit, as I was deputy city marshal, and commenced to back him off the sidewalk. Frank and Tom McLowry and Billy Clanton came to the door. Billy Clanton had his hand on his six-shooter. Frank McLowry took hold of the horse's bridle. I said, "you will have to get this horse off the sidewalk." He backed him off on the street. Ike Clanton came up about that time and they all walked into the gunsmith's shop. I saw them in the shop changing cartridges into their belts. They came out of the shop and walked along Fourth street to the corner of Allen street. I followed them as far as the corner of Fourth and Allen streets and then they went down Allen street and over to Dunbar's court. Virgil Earp was then city marshal; Morgan Earp was a special policeman for six weeks, wore a badge and drew pay. I had been sworn in in Virgil's place to act for him while Virgil had gone to Tucson on Stilwell's trial. Virgil had been back several days but I was still acting. I knew it was Virgil's duty to disarm these men. I expected he would have trouble in doing so and I followed up to give assistance if necessary especially as they had been threatening us, as I have already stated. About ten minutes afterwards, and while Virgil, Morgan, Doc Holliday and myself were standing on the corner of Fourth and Allen streets, several people said, "There is going to be trouble with those fellows," and one man named Coleman, said to Virgil Earp, "they mean trouble. They have just gone from Dunbar's corral into the O. K. Corral, all armed. I think you had better go and disarm them." Virgil turned around to Doc Holliday, Morgan Earp and myself and told us to come and assist him in disarming them. Morgan Earp said to me, "they have horses, had we not better get some horses ourselves, so that if they make a running fight we can catch them?" I said, "No, if they try to make a running fight we can kill their horses and then capture them." We four then started through Fourth to Fremont street. When we turned the corner of Fourth and Fremont we could see them. We had walked a few steps further when I saw Behan leave the party and come towards us; every few steps he would look back as if he apprehended danger. I heard Behan say to Virgil Earp, "for God's sake don't go down there or you will get murdered." Virgil replied, "I am going to disarm them"—he, Virgil Earp being in the lead. When I and Morgan came up to Behan he said, "I have disarmed them." When he said this I took my pistol which I held in my hand under my coat and put it in my overcoat pocket. Behan then passed up the street and we walked on down. We came up on them close—Frank McLowry, Tom McLowry and Billy Clanton standing all in a row against the east side of the building on the opposite side of the vacant space west of Fly's photograph gallery. Ike Clanton and Billy Claiborne and a man I did not know were standing in the vacant space about half way between the photograph gallery and the next building west. I saw that Billy Clanton and Fred McLowry and Tom McLowry had their hands by their sides, and Frank McLowry's and Billy Clanton's six-shooters were in plain sight. Virgil said, "Throw up your hands I have come to disarm you." Billy Clanton and Frank McLowry laid their hands on their six-shooters. Virgil said, "Hold, I don't mean that; I have come to disarm you." They—Billy Clanton and Frank McLowry—commenced to draw their pistols, at the same time Tom McLowry threw his hand to his right hip and jumped behind a horse. I had my pistol in my overcoat pocket where I had put it when Behan told me he had disarmed the other party. When I saw Billy and Frank draw their pistols I drew my pistol. Billy Clanton leveled his pistol at me but I did not aim at him. I knew that Frank McLowry had the reputation of being a good shot and a dangerous man and I aimed at Frank McLowry. The first two shots which were fired were fired by Billy Clanton and myself; he shot at me and I shot at Frank McLowry. I do not know which shot was first; we fired almost together. The fight then became general. After about four shots were fired Ike Clanton ran up and grabbed my right arm. I could see no weapon in his hand and thought at the time he had none and I said to him. "The fight has now commenced; go to shooting or get away;" at the same time I pushed him off with my left hand. He started and ran down the side of the building and disappeared between the lodging house and the photograph gallery. My first shot struck Frank McLowry in the belly. He staggered off on the sidewalk but first fired one shot at me. When we told them to throw up their hands Claiborne held up his left hand and then broke and ran. I never saw him afterwards until late in the afternoon, after the fight. I never drew my pistol or made a motion to shoot until after Billy Clanton and Frank McLowry drew their pistols. If Tom McLowry was unarmed I did not know it. I believe he was armed and that he fired two shots at our party before Holliday, who had the shotgun, fired at and killed him. If he was unarmed there was nothing in the circumstances, or in what had been communicated to me, or in his acts or threats that would have led me even to suspect his being unarmed. I never fired at Ike Clanton, even after the shooting commenced because I thought he was unarmed. I believed then and believe now from the acts I have stated and the threats I have related and other threats communicated to me by different persons, as having been made by Tom McLowry, Frank McLowry and Isaac Clanton, that these men last named had formed a conspiracy to murder my brothers Morgan and Virgil and Doc Holliday and myself. I believe I would have been legally and morally justifiable in shooting any of them on sight, but I did not do so or attempt to do so; I sought no advantage. When I went as deputy marshal to help disarm them and arrest them, I went as part of my duty and under the direction of my brother the marshal. I did not intend to fight unless it became necessary in self defense and in the performance of official duty. When Billy Clanton and Frank McLowry drew their pistols I knew it was a fight for life and I drew and fired in defense of my own life, and the lives of my brothers and Doc Holliday.

I have been in Tombstone since Dec. 1, 1879. I came here from Dodge City, Kansas, where against the protests of business men and officials I resigned the office of City Marshal which I held there from 1876. I came to Dodge City from Wichita, Kansas. I was on the police force in Wichita from 1874 until I went to Dodge City.

The testimony of Isaac Clanton that I had anything to do with any stage robbery, or any other criminal enterprise, is a tissue of lies from beginning to end. Sheriff Behan made me an offer in his office on Allen street, and in the back room of a cigar store, that if I would withdraw and not try to get appointed sheriff of Cochise county that we would hire a clerk and divide the profits. I done so and he never said another word to me afterwards in regard to it. The reasons given by him here for not complying with his contract are false.

I give here as a part of this statement, a document sent me from Dodge City, since my arrest and marked Exhibit A, and another document sent me from Wichita, since this arrest which I wish attached to this statement; and marked Exhibit B.

Exhibit "A"

To All Whom it May Concern, Greeting: We, the undersigned citizens of Dodge City, Ford County, Kansas, and vicinity do by these presents certify that we are personally acquainted with Wyatt Earp, late of this city; that he came here in the year 1876, that during the years 1877, 1878 and 1879, he was Marshal of our city; that he left our place in the fall of 1879; that during his whole stay here he occupied a place of high social position and was regarded and looked upon as a high-minded, honorable citizen; that as Marshal of our city he was ever vigilant in the discharge of his duties, and while kind and courteous to all, he was brave, unflinching, and on all occasions proved himself the right man in the right place. Hearing that he is now under arrest, charged with complicity in the killing of three men termed cowboys, from our knowledge of him we do not believe that he would wantonly take the life of his fellow man, and that, if he was implicated, he only took life in the discharge of his sacred trust to the people, and earnestly appeal to the Citizens of Tombstone, Arizona, to use all means to secure for him a fair and impartial trial, fully confident that when tried he will be fully vindicated and exonerated of any crime.

This exhibit was signed by sixty judges, county officers, city officials, lawyers, clergymen, and other citizens, and notarized by the clerk of the district court.

Exhibit "B"

State of Kansas, County of Sedgwick, City of Wichita.—We, the undersigned citizens of Wichita, in the county and state aforesaid, are well acquainted with Mr. Wyatt S. Earp, and that we were intimately acquainted with him while he was on the police force of this city in the years A. D. 1874, 1875 and part of 1876. We further certify that said Wyatt S. Earp was a good and efficient officer and was well known for his honesty and integrity, that his character while here was of the best, and that no fault was ever found with him as an officer or as a man. (Signed) George E. Harris, Mayor in 1875; M. Zummerly, councilman in 1875; C. M. Garrison, councilman in 1875; R. Cogden, ex-city marshal; J. M. Stove, ex-city treasurer; Fred Schlattner, city clerk; James Cauns, city marshal, etc. etc.

Wyatt Earp then continued his testimony.

Myself and Doc Holliday happened to go to Charleston the night that Behan happened to go down to subpoena Ike Clanton. We went there for the purpose of getting a horse that had been stolen from us a few days after I came to Tombstone. I had heard several times that the Clanton's had him. When I got there that night I was told by a friend of mine that the man who carried the dispatch from Charleston to Ike Clanton's ranch had rode my horse. At this time I did not know where Ike Clanton's ranch was. A short time afterwards I was in the Huachuca's, locating some water rights. I had started home to Tombstone and had got within twelve or fifteen miles of Charleston when I met a man named McMasters. He told me if I would hurry up I would find my horse in Charleston. I drove to Charleston and saw my horse going through the streets toward the corral. I put up for the night at another corral. I went to Barnett's office to get out papers to recover the horse. He was not at home, having gone to Sonora to see some coal fields that had been discovered. I telegraphed to Tombstone to James Earp, and papers were made out and sent to Charleston that night. While I was in town, waiting for the papers, Billy Clanton found out I was there. He went and tried to take the horse out of the corral. I told him he could not take him out; that it was my horse. After the papers came he gave the horse up without the papers being served, and asked me "if I had any more horses to lose." I told him I would keep him in the stable after this and not give him a chance to steal him.

In one of the conversations I had with Ike Clanton about giving away Leonard, Head and Crane, I told him one reason why I wanted to catch them was to prove to the citizens of Tombstone that Doc Holliday had nothing to do with it [Note: Earp refers here to the holdup of the Benson stage and the murder of Philpot.] as there were some false statements circulating to that effect. In following the trail of Leonard, Head and Crane, we struck it at the scene of the attempted robbery and never lost the trail of hardly a footprint from the time that we started from Drew's ranch, on the San Pedro, until we got to Helm's ranch in the Dragoons. After following about eighty miles down the San Pedro river, and capturing one of the men named King, that was supposed to be in with them, we then crossed Catalina mountains within fifteen miles of Tucson, following their trail around the front of the mountain after they had crossed over to Tres Alamos, on the San Pedro river. We then started out from Helm's ranch and got on their trail. They had stolen fifteen or twenty head of stock so as to cover their trail. Wyatt Earp, Morgan Earp, H. R. Paul, Breakenridge, Johnny Behan and one or two others still followed the trail up into New Mexico. The trails never led south from Helm's ranch, as Ike Clanton has stated. We used every effort we could to capture these men. I was out ten days. Virgil Earp and Morgan Earp were out sixteen days, and we done all we could to capture these men, and I safely say that if it had not been for myself and Morgan Earp, they would not have got King, as he started to run when we rode up to his hiding place, and was making for a big patch of brush on the river, and would not have got him if it had not been for us.—(Nov. 17, 1881).

This testimony revealed many facts and undercurrents for the first time, but the court thought them extraneous.

Judge Spicer, however, considered the fact that the Cowboys had threatened the Earps and refused to give up their guns unless the officers of the law were also disarmed, of great importance and in a clearly worded opinion he discharged the defendants.

Opinion of Justice Wells Spicer

The case has now been on hearing for the past thirty days during which time a volume of testimony has been taken and eminent legal talent employed on both sides.

The great importance of the case as well as the general interest taken in it by the entire community, demand that I should be full and explicit in my findings and conclusions and should give ample reason for what I do.

From the mass of evidence before me—much of which is upon collateral matters—I have found it necessary for the purposes of this decision to consider only those facts which are conceded by both sides or are established by a large preponderance of the testimony.

Viewing it in this manner I find that on the morning of the 26th day of October, 1881, and up to noon of that day, Joseph I. Clanton, or Isaac Clanton, the prosecuting witness in this case was about the streets and in several saloons of Tombstone armed with revolver and Winchester rifle, declaring publicly that the Earp brothers and Holliday had insulted him the night before when he was unarmed, and now he was armed and intended to shoot them or fight them on sight. These threats were communicated to defendants Virgil Earp and Wyatt Earp. Virgil Earp was at the time Chief of Police of the city of Tombstone, and charged, as such officer, by the city ordinances, with the duty of preserving the peace, and of arresting, with or without warrant, all persons engaged in any disorderly act whereby a breach of the peace might be occasioned and to arrest and disarm all persons violating the city ordinances which declare it to be unlawful to carry on the person any deadly weapon within the city limits without first obtaining a permit in writing.

Shortly after noon of October 26th the defendant, Virgil Earp, as chief of police, assisted at the time by Morgan Earp who was also at the time a special policeman in the pay of the city and wearing his badge, arrested and disarmed Isaac Clanton, and in such arrest and disarmament inflicted upon the side of his head a blow from a pistol. Whether this blow was necessary or not is not material here to determine. Isaac Clanton was then taken to Justice or Recorder Wallace, where he was fined and his arms, consisting of a revolver and Winchester rifle, taken from him and deposited at the Grand Central Hotel subject to his order.

While at Justice Wallace's court and awaiting the coming of Judge Wallace some hot words passed between Isaac Clanton and Wyatt Earp—Earp accusing Clanton of having previously threatened to take his life and then proposed to make a fight with him anywhere, to which Isaac Clanton assented and then declared that "fight was his racket," and that when he was arrested and disarmed, if Earp had been a second late there would have been a coroner's inquest in town. Immediately subsequent to this a difficulty occurred in front of Judge Wallace's court room between Wyatt Earp and the deceased Thomas McLowry in which the latter was struck by the former with a pistol and knocked down.

In view of these controversies between Wyatt Earp and Isaac Clanton and Thomas McLowry, and in further view of the quarrel the night before between Isaac Clanton and J. H. Holliday, I am of the opinion that the defendant, Virgil Earp, as chief of police, by subsequently calling upon Wyatt Earp and J. H. Holliday to assist him in arresting and disarming the Clantons and McLowrys committed an injudicious and censurable act; and although in this he acted improperly and without circumspection, yet when we consider the conditions of affairs incidental to a frontier county; the lawlessness and disregard for human life; the existence of a law-defying element in our midst; the fear and feeling of insecurity that has existed; the supposed prevalence of bad, desperate and reckless men who have been a terror to the county and kept away capital and enterprise, and considering the many threats that had been made against the Earps, I can attach no criminality to his unwise act. In fact, as the results plainly prove, he needed the assistance and support of staunch and true friends, upon whose courage, coolness, and fidelity he could depend in case of an emergency.

Considering all the testimony together I am of the opinion that the weight of evidence sustains and corroborates the testimony of Wyatt and Virgil Earp that their demand for surrender was met by Wm. Clanton and Frank McLowry drawing, or making motions to draw their pistols. Upon this hypothesis my duty is clear.

The defendants were officers charged with the duty of arresting and disarming brave and determined men who were experts in the use of firearms, as quick as thought and certain as death, and who had previously declared their intention not to be arrested or disarmed.

In coming to this conclusion I give great weight to several particular circumstances connected with the affray. It is claimed by the prosecution that the deceased were shot while holding up their hands in obedience to the demand of the chief of police, and on the other hand the defense claims that Wm. Clanton and Frank McLowry at once drew their pistols and began firing simultaneously with the defendants. William Clanton was wounded on the wrist of the right hand on the first fire and thereafter used his pistol with his left. This wound is such as could not have been received with his hands thrown up, and the wound received by Thomas McLowry was such as could not have been received with his hands on his coat lapels. These circumstances being indubitably facts, throw great doubt upon the correctness of statements of witnesses to the contrary.

The testimony of Isaac Clanton that this tragedy was the result of a scheme on the part of the Earps to assassinate him, and thereby bury in oblivion the confessions the Earps had made to him about "piping" away the shipment of coin by Wells, Fargo & co., falls short of being a sound theory because of the great fact, most prominent in the matter, to wit, that Isaac Clanton was not injured at all, and could have been killed first and easiest. If it was the object of the attack to kill him he would have been the first to fall; but as it was, he was known or believed to be unarmed, and was suffered, and, so Wyatt Earp testifies, to go away and was not harmed.

I also give just weight in this matter to the testimony of Sheriff Behan, who said, on one occasion, a short time ago, Isaac Clanton told him that he (Clanton) had been informed that the sheriff was coming to arrest him, and that he (Clanton) armed his crowd with guns and was determined not to be arrested by the sheriff, or words to that effect. And Sheriff Behan further testifies that a few minutes before the Earps came to them, that he, as sheriff, had demanded of the Clantons and McLowrys that they give up their arms, and that they demurred, as he said, and did not do it and that Frank McLowry refused and gave as a reason that he was not ready to leave town just then, and would not give up his arms unless the Earps were disarmed, that is the chief of police and his assistants should be disarmed.

The *Epitaph,* or Judge Spicer, apparently was in error here, as the statement regarding the attempted disarmament of Frank McLowry, appears in Ike Clanton's testimony, not Sheriff Behan's.

In view of the past history of the county and the generally believed existence at this time of desperate, reckless and lawless men in our midst, banded together for mutual support, and living by felonious and predatory pursuits, regarding neither lives nor property in their career, and at this time for men to parade the streets armed with repeating rifles and six-shooters and demand that the chief of police of the city and his assistants should be disarmed is a proposition both monstrous and startling. This was said by one of the deceased only a few minutes before the arrival of the Earps.

Another fact that rises up preeminent in the consideration of this sad affair, is the leading fact that the deceased from the very first inception of the encounter were standing their ground and fighting back, giving and taking death with unflinching bravery. It does not appear to have been a wanton slaughter of unresisting and unarmed innocents, who were yielding graceful submission to the officers of the law, or surrendering to or fleeing from their assailants, but armed and defiant men, accepting the wager of battle and succumbing only in death.

The prosecution claim much upon the point that the Earp party acted with criminal haste; that they precipitated the triple homicide by a felonious anxiety and quickness to begin the tragedy; that they precipitated the killing with malice aforethought, with the felonious intent then and there to murder the deceased and that they made use of their official character as a pretext.

I cannot believe this theory and cannot resist firm conviction that the Earps acted wisely, discreetly and prudentially to secure their own self-preservation—they saw at once the dire necessity of giving the first shot to save themselves from certain death. They acted; their shots were effective, and this alone saved all the Earp party from being slain.

In view of all the facts and circumstances of the case; considering the threats made, the character and position of the parties, and the tragical results accomplished, in manner and form as they were, with all surrounding influences bearing upon the result of the affair, I cannot resist the conclusion that the defendants were fully justified in committing these homicides; that it was a necessary act done in the discharge of official duty.'— (Dec. 1, 1881.)

The Earps and Doc Holliday were free men but they walked with death when they strode the streets of Tombstone. The Cowboys were their sworn and open enemies, and the town knew another chapter must eventually be written in blood and gunfire.

10 Vengeance

In the stubborn caliche at the brow of Boot Hill Cemetery, where the eye sweeps across the desert valley to the Dragoon and Whetstone mountains, there were two new graves, which held the bodies of three enemies of the Earp clan.

The Cowboys had made one effort to drive the Earps out in an open battle and had found the price of that kind of warfare too high. But they had no intention of leaving the Earps and the law and order forces in control of Tombstone if they could prevent it.

Judge Spicer soon received a threatening message warning him to leave, and on December 15, the Tucson night stage, in which Mayor Clum was riding was fired upon by highwaymen. These efforts having failed, the next move was an attempt at assassination. Virgil Earp, now a deputy United States Marshal, was the victim, and while he escaped death he was crippled for life. The *Epitaph* had this story.

MIDNIGHT ASSASSINS

U. S. Deputy Marshal Virgil W. Earp Shot in the Back
The Facts as Far as Learned

About 11:30 o'clock last night, U. S. Deputy Marshal Virgil Earp, was proceeding from the Oriental Saloon from the northeast corner of Allen and Fifth streets to his room at the Cosmopolitan hotel, and when he was about the middle of the crossing of Fifth street, five shots were fired in rapid succession by unknown men who were standing in the old Palace saloon that is being rebuilt next door above Trasker and Pridham's store, on the southwest corner of the same streets. Immediately after the firing the assassins ran rapidly down Fifth past the Combination shaft and disappeared in the darkness beyond Tough Nut street.

Two of the shots took effect on Mr. Earp, one badly shattering his left arm, and the other entered his left side, producing a wound the nature of which has not been ascertained at the present writing. Three of the shots went through one of the windows of the Eagle Brewery saloon on the northeast corner in range with which Mr. Earp happened to be at the time of the firing. The holes in the windows were about at the height of four, six and seven feet respectively above the sidewalk; but fortunately none of the inmates of the saloon were injured, the shots impinging harmlessly upon the opposite wall of the room.

Later Particulars

Since the above was written it has been learned that immediately after the shooting three men ran past the ice house on Tough Nut street and sung out to the man in attendance who had his door open at the time, "Lock your door." The same three men were seen by a miner a few minutes later making down into the gulch below the Vizina hoisting works. The shots were evidently fired from double barreled shotguns, loaded with buckshot, and there must have been three men as five shots were fired in rapid succession. It is simply a miracle that Mr. Earp was not instantly killed, as in the darkness, with the simple aid of a bit of lighted paper the marks of nineteen shots were found on the east side of the Eagle brewery and in the awning posts, three of them passing through a window on that side of the house.

Mr. Earp walked into the Oriental and told his brother Wyatt that he was shot. His friends escorted him to his room at the Cosmopolitan hotel and Drs. Matthews and Goodfellow were immediately called in to attend upon him. It was learned before going to press that his left arm received the principal damage, the shot taking effect just above the elbow, producing a longitudinal fracture of the bone between the shoulder and elbow. So far as could be learned the wound in his back is not necessarily dangerous, though painful.

This further proves that there is a band of assassins in our midst, who, having threatened the lives of Judge Spicer, Mayor Clum, Mr. Williams, the Earp brothers and Holliday, have attempted upon two occasions to carry their threats into execution, first upon Mayor Clum and second upon Virgil Earp. The question naturally arises, who will be the next subject? and a further question, How long will our people stand for this sort of thing? It is no fault of these damned assassins that several persons were not killed in their dastardly attempt to murder a United States

> officer last night; for there were many people in the Eagle Brewery, over the heads of whom the passing shots flew on their course. A few inches lower and there would have been corpses prostrate upon the floor in place of frightened people wondering what had happened to cause this bombardment.— (Dec. 29, 1881.)

The *Epitaph's* closing paragraph points up a period which has apparently been given too little attention. Something approaching terror was abroad, and the *Epitaph* asks a question which many people must have been asking, "Who will be next?" Then it asks another, even more significant question, "How long will our people stand for this sort of thing?"

This was the second time since the fight at the OK Corral that Clum referred to the possibility of direct action by the people. It is doubtful, however, that his intention was to awaken a mob. He was too strongly committed to law and order to countenance that course. What seems probable is that he was referring to the Vigilantes. That they existed there is no doubt, although the *Epitaph* did not mention them openly at any time.

Breakenridge, however, speaks, in *Helldorado* of "a law and order committee formed in Tombstone that stood in with the gang that was opposed to the sheriff." He also refers with apparent relish to one occasion on which the district judge gave several members of "a so-called law and order committee" a warrant for the arrest of Curly Bill and members of his gang. Breakenridge heard of it and released Johnny Ringo, whom he had just arrested, and Ringo rode to Galeyville to warn his friends.

Earp's biographer, Stuart Lake, goes much farther than Breakenridge in clearing up the status of the Vigilantes. He says that after the holdup of the Bisbee stage, Acting Governor John J. Gosper and United States Marshal Crawley P. Dake, held a conference with certain Tombstone citizens at which Wyatt Earp was made a special officer and given command of a posse of seven deputies, among whom were his brothers, Morgan and Warren, and Doc Holliday. Lake says also that the sum of $15,000 was raised and placed to Earp's credit so that he might pay his deputies who were to serve warrants issued by Judge William H. Stilwell of the district court.

This version is supported by a proclamation which was published in the *Epitaph* two months after the attack on Virgil Earp. It appears later in this chapter.

Three months after the attack on Virgil Earp the outlaws struck again from the dark, firing at Wyatt and Morgan Earp through the glass in the rear door of a billiard parlor. The bullet intended for Wyatt missed its target but Morgan was mortally wounded.

The *Epitaph* used its biggest one-column headline on the story.

THE DEADLY BULLET

The Assassin at Last Successful in His Devilish Mission Morgan Earp Shot Down and Killed While Playing Billiards

At 10:50 Saturday night while engaged in playing a game of billiards in Campbell & Hatch's billiard parlor, on Allen street between Fourth and Fifth, Morgan Earp was shot through the body by an unknown assassin. At the time the shot was fired he was playing a game of billiards with Bob Hatch, one of the proprietors of the house and was standing with his back to the glass door in the rear of the room that opens out upon the alley that leads straight through the block along the west side of A. D. Otis & Co.'s store to Fremont street. This door is the ordinary glass door with four panes in the top in place of panels. The two lower panes are painted, the upper ones being clear. Anyone standing outside can look over the painted glass and see anything going on in the room just as well as though standing in the open door. At the time the shot was fired the deceased must have been standing within ten feet of the door, and the assassin standing near enough to see his position, took aim for about the middle of his person, shooting through the upper portion of the whitened glass. The bullet entered the right side of the abdomen, passing through the spinal column, completely shattering it, emerging on the left side, passing the length of the room and lodging in the thigh of Geo. A. B. Berry, who was standing by the stove, inflicting a painful flesh wound. Instantly after the first shot a second was fired through the top of the upper glass which passed across the room and lodged in the wall near the ceiling over the head of Wyatt Earp, who was sitting a spectator of the game. Morgan fell instantly upon the first fire and lived only about one hour. His brother Wyatt, Tipton, and McMasters rushed to the side of the wounded man and tenderly picked him up and moved him some ten feet away near the door of the card room, where Drs. Matthews, Goodfellow and Millar, who were called, examined him and, after a brief consultation, pronounced the wound mortal. He was then moved into the card room and placed on the lounge where in a few brief moments he breathed his last, surrounded by his brothers Wyatt, Virgil, James and Warren with the wives of Virgil and James and a few of his most intimate friends. Notwithstanding the intensity of his mortal agony, not a word of complaint escaped his lips, and all that were heard, except those whispered into the ears of his brother and known only to him were, "Don't, I can't stand it. This is the last game of pool I'll ever play." The first part of the sentence being wrung from him by an attempt to place him upon his feet.

His body was placed in a casket and sent to his parents at Colton, Cal., for burial, being guarded to Contention by his brothers and two or three of his most intimate friends. The funeral cortege started away from the Cosmopolitan hotel about 12:30 yesterday with the fire bell tolling out its solemn peals of "Earth to earth, dust to dust."—(March 20, 1882.)

Wyatt Earp testified before the coroner's jury. He knew who had murdered his brother and, without waiting for the verdict, he took the road for Contention with Morgan's body. Virgil Earp, still crippled from the effect of gunshot wounds, went with him and so did Doc Holliday, Warren Earp, and other members of the Vigilante group. At Contention the party boarded the train for Tucson, and Colton, California.

There are conflicting stories of what transpired when Wyatt and his party reached the Tucson railroad yards. The *Epitaph's* story came by wire and carried three possible versions. One thing was certain: when the train pulled out of Tucson for California only Virgil Earp was aboard with the body of Morgan, and Frank Stilwell lay dead between the tracks in the Tucson yard.

Here is the story which Tombstone read.

ANOTHER ASSASSINATION

Frank Stillwell Found Dead This Morning
Another Chapter in the Earp-Clanton Tragedy

Special to the Epitaph.

Tucson, March 21—This morning at daylight the track man from the Southern Pacific railroad found the body of Frank Stilwell, about one hundred yards north of Porter's hotel at the side of the track, riddled with bullets. The circumstances of the case, so far as learned, are as follows: Stilwell arrived here Sunday to appear before the grand jury on a charge of stage robbery near Bisbee last November. He was under bonds for his appearance. Last night when the westbound passenger train arrived it brought the

Remains of Morgan Earp

who had been killed Saturday night at Tombstone and his three brothers, accompanied by Sherman McMasters, Doc Holliday and a man known as Johnson, all heavily armed with shotguns and revolvers. A few minutes before the train started Stilwell and Ike Clanton (brother of Wm. Clanton who was killed in Tombstone by the Earps) went to the depot to meet a man by the name of McDowell who was to have come in as a witness before the grand jury. On their arrival at the depot they saw the Earp party walking on the platform. Stilwell advised Clanton to leave at once saying they wanted to kill him. Clanton left a few minutes later. Stilwell was seen

Walking Down the Track

in the direction where his body was found. Four of the armed men who were on the platform soon followed. One was described as a slender, light complexioned man wearing a white hat. Just as the train was leaving six shots were heard in the locality of the assassination, but attracted no particular attention and nothing was known of the tragedy until this morning when the body was discovered. Six shots went into his body—four rifle balls and two loads of buck shot. Both legs were shot through and

A Charge of Buckshot

in his left thigh and a charge through his breast, which must have been delivered close, as the coat was powderburnt, and six buckshot holes within a radius of three inches. Stilwell had a pistol on his person which was not discharged. He evidently was taken unaware as he was desperate in a fight and a quick shot. His watch was taken in the hurry of which a part of the chain was left. There is much excitement here concerning the assassination and many speculations are rife. Some say that he was

Decoyed to the Spot,

where he fell as he possessed strong evidence against certain stage robbers. Others think he was trying to get away from the Earp party and was overtaken, while it is thought by some he went down the track to shoot one or more of the Earp party as the train was moving out, two of them being on board. The killing is thought to have been done by four of the party who accompanied the Earps here, as the four men who followed the deceased down the track

Were Not Seen Again.

This morning at one o'clock as the east bound train approached Papago, nine miles east of here, it was flagged and four armed men got on the train. They are strongly suspected. The deceased was 27 years of age; was a native of Texas; is a brother of the famous scout Jack Stilwell. He has been in Arizona four years; was a teamster at Signal for some time and lately has been keeping a livery stable at Charleston and Bisbee, and was an ex-deputy sheriff of Cochise county. Yesterday Ike Clanton received several dispatches from Tombstone warning him to look out—that a party was coming down to put him out of the way, which put him

On His Guard

The authorities here are determined to go to the bottom of the affair, and if the parties are apprehended there will be no sham examination, but a trial on merits, and the guilty parties, whoever they may be, will suffer the penalty of the law.

About the time Stilwell's body was found in Tucson, Wyatt Earp and his friends got off a train in Contention, where they were met by Vigilantes, who escorted them to Tombstone.

The *Epitaph* carried the verdicts of two coroner's juries that day, one of which sat in Tombstone, the other in Tucson. The Tombstone jury said that Morgan Earp came to his death by a gunshot wound inflicted by Frank Stilwell, Pete Spence, and

Indian Charley, a halfbreed. It based its finding on the testimony given by Spence's wife.

The *Epitaph* thought the testimony of Mrs. Spence so important that it published her statement in full. Since Wyatt Earp knew of this testimony before he found Stilwell in the railroad yards in Tucson, it seems necessary to insert it here.

Marietta D. Spence, being sworn, testifies as follows: Reside in Tombstone and am the wife of Peter Spence; on last Saturday, the 18th of March, was in my home on Fremont street; for two days my husband was not home, but in Charleston, but came home about 12 o'clock p. m. Saturday. He came with two parties, one named Freis, a German; I don't know the other's name but he lives in the house of Manuel Acusto. Each one had a rifle. Immediately after arriving he sent a man to take care of the horses and take them to the house of Manuel Acusto. Then they entered the front room and began to converse with Frank Stilwell. When they had finished, Frank Stilwell went out and Spence went to bed. This all happened that night. Spence remained in bed until 9 o'clock a. m. Sunday. Freis slept there. The other man went to his house on Friday and stayed all day; went out Friday night but returned in a short time to sleep. Saturday he was out all day and up to 12 o'clock at night, when Spence came in. There was an Indian with Stilwell called Charley. He was armed with a pistol and a carbine. He left Saturday morning with Stilwell and came back with him at 12 o'clock at night. Both Charley and Stilwell were armed with pistols and carbines when they returned to the house Saturday night. The conversation between Spence and Stilwell and the others was carried on in a low tone. They appeared to be talking some secret. When they came in I got out of bed to receive them and noticed they were excited, why I don't know. Stilwell came into the house about an hour before Spence and the other two. Stilwell brought me a dispatch from Spence, saying he would be up from Charleston that night, Saturday; (received it about two o'clock in the day). Think Spence left last night, the 20th, for Sonora. Don't know positively that he went. On Sunday morning Spence told me to get breakfast about six o'clock—which I did, after we had a quarrel during which he struck me and my mother and during which he threatened to shoot me, when my mother told him he would have to shoot her too. His expression was that if I said a word about something

I knew that he would kill me; that he was going to Sonora and would leave my dead body behind him. Spence didn't tell me so but I know he killed Morgan Earp; I think he did it because he arrived at the house all of a tremble, and both the others who came with him. Spence's teeth were chattering when he came in. I asked him if he wanted something to eat and he said he did not. Myself and mother heard the shots and it was a little after when Stilwell and the Indian, Charley, came in, and from one-half to three-quarters of an hour after Spence and the other two men came. I think that Spence and the other two men, although they might have arrived during the night, had left their horses outside of town, and after the shooting had gone and got them. I judged they had been doing wrong from the condition, white and trembling, in which they arrived. Spence and the two men had been for several days in the habit of leaving home in the middle of the day and returning in the middle of the night, but they never returned in the same condition as they did on that night, and after hearing the next morning of Earp's death, I came to the conclusion that Spence and the others had done the deed. Have not seen the Indian, Charley, since that night; do not know where he is. Four days ago while mother and myself were standing at Spence's house, talking with Spence and the Indian, Morgan Earp passed by, when Spence nudged the Indian and said "That's him; that's him." The Indian then started down the street so as to get ahead of him and get a good look a him. Freis is a German who works for Acusto as teamster. Think he was with Spence, Saturday night and assisted in killing Earp, also Stilwell and Indian Charley.

Warrants were immediately issued but Frank Stilwell was beyond the reach of the law.

The verdict of the Tucson jury appeared in a telegraphic dispatch. It found that Stilwell came to his death "from shots fired by Wyatt and Warren Earp, Doc Holliday, Texas Jack, alias Johnson, and McMasters." Warrants for their arrest were to be issued.

Later that afternoon the Earp party left the Cosmopolitan Hotel, brushed Sheriff Behan aside, and, mounting their horses, rode down Allen Street into the desert.

The *Nugget* carried a sensational story the next day in which it charged that Sheriff Behan had attempted to arrest Wyatt Earp, and had been immediately confronted by six-shooters.

The *Epitaph* published a calmer report in which it took a passing shot at its contemporary. As the *Epitaph* reported the departure this is what happened.

DOES MISREPRESENTATION PAY?

The mission of a journal is to give news in a plain, intelligent manner, devoid of distortion and misrepresentation. In deviating from such a course it ceases to be a newspaper and becomes a medium for the communication of personal malice and doing grave public injustice. The *Nugget* this morning was guilty of a gross mis-statement in reporting a matter of news that the public were entitled to have in all its nakedness and truth. It states in the most positive terms that the sheriff made an attempt to arrest the Earp party at the Cosmopolitan hotel and was instantly confronted by a six-shooter in the hands of each one of the six men composing the party. Now the facts of the case are, as derived from eye-witnesses and as good and reliable men as there are in Tombstone, that all that passed between the sheriff and the Earp party was this; Sheriff Behan was standing in the office of the Cosmopolitan hotel, when Wyatt Earp and the others composing the party came into the office from the rear entrance, each one having a rifle in his hands, in the ordinary manner of carrying a gun, and passed through the room to the street. As Wyatt advanced to the front and approached Sheriff Behan, the sheriff said to him, "Wyatt, I want to see you." Wyatt replied, "You can't see me; you have seen me once too often," or words to that effect. He passed out into the street and turned around and said, "I will see Paul," [Note: Sheriff Paul of Tucson] and then the party passed on down the street. These gentlemen say that no word was spoken by the sheriff that implied a demand for an arrest and that no weapons were drawn or pointed at the sheriff. Furthermore, one of these gentlemen says that he considers the sheriff did well in not attempting to make the arrest last night, under the circumstances; that he expects the Earp party will surrender themselves to Sheriff Paul, of Pima County, when he arrives. These are the plain, unvarnished facts, that can be substantiated, as before said, by some of the best men in Tombstone.—(March 22, 1882.)

A telegraphed warrant for Wyatt Earp and others named by the coroner's jury reached Tombstone, and Sheriff Behan raised a posse and began to scour the desert for the missing men. As deputies he swore in many of the tough characters whom he knew were Earp's deadliest enemies. Among them were Ike Clanton, Johnny Ringo, and Curly Bill.

The town seethed with condemnation of the sheriff but the *Nugget* said the men were all "honest ranchers." It was to prove a stupid act on Behan's part.

There was a touch of the comic opera in the way Behan's men rode in and out of town, spurs jingling, guns glinting, without ever coming within shooting distance of Wyatt Earp.

But there was no comic opera about Earp's actions. One of the men named as his brother's killer was dead. Now the half-breed, Florentine, alias Indian Charley, met the same fate.

The *Epitaph* told this story.

STILL ANOTHER KILLING

A Mexican Found Dead This Morning
The Act Supposed to be the Work of the Earps

This afternoon Theodore D. Judah came in from Pete Spence's wood camp in the South Pass of the Dragoons and gave an Epitaph reporter the following information: Yesterday morning, about 11 o'clock, Wyatt and Warren Earp, Doc Holliday, McMasters, Texas Jack and Johnson, came into camp and inquired for Pete Spence and Indian Charley; also as to the number of men there and their whereabouts. Judah informed them that Spence was in Tombstone and that a Mexican named Florentine was looking for some stock which had strayed away. Judah indicated the direction taken by the Mexican and the party immediately left as directed, passing over a hill which hid them from view.

A few minutes later ten or twelve shots were heard. Florentine not returning, this morning Judah proceeded in search of him and found the body not far from camp, riddled with bullets. Judah immediately came to town with the news. He states that had the sheriff's posse come a mile further they would have had all the information they wanted.—(March 23, 1882.)

Some of the criticisms made of Wyatt Earp are based on the assumption that, after the death of Morgan, he took the law into his own hands and set out coldly to get the killers.

Even some of the people of Tombstone in 1882 might have wondered what powers he possessed. But if they did the *Epitaph* answered them the day after the shooting of Indian Charley, when it published this message and warning from the mayor of the town.

PROCLAMATION

To the citizens of the city of Tombstone: I am informed by his Honor, William H. Stilwell, Judge of the District Court of the First Judicial District, Cochise county, that Wyatt S. Earp, who left the city yesterday with a posse, was intrusted with warrants for the arrest of divers persons charged with criminal offenses. I request the public within this city to abstain from any interference with the execution of said warrants.

Dated January 24, 1882

JOHN CARR, Mayor.

This would seem to make it clear that the responsible citizens of Tombstone believed Earp was an honest officer of the law, and that he did have official support.

On this proclamation alone, were he alive today, Wyatt Earp might well rest his case at the bar of public opinion.

All Tombstone must have waited impatiently for the daily issues of the *Epitaph* during this brief period. No day passed without its moments of drama. The killing of Morgan Earp, the mysterious death of Stilwell, the departure of the Earps, the killing of Indian Charley, the publication of the mayor's proclamation took place in five days, and on the sixth day the *Epitaph* broke the most sensational story of all.

Clum, as might be expected, apparently had an open pipeline into Law and Order League headquarters. So the *Epitaph* scooped the *Nugget* on the killing of Curly Bill in a Wild West tale. As always, the *Epitaph* told the story with great deliberation, introducing the background first.

Here is the account of what the *Epitaph* called "one of the most desperate fights that ever took place on Arizona soil."

BATTLE OF BURLEIGH

The Earp Party Ambushed by Curly Bill and Eight Cowboys

A Hand to Hand Encounter in Which Curly Bill is Killed

The town has been full of reports the last two or three days as to the whereabouts of the Earp party, and their probable movements. No sooner had one report got well under way than another was issued which contradicted it. There has been marching and countermarching by the sheriff and his posse until the community has become so used to the ring of spurs and clank of steel that comparatively little attention is paid to the appearance of large bodies of horsemen in the streets. Yesterday afternoon the sheriff with a large force started down the road toward Contention, possibly to follow up the report that the party had been seen in the Whetstone mountains, west of the San Pedro river, with their horses completely fagged out and the men badly demoralized. This, like so many other reports, was as baseless as the fabric of a dream.

The Battle of Burleigh Springs

Yesterday afternoon as the sun was descending low down the western horizon, had a person been traveling on the Crystal or Lewis Spring road towards the Burleigh Spring, as our informant was, he would have seen one of the most desperate fights between the six men of the Earp party and nine fierce cowboys led by the daring and notorious Curly Bill, that ever took place between opposing forces on Arizona soil. Burleigh Springs is about eight miles south of Tombstone and some four miles east of Charleston, near the mine of that name, and near the short road from Tombstone and Hereford. As our informant, who was traveling on horseback leisurely along toward the Burleigh, came to a slight elevation in the road about a half mile south thereof, he observed a party of six men ride down to the spring from the east, where they all dismounted. They had not much more than got well upon their feet when there rose up at a short distance away

Nine Armed Men

who took deadly aim and fired simultaneously at the Earp party, for such the six men proved to be. Horrified at the sight that like a lightning stroke flashed upon his vision, he instinctively stopped and watched for what was to follow. Not a man went down under this murderous fire, but like a thunderbolt shot from the hand of Jove the six desperate men charged upon their assailants like the light brigade at Balaklava, and when within easy reach returned the fire under which one man went down never more to rise again. The remaining eight fled to the brush and regained their horses when they rode away towards Charleston as if the King of Terrors was at their heels in hot pursuit. The six men fired but one volley and from the close range it is supposed that several of the ambushed cowboys were seriously if not fatally wounded.

The Six Men

returned to their horses where one was found to be in the agony of death, he having received one of the leaden messengers intended for his rider. The party remained at the spring for some time refreshing themselves and their animals when they departed going southerly as if they were making for Sonora.

The Dead Man Curly Bill

After the road was clear our informant rode on and came upon the dead man, who, from the description given, was none other than Curly Bill, the man who killed Marshal White in the streets of Tombstone, one year ago last September. Since the above information was obtained it has been learned that friends of Curly Bill went out with a wagon and took the body back to Charleston where the whole affair has been kept a profound secret, so far as the general public is concerned.—(March 25, 1882.)

The following day Sheriff Behan and a large posse went after the Earps again, and the *Epitaph* scarcely bothered to veil its contempt over the fact that the Sheriff was back in town before the day was over. Its news account was very brief.

Search for the Earp Party

Sheriff Behan left with a posse of some fifteen or sixteen men, among whom were John Ringo, Fin Clanton and several others of the cowboy element, together with some of the permanent residents of Tombstone. They went as far out as the Dragoons where they got track of the party they were after and tracked them back (so they say) to within four miles of town, where the trail became obliterated by the passing travel. It is supposed by some they are now within easy reach of Tombstone.—(March 27, 1882.)

Tombstone rocked with rumors after news came of the Battle of Burleigh and there were endless arguments over whether Wyatt Earp had actually killed Curly Bill.

While the *Epitaph* had no doubt of the accuracy of its account, it was too good a newspaper to refuse to print a contradictory report. It did this in what it called

Second Version of the Battle of Burleigh Springs.

On Friday last, Dick Wright, better known in Tombstone as "Whistling Dick" and Tony Kraker were out on the mesa west of Drew's ranch below Contention, in search of strayed mules, and just at evening they rode down to the spring when they were suddenly confronted by four men with leveled guns pointed directly at them. Tony sung out, "what are you doing there you lop-eared Missourian?" This original salutation disarmed the cowboys, who lowered their guns and invited Tony and Dick to get down and make themselves at home, which they did. Sitting around the campfire the four cowboys told them their version of the story which was as follows: They said they were camped at the spring when they saw the Earp party ride down, and not knowing how they stood with them they thought that they would

Give Them a Shot

just for luck so they blazed away and shot off the pommel of Wyatt Earp's saddle and killed the horse that Texas Jack was riding. They said that not one of the Earp party charged upon them but Wyatt, the balance all running away. Wyatt dismounted and fired his gun at them but without effect. Texas Jack is said to have jumped up behind one of the other boys a la Mexicana, and off they went as rapidly as they could. These are about as near the two sides of the fight as can be got at this time.—(April 3, 1882.)

There was no more news from the Earps for several days. Then the *Epitaph* received a letter which it printed with an editor's note.

THE EARP PARTY

Journal of Their Adventures and Wanderings

The following letter was received today written upon detached leaves from an account book, and post-marked Willcox. It may be genuine and may not be; each reader may judge for himself.

In Camp, April 4, 1882

Editor Epitaph:—In reply to the article in the Nugget of March 31, relating to the Earp party and some of the citizens of Graham and Cochise counties I would like to give you the facts in this case concerning our trip in Cochise and Graham counties. Leaving Tombstone Saturday evening, March 25.

We Went Into Camp

six miles north of town. Next morning we were overtaken by six prospectors on their way from Tombstone to Winchester district who asked us to partake of their frugal meal, which we ate with relish, after which we traveled in company with them on the main road to Summit station, where we had dinner and awaited the arrival of the passenger train from the west, expecting

A Friendly Messenger.

From here we continued our journey on the wagon road to Henderson's ranch where we had refreshments for ourselves and horses. Here we were informed that a gentlemanly deputy sheriff of Cochise county, Mr. Frank Hereford (for whom we have the greatest respect as a gentleman and officer) was at the ranch at the time of our arrival and departure and have since learned the reason for not presenting himself was fears for his safety, which we assure him were groundless. Leaving this ranch we went into camp in good grass one mile north. At seven next morning we saddled and went north to

Mr. H. C. Hooker's Ranch

in Graham county where we met Mr. Hooker and asked for refreshments for ourselves and stock, which he kindly granted us with the same hospitality that was tendered us by the ranchers of Cochise county. As regards to Mr. Hooker outfitting us with supplies and fresh horses as was mentioned in the Nugget, it is false and without foundation, as we are riding the same horses we left Tombstone on, with the exception of Texas Jack's horse, which was killed in the

Fight With Curly Bill

and posse, which we replaced by hiring a horse on the San Pedro river. In regard to the reward paid by Stock Association which the Nugget claims Mr. Hooker paid to Wyatt Earp for the killing of Curly Bill, it is also false as no reward has been asked for or tendered.

Leaving Hooker's ranch on the evening of that day we journeyed north to within five miles of Eureka Springs. There we camped with a freighter and was cheerfully offered the best his camp afforded. Next morning, not being in a hurry to break camp, our stay was long enough to notice the

Movements of Sheriff Behan

and his posse of honest ranchers, with whom, if they had possessed the trailing abilities of an average Arizona ranchman, we might have had trouble, which we are not seeking. Neither are we avoiding these honest ranchers as we thoroughly understand their designs.

At Cottonwood we remained overnight and here picked up the trail of the

Lost Charley Ross

"and a hot one." We are confident that our trailing abilities will soon enable us to turn over to the "gentlemen" the fruits of our efforts so that they may not again return to Tombstone empty-handed. Yours respectfully,

One of them.

Perhaps this heavy sarcasm burned Behan, for he took the trial again, and the *Nugget's* report of what happened exasperated the *Epitaph* to a point where it finally adopted the parallel column device. In one column it reprinted the *Nugget* story. In the next column was its own version.

The *Epitaph* account is significant because it reveals the attitude of the ranchers and the United States Army towards the "honest ranchers" in Behan's posse. Since the principals never denied the following *Epitaph* report it may be accepted as accurate.

FACTS OF HISTORY

"Truth Crushed to Earth Shall Rise Again."

Fortunately for the facts of history the Epitaph has a correspondent at the Sierra Bonita ranch, who vouches for the truth of the following narrative of what did occur there during the visits of both the Earp and Sheriff parties.

The Earp party reached Hooker's ranch Monday afternoon, March 27th, where they asked for refreshments for themselves and their horses, which was cheerfully granted them by the proprietor. About seven o'clock in the evening they left the ranch without giving any indication as to what direction they were going that night or in the future. The next morning the sheriff and his posse rode up to the house of Mr. Hooker and DEMANDED refreshments for themselves and beasts which was freely granted them.

After Occurrences

The following is a brief digest of the occurrences at the ranch: Sheriff Behan asked Mr. Hooker if he knew the whereabouts of the Earp party. Mr. Hooker replied that he did not know and that if he did he would not tell him. Sheriff Behan then said, "You must be upholding murderers and outlaws then." Hooker said, "No sir, I am not; I know the Earps and I know you and I know they have always treated me like gentlemen; damn such laws and damn you, and damn your posse; they are a set of horse thieves and outlaws." At this one of the "honest farmers" (?) of the posse spoke up and said, "Damn the son of a b----, he knows where they are and let us make him tell." At this Hooker's hostler stepped away for a moment and returned with a Winchester and drawing a bead on the honest granger said, "You can't come here into a gentleman's yard and call him a son of a b----! now you skin it back! skin it back! If you are looking for a fight and come here to talk that way you can get it before you find the Earps; you can get it right here."

Mr. Hooker then turned to Sheriff Behan and said, "These are a pretty set of fellows you have got with you; a set of horse thieves and cut-throats." Behan and Woods both spoke up and said, "They are not our associates, they are only here on this occasion with us." Hooker then replied, "Well, if they are not your associates I will set an extra table for you and set them by themselves," which he did.

That Diamond Stud

After breakfast Sheriff Behan went out to the stable and spoke to the hostler saying, "Don't say anything about this," at the same time taking a diamond stud from his shirt bosom and presenting it to the hostler, saying as he did so, "Take this, it cost a hundred dollars, but don't say anything about what occurred here." He then turned to Mr. Hooker and remarked, "If I can catch the Earp party it will help me at the next election."

Leaving the ranch, they started off on the trail and crossed the valley to the foot of the mountains and then took up the valley and around to Fort Grant, where they tried to get Indian scouts. Behan offered $500 for the services of the scouts to Col. Bidwell, and during the negotiations remarked that he wanted them to hunt down the Earp party, saying, "I have just come from Hooker's ranch and I asked Mr. Hooker if he knew where the Earps were, and he said, 'No and I would not tell you if I did.' " Col. Bidwell, stroking his beard with his left hand, looked straight at the sheriff and said, "Hooker said he didn't know, and would not tell you if he did? Hooker said that, did he? Well if he did

You Can't Get Any Scouts Here."

This ended the interview.

It will be seen by a comparison of the foregoing with the Nugget report that there is the traditional grain of truth in that garbled statement; just enough, in fact, to swear by. Anyone doubting the truth of the Epitaph correspondent's report of what occurred at Mr. Hooker's are referred to Mr. Lou Cooley, who will supply all the evidence needed to convince the most skeptical.

The Epitaph was the first paper to obtain the news of the attack on the Earp party by nine cowboys and the death of Curly Bill, which fact the Nugget most strenuously denied, as did all the cowboy element. The Nugget went so far as to publish a challenge for the payment of $1,000 reward for the conclusive evidence of the death of Curly Bill, but upon a demand that the money be placed in escrow subject to payment: upon the truth being adduced it backed down. The Epitaph offered to pay $2,000 to any worthy charity provided Curly Bill would put in an appearance, alive and well. Up to the present time he does not materialize to claim the forfeiture of the reward, nor will he, as his friends have been reluctantly forced to concede the fact of his death in the battle of Burleigh, so-called.—(April 14, 1882.)

This was the last story published by the *Epitaph* of the whereabouts of Earp and his men. The *Nugget,* for a time, carried wild tales of desperate battles on the desert, and capped them with a story that Wyatt himself had been killed.

The truth was that the Earps had vanished into the far reaches of deserts and mountains and no man saw them or cut their trail. So, eventually, the sheriff's posse stopped galloping in and out of town and the excitement boiled down to one question—"Where are they?"

In his own good time Wyatt Earp supplied the answer. He and his men had ridden out of the territory and were in Colorado. Wyatt wired his friend, Sheriff Paul, of Tucson, of his whereabouts and went on to Denver, where he waited for the Territory of Arizona to begin extradition proceedings.

The one thing Earp had to fear was being returned, defenseless, to the sheriff of Cochise County and he apparently felt his chances of getting a fair hearing from Governor F. W. Pitkin of Colorado were better than from the political ring in Arizona.

Governor Pitkin heard the case when Sheriff Paul arrived, and refused to honor the extradition papers. He said the warrant charging Earp with the murder of Stilwell was an obvious trick.

By this time the *Epitaph* had been sold and Clum had left. The new owners apparently wanted no part of the fight and, too, they had something else to engage their attention. President Arthur was threatening to send the Army in to take control of Cochise County.

Wyatt Earp never returned to Arizona, although with the political demise of Johnny Behan there was no one who cared to press a charge against him. He died, well-to-do, in Los Angeles in 1929, but he lives on in the Southwest as the most dramatic personality in the history and literature of his time.

And the mining camp which is the scene of his story lives on too in the reflected glory of the man they call—The Lion of Tombstone.

11 Hangings – Legal and Otherwise

In the entire red saga of Cochise County there is no single instance of cold-blooded killings which, for sheer savagery, can approach the infamous murders known as the Bisbee Massacre.

Five desperadoes held up a general store in the little copper camp of Bisbee one late December evening in 1883. While three of the men were plundering the store, two men stood on guard outside the door and wantonly killed three men and a woman.

The border blazed with anger, and this time the law got the killers. In six weeks' time the five men and their undercover leaders were in the Tombstone jail.

Johnny Behan was no longer sheriff, having been overwhelmingly defeated in his party's first Cochise County convention. He got only four votes in the early ballots and finally withdrew. This was the only time Behan ran for the office, his previous terms having been by appointment. J. H. Ward, the Republican nominee, won the election and he seems to have been able to find deputies who were allergic to outlaws.

The five participants got a quick trial, were convicted, and sentenced to be hanged. Their mastermind, John Heath, asked for a separate trial and was saved temporarily from the same fate when the jury brought in a verdict of second degree murder.

This did Mr. Heath very little good for a group of Bisbee men rode into town three days later, took Heath from his cell, and lynched him from a telegraph pole.

The story has been told and written many times, but never with the flavor and the details furnished by the pages of the *Epitaph* and *Republican* which, at that time, were operated by one management.*

The five men were hung simultaneously from one gallows,

* University of Arizona Bulletin: "Newspapers and periodicals of Arizona."

and the news story of the event covered the holdup and murders, the chase, capture, trial and sentencing, the last hours of the condemned, and finally, the scenes on the scaffold.

It is an interesting example of the way border newspaper men organized and wrote a big story.

DANCING ON AIR

The Bisbee Bandits Atone for Their Crimes on the Scaffold; An Ignominious but Well-Merited Fate Bravely Met

The "Final Launch Into Eternity" Successfully Accomplished by Sheriff Ward

Scenes at the Jail Before the Execution—Brief Resume Of the Crime—etc.

THE CRIME

The horrible tragedy which was enacted at Bisbee on the evening of December 8, last has been summarily avenged, and the last of the perpetrators and participants have made atonement with their lives for the dastardly crime then and there enacted. The facts concerning the crime for which five men today perished ignominiously on the scaffold are well known to all readers of the Republican, and yet a brief resume of the same in this connection will prove of interest. At 7:00 o'clock p. m., on the day above mentioned five men rode up the canyon at Bisbee, dismounting and hitching their horses about 100 yards below the main portion of the town. They then proceeded leisurely up the street until the store of A. A. Castanada was reached when three of the strangers entered the store, in which were seven or eight persons at the time. The intruders wore heavy blanket-lined, thick overcoats, and each was armed with a magazine rifle and a brace of six-shooters. Two of them were masked while the face of the third was exposed to view. As they entered the store they drew their weapons and commanded all present to

Throw Up Their Hands

which was promptly complied with. Since proven to be James Howard, alias "Tex" then held up the frightened inmates of the store while the other two, Kelley and Sample, proceeded to go through the same, securing cash which has been variously stated to amount to from $900 to $3,000. Meanwhile the other two bandits, believed to be Dowd and Delaney, remained on guard in front of the store, and as any citizen chanced to come that way he was immediately ordered to enter the store. The first to disobey the order and attempt a retreat was J. C. Tappenier, who was ruthlessly shot down and instantly killed. The shots caused a rush of citizens into the street, whereupon the guardian bandits began shooting indiscriminately up and down the street. The result was the killing of D. T. Smith, J. R. Nolly and Mrs. R. H. Roberts in addition to J. C. Tappenier, before mentioned. The store being thoroughly plundered, the robbers left with their booty. As they were going in the direction of their horses, Deputy Sheriff Daniel opened fire upon them and, as was subsequently developed, wounded one them, Sample.

The Pursuit

Then followed the pursuit. A posse headed by Daniel, left shortly after the robbery, one John Heath, who had for some days previous been a resident of Bisbee, being especially active in organizing the posse, of which he was a member. News of the tragedy was also sent immediately by courier to this city, and before daylight, Deputy Sheriff Bob Hatch, Si Bryant, and other determined men, were also in the field. Daniel's posse remained out scouring the country until all trace of the robbers was lost. However, from ranches where they stopped, full description of the men, together with their names were obtained. Evidence was also obtained implicating Heath as the prime mover in the affair and immediately upon Daniel's return the former was arrested. The whole country was, of course, aroused at the peculiar atrocity of the murders, as it was generally conceded the robbery could just as well have been committed

Without the Shedding of Blood.

Rewards were offered by the territory, county and citizens of Tombstone aggregating $1,500 to the man. Descriptions of the men were broadcast all over the country and circulars printed in Spanish were distributed in all towns of northern Mexico. Such was the vigor and tenacity of the pursuit maintained by Sheriff Ward and his deputies that, contrary to all expectations, complete success crowned their efforts and the last of the bandits was run to earth within a comparatively short time. The first one captured was Kelley, who was arrested disguised as a tramp at Deming. He was evidently working his way east. Then followed the arrest of Howard and Sample in Graham County by Deputy Sheriff Hovey of that county. Meanwhile Deputy Sheriff Daniel had ascertained that Dowd and Delaney had gone to Mexico, and thither he followed them, capturing the former at Corralitas, in the state of Chihauhua. Delaney, the last of the gang, was soon afterwards run down at Minas Prietas, in the state of Sonora, and on January 22, just 45 days after the perpetration of the crime, every participant was securely lodged behind the bars.

Trial, Conviction and Sentence

Judge Pinney, in response to a universal call of the people of the territory as voiced in the Republican at the time called a special term of the district court. The special term convened on February 4th, the prisoners arraigned on the 8th, indictments charging them with murder having meanwhile been found by the grand jury, to which they pleaded not guilty. Separate trials were waived by all except Heath and the trial of the five men who this afternoon expiated their crimes upon the gallows was commenced on February 9th. They were defended by some of the ablest members of the Tombstone bar, but the evidence which had been chiefly worked up by Deputy Sheriff Daniels and Assistant District Attorney Robinson was overwhelmingly against the prisoners and on the 11th of February a verdict of murder in the first degree was rendered against all the defendants. A motion was made for a new trial which was over-ruled by the court, and sentence of death was passed on the culprits on the 19th of the same month.

To keep the picture clear, the *Republican's* story is broken at this point to insert the *Epitaph's* account of the courtroom scene when sentence of death was passed on the five men.

Heath was on trial that day and the judge recessed the case while the convicted men were brought before him. This is the way the *Epitaph* saw the dramatic moment.

To say that the courtroom was crowded at the appointed hour would but idly convey the idea. It was literally packed to suffocation, the crowd even pressing on the diaz leading to the judge's seat. The prisoner's dock was

Crowded With Ladies

and large delegations were also present upon the main floor inside the rail. Many of those present were representatives of the wealth, beauty and culture of this city, and it is but fair to presume that a desire to hear the eloquence of Messrs. Herring and Smith, was the motive prompting attendance, and not that of morbid curiosity to see five unfortunate victims of their own evil passions sentenced to die an ignominious death on the scaffold. Soon the clank, clank, clank of the manacles was heard, and the doors swung open to admit the prisoners, closely guarded by the sheriff and his deputies. Slowly they advanced up the aisle and took seats facing Judge Pinney. The silence was painful when the latter told the five men to stand up, and, questioning each in turn, asked him if he had anything to say why sentence of death should not be passed on him.

None of the five made a statement, and the judge pronounced the death sentence.

Now the *Republican's* story is resumed.

Subsequently the condemned men inclosed a handsome retainer to Colonel Herring with the request that he endeavor to get an appeal. The learned advocate said he could see no grounds for an appeal in the case and accordingly refused to accept the retainer. Thus were the doomed men deprived of the last vestige of hope and the conviction that an ignominious death must expiate their crimes was forced upon their consciousness.

The Eve of Eternity

For some time after all hope had departed from the condemned men their terrible position was apparently not realized by themselves and crimination followed by recrimination was of frequent occurrence in the jail where they were confined. But as the dread day which was to be their last on earth approached more serious thoughts appeared to harass their minds. Father Gallagher was a frequent visitor in the cells of the condemned and his spiritual administrations were received with favor by the condemned men. Father Antonio Jovencean came from Tucson a few days ago and has since labored assiduously in behalf of the prisoners. Delaney, Sample and Kelley were the first to listen to the holy counsel of the reverend fathers they having previously received the ordinance of baptism in the Catholic church. Then Dowd and Howard, who had remained somewhat obdurate, yielded to the comforting assurances of their spiritual advisors, and the rite was conferred upon them in the presence of a number of ladies and gentlemen in the jail.

How the Last Night Was Passed.

The prisoners last night regaled themselves with a hearty supper of oysters and other delicacies furnished by the sheriff. A Republican reporter visited the jail at midnight and found the doomed men restless and uneasy, being unable to sleep which they attributed to the hearty supper eaten. The remainder of the night was passed in a similar manner, and only occasionally relieved by short periods of disturbed slumber. This morning

At an Early Hour

Will Baron with his shaving utensils was admitted to the jail and the prisoners were submitted to his tonsorial manipulations. They were then dressed in neat suits of black furnished for the occasion by Sheriff Ward. As they were being attired in grave clothes an occasional grim joke at the appearance of some of their comrades was indulged in by the bandits. The reverend fathers and Miss Nellie Cashman were in constant attendance and the forenoon gradually wore away, the prisoners bearing up bravely, and conversing upon ordinary topics with greatest nonchalance. At the request of the condemned the death warrant was read in the cell by Sheriff Ward and was listened to attentively by the unfortunate men. The reading was commenced in a clear, firm voice, but when that portion was reached commanding him to hang until they were dead the listening men standing before him it is no discredit to our sheriff to say that his voice became tremulous and husky with emotion. The reading was finished at 12:55 when the sheriff said:

"Boys, you have asked the privilege of going to the scaffold free from straps or manacles. This privilege I grant you, but each of you will be taken by the arm of an officer."

"I'd rather be strapped than packed up to the scaffold," said Sample.

"So would I," echoed the other four.

The sheriff assured them that they would be allowed to walk from the jail to the death-trap free and untrammeled, after which some strong coffee was served, stronger stimulants being refused.

The Crime Expiated

Over 500 tickets of admission to the jail yard to witness the execution were issued by Sheriff Ward and they were nearly all represented. The gate to the jail was thrown open at 12 o'clock and in a few minutes the waiting multitudes were inside. The procession moved from the jail door to the foot of the gallows and the nine steps leading to the platform were ascended in silence, the prisoners going to their doom with light springy steps. The broad brimmed sombreros with which the

Doomed and Daring Rustlers

were wont to shield themselves from the inclemencies of the weather while scouring the mountains and mesa, were quickly exchanged for the horrible black caps. The prisoners glanced anxiously around, first at the crowd surrounding them and then at the dangling nooses and other ghastly paraphernalia which were to be the means of their death. Delaney, Kelley and Sample recognized familiar faces in the crowd and shouted out cheerily, "Good-bye." A series of handshakes followed between the men standing on the very threshold of death and the attending officers and priests, after which their arms and legs were quickly strapped, when Sheriff Ward said, "stand up, boys."

The five men arose as with one accord, and the chairs were removed from the trap on which they had been resting. Sample, who occupied the west end of the scaffold, then said in a loud and firm tone of voice:

"Gentlemen, before I die I wish to say a few words. I die innocent of the murders and robbery committed at Bisbee on the 8th of December and, so far as I know, John Heath had nothing to do with the affair. He never put up any such job with me. I die in a firm belief in the Catholic church and request a Christian burial."

James Howard whose position was next in order on the death trap asserted his innocence of any complicity in the affair and also his belief in the innocence of Heath.

Dan Dowd, the next in order, reiterated the statements already made and also requested a Christian burial.

W. E. Delaney said, "Gentlemen, I expect in a few minutes to meet my God. I am entirely innocent of the crime of which I was convicted and if I had had a fair trial I would not be here to hang today. I request a Christian burial and I hope that Father Gallagher will conduct the services and look after our bodies."

Kelley, whose position was on the extreme east end of the scaffold, remained silent, when several voices in the crowd shouted, "Kelley, Kelley." The poor wretch, whose face was already as pallid as that of a corpse, responded as follows: "I am innocent of the murders committed at Bisbee on the evening of December 8th. I have never yet murdered a human being. I have only one request to make and that is a Christian burial."

In response to a question from Sheriff Ward if they had anything more to say, they all answered, "no." The nooses were then adjusted to their necks by the attending officials, the priests meanwhile whispering words of consolation in the ears of the doomed murderers, who each and all stood firm as adamant throughout the trying ordeal.

"This is a Regular Choking Machine"

remarked Dowd as the rope was being placed around his neck, and the result showed that he spoke too truly. The caps were then pulled down over their faces and the nooses tightened.

"Let her go," said Kelley in a muffled voice.

At precisely 1:18 Sheriff Ward with a quick movement cut the cord by which a 250-pound weight was suspended and the ponderous trap fell with a "swish." When the ropes became taut the framework quivered with the descending weight, while every joint in the timbers creaked mournfully. The suspended forms of Sample, Howard, Delaney and Kelley never moved a muscle after the fatal drop, but the legs of Dowd were drawn up convulsively several times, and his whole body was shaken as with the mortal agony of suffocation. Pulsation was perceptible after the drop as follows: Howard, 7 minutes; Dowd, 7½ minutes; Sample, 5½ minutes; Delaney, 7½ minutes; Kelley, 9 minutes. The bodies were allowed to hang thirty minutes when, being pronounced dead by the attending physicians, they were cut loose and placed in neat but plain coffins. They were then taken to the morgue where the physicians viewed the bodies and concluded that with the exception of Sample the necks of the executed felons had not been dislocated.—(March 28, 1884.)

Here the story must cut back to February 19, and the trial of Heath.

Like the people of Bisbee and Tombstone, the *Epitaph* was convinced that Heath had master-minded the fatal holdup.

So, on the second day of the trial it predicted a hanging verdict before the jury came in. Its headline and story follow.

WILL HANG

The Conviction of Heath a Foregone Conclusion

Col. Herring resumed his argument for the defense in the Heath case, occupying a little more than an hour in addition to the time taken up by him in the morning. At the conclusion merited applause greeted the distinguished advocate, for the very skilful manner in which he had made the worse appear the better cause. It was evident that his cunning sophistries and ingeniously spun themes had made more than a passing impression on some of the jury, and all the efforts of District Attorney Smith, who followed him, were brought to play to disabuse the minds of that body. For the space of an hour he hurled the weight of his logic, satire, invective and legal eloquence at the legal barriers erected by Colonel Herring in his client's defense, and carried his audience with him as he pictured in glowing colors the depth of depravity into which he claimed Heath had fallen. The argument was an universally forceful one, and did much to counteract the impression made by the preceding counsel. At the close of the district attorney's argument, the jury were charged by the judge, and retired to deliberate upon a verdict. After an absence of about five hours they came into court and announced they had agreed. Upon the reading of the clerk, it was discovered that the defendant has been found guilty of

Murder in the Second Degree

That this verdict gave almost universal dissatisfaction, is but stating the naked truth. Such a thing as a compromise verdict was not warranted by either the law or the evidence. John Heath was either guilty or not guilty of the crime of murder charged against him. If he was guilty of murder at all it was murder in the first degree. If not guilty of murder in the first degree he was not guilty of murder in any degree and should have been acquitted. As previously stated the verdict was a compromise one, it being stated that on the first ballot the jury stood six for murder in the first degree, four for acquittal and two for murder in the second degree.—(Feb. 19, 1884.)

Here again the researcher is checked by a break in the *Epitaph's* files. This time it is a real loss. For there is no spot news story of the formation of a group of one hundred armed, mounted and angry men in Bisbee, or of their long night ride through a high pass and over the starlit deserts.

No one tells what the people of Tombstone thought when they were awakened in the early hours of the morning by a cavalcade riding furiously through the city.

One is fortunate, however, to find an eye-witness story of the lynching, written by S. C. Bagg, a former editor, even though it was published years later in the *Epitaph*. This is the way he remembered an hour which was high drama, even for Tombstone.

> I believe in all the murders and lynchings I have ever known in the west, and I have seen a few in my time, I never saw more real down right nerve displayed by the chief actor on the program, than in the case of Jack Heath, who was hung by the Vigilance Committee, Feb. 22, 1884. I remember the date because we afterwards celebrated Washington's birthday and lassoed steers with the same rope that hung the rustler. It was a bright spring morning, such as is only known in this season in the mountain towns of Arizona, that Heath was hung to a telegraph pole, about three blocks from the Courthouse in the best mining camp Arizona ever saw.
>
> When the news was carried to Bisbee that Heath had been found guilty of manslaughter, a meeting of citizens was called and it was decided that the mines would be shut down for twenty hours and all citizens who could secure horses were requested to be in Tombstone by daylight. The hundred horsemen who filed up in front of the Courthouse made short work of getting to their man. The sheriff was disarmed and lifted over the heads of the determined men down the stairs to the sidewalk and Heath soon appeared with a rope around his waist.
>
> "I suppose you want me, gentlemen," was his greeting as they came to his cell. He was clad in a pair of broadcloth pants, white flannel undershirt, and calf-skin boots.
>
> "Don't drag me and I'll go with you," he added; he kept his word for he started down the street like a deer, with 50 feet of rope behind him held by as many hands. "Where shall I stop,"

he asked, when he was under the pole selected for his gallows. A thousand people had gathered by this time, and he stood in the center of the crowd, the coolest one among them.

It was short work to throw the rope across a bar and slip the noose around the doomed man's neck, and then was exhibited the most wonderful show of bravery the oldest follower of Western mining camps ever witnessed.

"Have you anything to say?" shouted the leader. Heath's only answer was a motion to his pocket, from which he pulled a silk handkerchief and placed it over his eyes and face, asking a bystander to tie it behind. "Now, gentlemen, will someone tie my legs?" and when his request was granted, he asked to have still another handkerchief tied around his knees. This being accomplished he remarked that he was ready.

"Gentlemen, you are hanging an innocent man, but I am not afraid to die," he said. "I have two requests to make. Promise me not to shoot into my body when I am strangling and give me a decent burial. I am ready." And the body of the nerviest desperado who ever trod the soil of Arizona dangled between the earth and the sky, as the last word was finished. The coroner's jury decided that "the deceased came to his death from lack of breath," and as the coroner and jurymen were all witnesses of the affair, no testimony was necessary.

The Halderman Brothers

Men killed and escaped in Tombstone but some of them were caught and some were hanged.

The *Epitaph* gave better than three columns of type on page one, November 18, 1900, to an account of the hanging of the Halderman brothers. They were convicted of murdering a constable and an eighteen-year-old boy and of shooting the constable's assistant.

According to the *Epitaph* the family of the Halderman brothers spent a large sum in their defense and when the brothers were convicted, carried the case to President McKinley, who delayed their execution until the governor of the territory had made a complete investigation of the trial. The governor being satisfied, a new date was set for the execution.

The story which follows does not cover the long legal battle but does contain the highlights of the hanging, as an *Epitaph* reporter saw it.

PAID THE PENALTY

Thomas and William Halderman Sent to their Doom

All that human agency and legal skill could do to save those whom the mandate of the law had marked as its own was done in behalf of Thomas Halderman and William Halderman, but Justice wept and would not be comforted; the blood of two peace officers of Cochise county cried aloud and hushed the voice of mercy, and at 12:40 o'clock these two young men forfeited their lives to satisfy the ends of the law. The importance of this case caused the bringing to bear upon those in power the strongest of influence both from those in high public station and in private life. But the pardoning power was satisfied after a most thorough examination, that the men had a fair and impartial trial; were defended by able attorneys and their conviction and sentence was legal, although twice the gallows, with its ghostly shadows flung across the prison windows, was in readiness and twice was the hand of mercy stretched forth to give them a small respite from their impending fate. The first respite was given them when the appeal to the supreme court was taken, the next was granted by President McKinley and lastly by Governor Murphy, who fixed today as the time which was the last.

All the windows in the court house on the second floor facing and overlooking the prison yard were lined with people to witness the execution. When the iron door leading to the jail was swung open a solemn hush prevailed and all eyes turned in that direction. Shortly afterwards the condemned men appeared, Thos. Halderman in the lead in charge of Deputy Sheriff Johnson and Wm. Halderman in charge of Deputy Sheriff Bravin while Sheriff Scott White and Rev. Elliott followed closely in the line down the narrow steps to the scaffold. Thos. Halderman, the younger prisoner had just emerged from the jail door and facing the crowd said, "Hello hombres," then placing his hand to his eyes to shed them from the sun's rays said, "the sun's hot ain't it?" . . .

Wm. Halderman stepped to the front under the dangling noose and surveying the crowd below said with a wave of his hand, "Nice looking crowd." He even smiled and remarked "Some of you fellers are shaking already." Thos. Halderman who was equally nervy held the rope and also looked over the crowd below and turning to his brother said, "Those people look all right." He looked at the noose and mechanically placed it over his own head. He then listened attentively to the reading of the death warrant by Sheriff Scott White. At the conclusion of the reading Sheriff White asked if they wished to make a statement. Thomas Halderman spoke up promptly and in a clear voice said:—"I have nothing to say and guess it would not do any good anyway, I forgive you all and hope you will forgive me." Wm. Halderman said, "This will be an experience that ought to benefit all of you. I hope I will meet you all. I pray for you and hope you will pray for me."

The black caps were then drawn over the heads of the prisoners and as it shut them out from sight of the faces below, both men said in chorus "Goodbye boys. Pray for us." Each said "Good bye," and the crowd answered "Good bye." The trap was sprung at exactly 12:40. The bodies were cut down just 28 minutes after the trap was sprung.—(Nov. 18, 1900.)

12 Double Crossing Desperado

The Earps played the leads, and the Clantons and McLowry's, Johnny-Behind-the-Deuce, Curly Bill, and others of the Cowboy gang were the heavies, in the dramas of early Tombstone days.

But they were not the only actors who played long engagements and whose names and deeds occupied columns of *Epitaph* space. Others followed them, and one held the stage for four years. In that time he wrote a record of daring, cunning, and treachery unmatched in the history of the Southwest. He was William (Billy) Stiles.

From 1899 to 1903, Stiles and his sometimes pal, Burt Alvord, were public enemies numbers one and two of the territory. In the beginning of their careers they were constables and deputy sheriffs. Stiles was also a rancher, and had served as an express messenger. They had good names in Tombstone and its nearby settlements.

Then they went bad and under the cloak of their reputations they organized a train robbery at nearby Cochise. It was a daring and perfectly executed holdup and it sent the posses over the trails in all directions.

This was the *Epitaph's* first story in what was to be a four-year serial.

THE HOLD UP

How it Was Done—Posses On the Trail

About 1:30 a. m. yesterday morning the west bound S. P. passenger train was held up at Cochise station in this county and three masked robbers succeeded in securing considerable booty the amount of which is variously estimated at from $5,000 to $30,000. The three men uncoupled the express car from the train and had the engineer pull forward a short distance. When the express messenger refused to open the door the robbers immediately set off some giant powder under the car and soon forced an entrance. A fusillade of shots was continually fired by the robbers and no one was permitted to come out of the passenger coaches. The robbers were cool and deliberate and perfectly understood the handling of giant powder. The robbers stated at the outset that the express car would be the only car robbed and the passengers would not be molested, which was faithfully carried out.

Having secured their booty the trio, after firing a parting shot, left the train afoot, one robber carrying the sack. The train was delayed a little over a half hour by the robbery.

Immediately after information was had here, Sheriff White had two posses in the field, and the sheriff left here yesterday with a Tombstone posse besides.

Two suspicious looking characters were at Cochise for a day or two before the robbery, pretending to be hunting for work, and it is now believed they are the parties who committed the robbery. As it was payday in Pearce today, the robbers doubtless figured on this money arriving with the express robbed. Whether they secured the money intended for the Pearce employes, some $25,000, it is not known nor will the Railroad or Wells, Fargo & Co. officials divulge.

Word received today from one of the Sheriff's posses to the effect that four horsemen were trailed from Cochise and posse are in pursuit. This would lend color to the theory that the fourth robber had charge of the horses while the three companions did the work.—(Sept. 11, 1899.)

Three posses galloped over the trails and searched the hideouts favored by outlaws. But the best the *Epitaph* could report after four weeks was that the sheriff was "hopeful of the final capture of the robbers and although his most diligent efforts at capture have been in vain thus far, the public nevertheless appreciates his prompt action in leaving nothing undone in an earnest and determined pursuit of the outlaws."

After that the *Epitaph* forgot about holdups and went on to other matters until February of the following year, when a second train was held up. This time the crime was staged at Fairbank, which was practically in Tombstone's back yard and the editor gave its readers this full account.

A HOLD UP

The N. M. & A. Train Held Up at Fairbank

Fairbank was the scene of a hold up last night, three masked men armed to the teeth making a raid on the N. M. & A. train just as the north bound passenger train pulled into and stopped at the station.

The movements of the robbers and their methods would indicate that they were no novices in their work, exhibiting plenty of nerve and reckless courage and during their brief stay made things very exciting as a hold up usually is. The robbers secured but little booty for their trouble and although various reports are given out as to the amount of money secured it is authentically stated that but one package, containing $17 in Mexican money, which happened to be out of the safe in the express car is missing.

The particulars as learned from several eye witnesses are to the effect that as soon as the train stopped and the agents and helpers were busy unloading mail and express matter, three men were seen to emerge from the side of the depot platform. One of the men went to the engine and the other two hurried to the express car, ordering everybody to throw up their hands and immediately began shooting by way of enforcing the order. The bystanders, with hands aloft, were somewhat scattered and the leader commanded all to "bunch up" punctuating his remark with comprehensive profanity. It is needless to say all hastened to obey. Presently the engineer and fireman came from their post, and were marched to the crowd where they were also commanded to remain with hands up. The first robber who stopped at the engine had marched the two railroaders to the crowd at the point of a pistol.

Meanwhile a fusillade of shots was kept up and the mail and express car was perforated with shots. Express messenger J. D. Milton appeared at the door of his car with a Winchester and began firing at the robbers. At the first fire from Milton one of the robbers was positively seen to fall to the ground. Whether he was wounded or not is not known but he returned the fire as did also the others, when suddenly Milton dropped having been shot in the right arm. At this exciting moment the horses on the Tombstone stage, which was nearby, became frightened from the shooting and started to run away. Driver Ed Tarbell who was in the "bunched" crowd started to head them off when one of the robbers sternly ordered him to halt. Ed wisely halted. Then the robber who had fallen to the ground as stated above, fired several shots at the fleeing animals, one bullet taking effect in the stifle of the horse and effectually stopping the runaway although at the probable cost of the horse which may die.

When it was evident that Milton was helpless one of the robbers climbed into the express car with a sack and hurriedly rummaged through papers, packages, etc. The through safe was locked and but little of value was to be found. Quite a number of things were overlooked in the hurry of the robber and no attempt was made to blow open or have the messenger unlock the iron box. It is said but one package containing $17 Mexican money is gone, although several bystanders claim the sack was fairly well filled when the robbers left the car.

The leader of the robbers then turned his attention to the depot and inquired of the "crowd" where the agent was. Agent Guy was in the "bunched crowd" but discreetly kept silent and none of the others cared to impart the fact of his whereabouts. With another voluminous outburst of profanity, the robber went to the door of the depot which was locked. He kicked down the door, walked in, found all the safes and drawers locked and came out empty handed. The three robbers then walked off together going west of the depot where it is presumed they had horses ready and in waiting.

The train immediately backed to Benson for medical attention for Messenger Milton. It is understood that the bones in his arm are so shattered that amputation will be necessary. The injury to Milton is to be regretted. He was a brave and efficient officer and well known here.

A sheriff's posse were organized last night in Tombstone and were at the scene as soon as possible. Trailing was impossible last night as no trails could be found. This morning more officers were sent out and notifications were dispatched in every direction to keep a sharp lookout. No clue whatever is had to the identity of the robbers thus far.—(Feb. 15, 1900.)

Later

Just as we go to press Deputy Sheriff George Bravin arrived with the information that one of the robbers was found and proved to be Three Fingered Jack, the notorious character who was recently released from the county jail here. Jack was found shot in the abdomen being the wound he received from Messenger Milton during the holdup. The rest of the robbers, now believed to be five in number, left their wounded comrade while they pushed on toward Tombstone or headed for Pearce. A posse is in close pursuit while Deputy Bravin came in for a conveyance to bring the wounded robber to town. The wounded man was found six miles from town. It is thought he cannot live.—(Feb. 16, 1900.)

Three Fingered Jack, dying in the county jail, grew bitter over being deserted by his gang and gave their names to the sheriff. Within a week deputies picked up George and Lewis Owints (later referred to as Owen, Owing, and Owings) and Tom Yoes, better known and referred to hereafter as Bravo John.

This, however, was nothing compared to the story which broke a week later—on page three, as usual. There is no issue of the *Epitaph* for this day and the *Prospector's* account is used here.

SENSATIONAL ARRESTS

The Prospector intimated a day or two since that a sensational surprise was in store for our citizens when several arrests of well known residents of the county would be made, charged with train robbery. The first installment of the surprises was effected Wednesday night in the arrest of Constable Burt Alvord and Wm. Downing, a well known cattleman, both charged with complicity in the train robbery at Cochise last August, the particulars of which are yet fresh in the minds of our readers.

The arrests were made by the sheriff's office and is the culmination of what the officers contend to be a strong case against the accused, the work of gathering evidence having been slowly and quietly carried on during the past few months. The particulars are being religiously guarded as more people connected with the affair are yet to be apprehended and the publicity of the facts at this time might seriously interfere with the officers.—(Feb. 25, 1900.)

The *Epitaph* did not have long to wait, for, within a week, Billy Stiles, deputy constable at Pearce and a member of the sheriff's own force, appeared as a surprise witness at the preliminary investigation of Alvord and Downing and sang like a desert canary. The busy reporter must have felt completely frustrated when he got no more than a one-column head on an inside page for this story.

SENSATIONAL CASE

Startling Testimony of a Confessed Train Robber

The preliminary investigation in the case of the U. S. vs Burt Alvord and Wm. Downing, on charge of obstructing U. S. mail was set for this afternoon before Court Commissioner Emanuel.

The announcement brought out a large crowd who were present to hear the trial. Deputy U. S. District Attorney Bennett assisted by Attorney Frank Cox appeared on behalf of the United States, and A. R. English in defense of the prisoners. The case was set for 2 p. m. but the arrangement of formal preliminaries delayed the hearing until 3:30 p. m. at which time court opened.

The proceedings developed some of the most sensational features ever brought out in the Cochise county court house.

The testimony of Chas. Adair, W. F. & Co. messenger on the train at the time of the Cochise robbery, Sept. 9th and C. R. McHaun, mail agent, who were placed on the stand, was merely as to details of the robbery. Mr. W. N. Stiles, deputy constable at Pearce, proved the sensational witness. He confessed to the "hold up" saying himself and Matt Burts did the work. And Constable Alvord and Wm. Downing were conspirators in that they were "in" on the booty and helped plot the hold up. The witness stated the matter had been considered between the four—Downing, Alvord, Burts and himself for two months. Downing was to furnish the horses. Alvord's duty was to provide men to swear to alibis if the two robbers were caught and Burts and himself were to "hold up" the train which they did, the two doing the work alone.

After the robbery Stiles and Burts went direct to Willcox and left the money in Alvord's house; later it was carried to Downing's house. After due time Alvord gave Stiles $430 stating it was his share of the proceeds. Stiles stated the powder and fuse was secured in Willcox, Alvord helping to get it by forcing the door at Soto Bros powder house, the caps were secured at a mine at Dos Cabezas the whole being secured without the knowledge of anyone.

The prosecution rested the case and postponement was had to 7 p. m. when the defense will make their stand.

Stiles, having decided that the law was closing in on him, had sold out on a promise of immunity and the sheriff was so delighted that he treated the star witness like a favorite boarder, and gave him the freedom of the jail.

Stiles then crossed the sheriff by engineering a jail break and escaping with the men he had just betrayed. The *Epitaph* told the colorful story this way.

JAIL DELIVERY

Bert Alvord, Bravo John and Stiles Get Away. . . .
Posse in Pursuit

About 3 p. m. Tombstone was thrown into a fever of excitement, the like of which has not visited our city since the days of the hanging of Heath by an indignant mob. The occasion for this was the news of a jail break at the county jail and the shooting of Deputy Sheriff Geo. Bravin who was wounded in an attempt to block the break for liberty.

Despite the most precautionary measures taken by the Sheriff's office to guard against any attack of friends of the prisoners in jail on charge of train robbery to secure their release by force, as was feared, the expected happened but from a source that was never suspicioned, the dastardly work being done by Wm. Stiles, the self confessed train robber, who turned state's evidence against his pals, then further proved his treachery by attempting to help them escape from jail, even at the sacrifice of the lives of any who might stand in the way. Fortunately the brave Deputy Sheriff, George Bravin, was not killed though he had a most narrow escape.

Last evening Matt Burts was brought over from the Tucson jail for his preliminary examination here for train robbery. W. Stiles, the principal witness who turned state's evidence, also arrived to testify. It was deemed advisable by the authorities and prosecution not to place Burts in jail in company with the other prisoners on some charge for reasons that are obscure. As a consequence Burts was under guard of two deputies. His trial was to be had today and he was again to be taken to the Tucson jail tomorrow.

Add Jail Delivery

While the guards were away from the jail with Burts, Deputy Sheriff Bravin was left alone in charge of the jail. Wm. Stiles, who up to this time had helped the officers in every way to prosecute his pals, and who was believed to be the last man to even think of aiding in a jail break, suddenly pushed a six-shooter at Deputy Bravin, while in the front jail room and commanded him to deliver the keys of the jail. Bravin was unarmed, having left his gun on the office desk, while stepping temporarily into the jail room. Instead of complying, Bravin pluckily knocked at the pistol of his assailant. At the same time Stiles shot and the Deputy fell. Stiles in an instant secured the keys and opened the main cell doors inviting all the prisoners to make a break for liberty. Burt Alvord and "Bravo John" both charged with train robbery came out and, rushing to the front with Stiles, took three Winchester rifles and two six-shooters, the whereabouts of which were known to Stiles, and hurriedly left, the three going down Fremont street to the ranch of John Escapule below town where they stole two horses, grazing near and rode off toward the Dragoons two of the men riding one horse.

The opportunity to escape was offered the entire 24 prisoners in jail. As the Halderman brothers came out Deputy Bravin spoke to them saying kindly that they had better not attempt escape as they would not have time to get away. Both of the condemned men said, "all right, George, we'll stay." Wm. Downing, one of the accused train robbers refused to go at all as was also the case of the Owen brothers under the same charge; Sid Page also remained inside. Several of the other prisoners started to go and one prisoner named Griffith, at the request of the deputy, closed the iron door.

The Halderman brothers seeing the wounded condition of the deputy, together with the other prisoners, carried him to a bed in the ante room and endeavored to relieve his pains.

A few minutes after the escape several posses were in pursuit and are believed to be but a short distance behind the three fugitives. Many determined men offered their services and were sent out. The feeling runs high and should the escapees be recaptured the probability for a lynching is exceedingly good.

Bravin is shot through the calf of his leg, the bullet passing below his knee through the leg and taking off two toes on the other foot. He is resting easily at his home under the care of Dr. Walter.

Up to the time of writing no news of the posse has been had.—(April 8, 1900.)

News was "had" three weeks later, however, when a rancher came to town with a strange tale, which the *Epitaph* reported in the following news story.

Exciting Experience

Harry Hughes was in town yesterday from his ranch in the Dragoons, near Granite Springs. Young Hughes was visited at his ranch by Alvord, Stiles and Bravo John on Friday last and he tells of his exciting experience with them. Hughes states that he was awakened about 2 a. m. by the trio who entered the house and ordered him, at the point of a gun, to get up and cook them breakfast. They were in a hurry and would brook no delay. The desired breakfast was hastily prepared. During the eating of the meal the outlaws volunteered much information of a jocular nature regarding the officers and defiantly offered to meet any posse. A fresh mount was desired and Hughes was ordered to round up the horses in the pasture. This he did with Stiles ever near him, having his Winchester ready. The outlaws held a consultation and not being familiar with a certain trail over the mountains Hughes was made to saddle his horse and lead them. Enroute the outlaws decided they needed some ammunition and resolved on another bold plan. It was thought at first that the three would ride into Pearce and hold up a store. On further discussion it was proposed to send Hughes for the cartridges and force him to do so at the peril of his life. After solemnly vowing no mercy or pity if he disclosed their whereabouts or failed to bring the ammunition Hughes was sent to Pearce on his mission. Stiles accompanied him to the edge of town and in plain sight of the store. Hughes did as he was admonished, fully believing the threat would be carried into effect if he did otherwise. Some $10 worth of ammunition was bought and taken back. Instead of meeting with a feeling of thankfulness, Hughes states Alvord and Bravo John wanted to kill him presumably on the theory that dead men tell no tales. Stiles interfered and Hughes was finally told to go to the Warren ranch, in an opposite direction from Pearce, and remain there until night. His six-shooter was returned to him and he left. A woman passing on the road saw the band of outlaws and reported them at Pearce. A posse was formed which Hughes joined later and tracked the three men back to the Dragoons where the trail was lost.—(April 29, 1900.)

In the issue with Hughes' story, the *Epitaph* also published this note from the outlaws, in which they taunted the sheriff and sent back the keys of the jail.

The Escapees Again

Today the keys of the Tombstone jail were returned to Sheriff White from Alvord, Stiles and Bravo John the three fugitives having sent the keys by a Mexican. With the keys came a letter addressed to the sheriff from the trio showing that they have developed a sense of humor bordering on the burlesque. The satirical composition is published in full as follows:—

On the Road
Friday, April 20, 1900

Scott White, Esq.—We send you the keys; we would have given them to Sid Mullen but he was too fast for us, we could not overtake him. We met the Mexicans that killed the gambler in Johnson camp but as we had no warrants we did not arrest them—and then we were afraid they would shoot, and we had no warrant and were afraid we could not collect the mileage.—Tell the boys that we are well and eating regular. Tell the man that I got the Studebaker saddle from will send it home soon. Yours truly

Juan Bravo
Stiles
Alvord

—(April 20, 1900.)

Stiles lost his bravado soon after this, and early in July surrendered at Casa Grande, a settlement 159 miles northwest of Tombstone. The *Epitaph* told the news in a story with a breathless, eighty-word lead.

STILES SURRENDERS

Indeed is truth stranger than fiction. Last evening Tombstone received a surprise in the announcement that William Stiles, the self confessed train robber and outlaw, is again in the hands of the law, the notorious gentleman having given himself up and surrendered to Chas. Hood and Bert Grover because he was tired of being an outlaw, and had reason to fear that his life was in danger not only from officers but his friends in crime, and therefore wanted protection.

Stiles was brought in on the stage last night under charge of Officers Hood and Grover, the prisoner having surrendered to them by agreement, and gave himself up at Casa Grande in Pinal county—the home of Stiles. Thus the man who confessed to the Cochise train robbery, implicating his pals who were all jailed, then in turn successfully holding up the jail to release them, even to shooting Deputy Bravin in the attempt; becoming an outlaw and defying officers and the law, is again in the hands of the authorities and declares a willingness to stand by his confession.

To the minds of the public Stiles is an enigma, whose actions are a puzzle and so variable and fickle that it is questionable if much reliance can be placed upon his assertions.

Stiles was put under guard last night and no one permitted to see him. Early this morning he was taken to Tucson to be placed in jail there for safe keeping, it being not deemed advisable to place him in the Tombstone jail. Stiles is fat and looks much better than when he left here so unceremoniously. He was very reticent and preferred not to talk further than saying he was tired of being an outlaw and therefore surrendered. Stiles was in conference with District Attorney Land and officers last night for several hours, the result of which is being kept secret.—(July 8, 1900.)

The government brought members of the Fairbank holdup gang to trial, and, with the help of the treacherous Stiles, convicted three of them. R. H. Brown was tried first and his case caused some commotion in the court, of which the *Epitaph* has this to say.

There was an unusual scene in the United States district court in Tucson Saturday when Judge Davis called in the jury in the case of Brown, on trial for the Fairbank train robbery. The jury had been out fifty hours. The judge asked how they stood and when he was informed it was eleven for conviction and one for acquittal he asked for the name of the man who hung the jury.

The judge pointed him out to the marshal and requested that he be discharged and hereafter not allowed to serve as a United States juror. The case will be tried again tomorrow.

Meanwhile, however, George Owints—now referred to as "Owings"—had decided the Government's case was too strong to fight, and he went on the stand and threw himself on the mercy of the court in a confession which was complete to the last detail. The *Epitaph* picked up the story from the Tucson *Citizen* and rewrote it as follows.

Owings' Story

According to the Citizen there was a sensation in District court in Tucson yesterday when George Owings confessed the charge of train robbery in which he was implicated with Brown and several others. It was during the trial of Brown, the man who is said to be the leader of the band. The Citizen says Owings took the step he did without solicitation, it was as much a surprise to the district attorney as to the crowd that assembled in the courtroom to witness the trial.

The confession was complete, the story was told with graphic effect, every detail and circumstance of the Fairbank holdup, the days of planning, the craftiness of Burt Alvord in providing protection for the men who were to take part in the affair, the preparation for the first nefarious work of the band which was to be but the beginning of a series of holdups. It was a scene which might form the foundation for a yellow-back novel, and the story would be of more than ordinary interest in thrilling scenes and picturesque description.

George Owings and Lewis Owings, were arrested along with Alvord, Stiles, Bravo John, Downing, Burts and Brown soon after the Fairbank hold-up. Very little was known of the Owing brothers and but for the confession made by Three Fingered Jack when he was found dying upon the trail of the fleeing bandits these men would probably not have been suspected.

The Citizen says that Owings told of the part taken by Alvord, how he organized the gang, commissioned Bravo John the captain of the crowd and secured men in Willcox who would give their testimony that the men were innocently playing cards in a saloon in some town or mining camp at the time of the hold-up. Every possible protection was made, every care of the successful consummation of the crime, and Alvord looked after the preparation to the last. But he remained behind and let the others do the work. Owings' confession left the defense of Brown in a precarious position for Owings, too, was to be tried for interfering with the United States mail. When he was taken back to his cell he told his brother what he had done, and Louis this morning came into court and pleaded guilty along with George.—(Oct. 11, 1900.)

The following day the *Epitaph* carried still another account of the confession, and this time the editor took advantage of the opportunity to work a little color into this story of the gang's final conference.

> From the Citizen more of Owings' confession is learned. Owings detailed carefully the movements of the men from the time they gathered together in the house of Brown at Pearce until the holdup.
>
> On the day before the plan was put into operation the men went to Brown's house in Pearce. From there they rode over to the Dragoon mountains and camped for the night. There about the campfire the band was organized with Bravo John as captain. Gathered in the recess of a canyon, with the flickering campfire throwing weird, distorted shadows all about, with the silent watchful stars above for witnesses, these desperate men swore a most solemn oath to kill the first man who showed fear when the crisis came. They were dangerous men embarked upon an enterprise whose penalty in case of failure and capture was death and no precaution possible was neglected. Having completed their arrangements they laid down to sleep.
>
> On the morning of the fifteenth they rolled their blankets and prepared to start. At first they were going as a body but Bravo John objected that such a move would create suspicion and it would be best for the party to divide and go to the rendezvous separately or in pairs.
>
> So the party divided, the two Owings brothers going together, Three Fingered Jack with Brown but Bravo John alone. Thus divided the band made its way to the meeting place down the long slope which drops to the San Pedro river valley. They gathered in the river bottom a few miles below Fairbank and waited for night and the coming train.
>
> When night fell the party went to the depot and attacked the train.—(Oct. 12, 1900.)

The jury which heard Brown's second trial must have been impressed by the public denunciation of a member of the hung jury, for they convicted him before the sun set behind the saw-toothed ridges of the Tucson Mountains.

This left Alvord and Bravo John the only ones of the holdup

gang at liberty, and Alvord finally decided to come up from his hideout in Mexico and surrender at the border.

This set in motion one of the strangest legal merry-go-rounds in border history.

The district attorney brought Alvord to trial in Tombstone on the original charge, which was assault to commit robbery, but immediately asked that the court dismiss the case. Conviction under the charge carried a sentence of death and the jury had already turned William Downing loose because it did not believe in a death penalty where no murder had been committed.

Uncle Sam then held Alvord on a charge of committing two train robberies. The witnesses were members of his old gang and again the jury failed to convict. Two members said they were not willing to accept the word of convicts.

So the Government looked up its old standby, Billy Stiles, and made another deal with him. He promised to help convict Alvord and part of his price, as usual, was immunity.

But when Stiles went before the grand jury to double cross Alvord he also tried to double cross the grand jury and told them practically nothing. So the grand jury indicted Stiles along with Alvord.

Now it was Alvord who decided to confess, which he did, but before they could get him out of the Tombstone jail and start him on the road to Yuma who should join him behind the bars but Stiles.

Stiles talked himself back into Alvord's confidence, sold him another bill of goods and, together, they executed a second jail break. The *Epitaph* had a fresh chapter to add to the Stiles-Alvord serial.

Stiles—Alvord—The Jail Delivery

Another jail delivery for Tombstone, the second that has been generalized by Bandits Stiles and Alvord, two of the most daring highwaymen that ever infested Cochise county.

Alvord and Stiles, who have been in prison for the last six

months pending a hearing before the United States court on charges of robbing the mails, the former having pleaded guilty and received a sentence of two years penal servitude, headed a jail delivery last evening, Dec. 20, 1903, by which seventeen others, not quite so notorious but fully as dangerous were liberated and are free to ply their nefarious vocations of robbing and pillaging the public.

This is the second successful jail delivery engineered by Stiles and Alvord during the first of which Jailor George Bravin was shot by Stiles. This occurred during Sheriff Scott White's administration. They made good their escape and found shelter in Mexico for about three years, finally surrendering of their own volition, being promised, it is understood, that they would be granted immunity and taken into the fold of respectability. Stiles was the first to return and was made a clandestine member of the Arizona Ranger force. After "fixing" matters, Alvord surrendered at Naco and was wined, dined and lionized, the receptions furnishing an optical assurance to the youth of the land that crime would meet with approval and reward. But a law-abiding element rebelled and the two pilgrims were indicted and incarcerated as self-confessed highwaymen. . . .

Jack Virgin, who was the last prisoner to come through the hall of the jail wall gave a graphic description of the delivery.

"The prisoners had been looking on the proposed escape for two days," said Virgin. "On Monday a knife blade and pocket knife were being nicked with which to saw one of the bars to admit prisoners from the east side to the west end. A clamp that had been previously sprung was cut in about twenty minutes. This bar was then pulled and used to batter down the hole in the brick wall above the cells. Water was used to dampen the mortar and deaden the sound of their work. About four o'clock the brick had all been removed except the last tier, and a blanket hung up as if to air same, concealing any view of the front. It was known among all the prisoners that the usual inspection would be held last night and opportunity was only awaited for dusk, while it was decided to leave about half an hour before 'closing up' time. It would have been worth the life of any prisoner to 'squeal.' At the time for leaving Stiles and Alvord were joined by James and Sailor Brown from the other side. The four pushed out the remaining tier of brick and the matter of leaving was but a few minutes. Stiles was the first man out. All the other prisoners who escaped followed the lead in quick succession. All but four prisoners in the entire jail had an opportunity to leave. These four were shut out in another portion of the jail. I was the last one to get out, the others being ten or fifteen minutes ahead. I went around to the front and informed Deputy McDonald that a jail delivery had occurred. McDonald run around to the opening and fired several shots to attract attention and get help. A crowd appeared shortly after.

"From what I can learn," said Virgin in answer to the inquiry, "they had no horses or guns outside, but the four prisoners, Stiles, Alvord, James and Brown were to meet below the town and head for the line."—(Dec. 21, 1903.)

Both men were trapped at the border six weeks later, and, in a night gun battle which followed, Alvord was wounded. Stiles took care of himself, as usual, and instead of remaining to fight it out, deserted his companion. According to the *Epitaph* this is the story.

News from Naco today is to the effect that much excitement and interest is aroused at the border town in consequence of the capture of Burt Alvord near there last night.

From all accounts officers and outlaws engaged in a desperate fight, and it appears that darkness only prevented considerable bloodshed.

It was dark when the officers arrived at the place of rendezvous and were as promptly recognized by the outlaws, an unknown Mexican being with Alvord and Stiles. The latter trio opened fire and the officers did likewise.

After a few volleys Alvord was found to have been shot and Stiles and the Mexican were seen to leave in the darkness and escape although it is thought Stiles also is wounded.

Alvord is under sentence of two years to Yuma for train-robbery, and Stiles has eleven indictments hanging over him for the same offense.—(Feb., 1903.)

There is no further news of Stiles until Nov., 1905. Then the *Epitaph* reprinted a story which it clipped from the Douglas *International-American.*

Pio Quinta, who owns a number of prospects in the district south of Montezuma, arrived in Douglas yesterday with a story to the effect that Billy Stiles, the partner of the notorious Burt Alvord, had been killed while fighting with a band of Yaquis against soldiers of the Mexican government.— (Nov. 5, 1905.)

As the months passed, Tombstone hoped the report was true but apparently it was false. Stiles was reported in Chihuahua, Mexico, in 1906, and later was spotted south of the border near San Diego. After that he dropped out of sight again.

Two years went by with no more news of Stiles and then his wife announced she had received word her husband had been killed in a fight with cattle rustlers in Wyoming. The only reason this received any credence was that it would be in keeping with Stiles' character for him to shift over to the side of law and order. Inquiry, however, failed to substantiate Mrs. Stiles' story.

But whether Stiles was dead or alive, Tombstone did not forget him, and for many years parents of children caught in little falsehoods warned their young, "Watch out or you'll grow up to be like Billy Stiles."

13 "Why Don't They Pump Out the Water?"

Every tourist who lingers in Tombstone for a few hours learns that there is still treasure lying under water in the depths of the hills of silver.

Tombstone likes to talk about the fact that the Arizona Bureau of Mines and the United States Geological Survey have said so.*

It is part of the diet of hope on which the camp has existed for seventy years.

Naturally, the tourists always ask, "Why don't they pump out the water?"

It seems like such an obvious solution. But the answer is that it has been tried twice and each time the effort has failed.

Arizona Bureau of Mines has made this report:

"It should be recognized that if mining is to be continued for long periods below the present water level, draining of the area to the depth of development will be necessary. Ore extraction below the water level, to be profitable, must be on a scale commensurate with the cost of pumping."

Mining experts have told the story of the struggle in the Tombstone mines as well as factual reports, tables, and charts can tell anything. But the pages of the *Epitaph* tell it as the people knew and lived it and as they remember the long, heartbreaking fight to recapture their fabulous past.

March is a pleasant month in Tombstone. The sun warms the rocky hillside where the town lies at an elevation of 4,500 feet, and there are seldom any clouds. So it was probably a sunny spring day when the *Epitaph* reporter sat down in his little office and scrawled out in longhand what he thought was a marvelously hopeful story about the mines.

* "Geology and Ore Deposits of the Tombstone District, Arizona," published by the University of Arizona, 1938.

What he could not know was that he was announcing the death sentence had been passed on Tombstone, and had he been told so he would not have believed it.

The year was 1881,* in which they took five million dollars worth of ore out of the mines. The camp was three years old and had six hundred houses and four thousand people. It was roaring with wealth and there were constant reports of new strikes.

But on the day the reporter wrote this story the miners had found something new. They struck water.

It seems ironical now, when one reads the *Epitaph's* later stories of the millions spent in a gigantic struggle to dry out the mines, that the paper could ever have greeted the news of water as a boon. Yet one can understand why the editor rejoiced if he realizes that enormous ore wagons capable of carrying ten tons of ore to a load, were hauling their cargoes eight and nine miles to the nearest water—the stamp mills on the San Pedro River at Contention and Charleston.

There had always been great need in the city for water. Here it was, gushing out from the rocks as though fate, which had smiled on Ed Schieffelin, had smiled again.

It was even "of a character to leave little doubt as to the permanency of the flow."

How often they were to wish in the years of struggle and frustration that lay ahead that the character was not so permanent.

Here is the *Epitaph's* story as it ran on that exciting spring day.

"HERE'S RICHNESS"

This past week has been a most important one in the history of Tombstone. Water has been struck in one of the leading mines in the district, of a character to leave little doubt as to the permanency of the flow. It has been the opinion of course of all our best mining men that if the veins of the camp did not "peter out" water would be struck sooner or later; but those men were few, if there were any at all, who believed that the water would be found at a less depth than 1,000 feet. So firm and general was this opinion that none of the hoisting works in the district, not even the later and more powerful ones, were built with any view of encountering the water problem, and there are only two shafts in the district that would not have to be re-cut were water to be encountered generally. The great importance of water in the mines especially here in Tombstone, is not overrated, and the late strike in the Sulphuret has been very generally discussed during the week. One well informed and very conservative mining man yesterday remarked to the Epitaph reporter that in his opinion the camp had been benefited 100 percent by the encountering of water in the Sulphuret. It would inspire renewed confidence in the permanency of the veins, it would relieve the mines of the expense of hauling ore so many miles to the river; it would tend to bring more capital to Tombstone district than would a dozen "big strikes" in the upper levels of the mines themselves. He regarded the discovery of water in the Sulphuret as of far greater importance than the developments of rich ore, extensive as they are, which were recently made in the same mine.—(March 25, 1881.)

With newspaper enterprise, the editor sent his reporter out to get an eye-witness account of this great boon. Sure enough the water was there, and they were hoisting it out in a bucket. So the reporter went back to the *Epitaph* and told what he saw and heard. This is what he wrote.

The Water Strike

An Epitaph reporter was yesterday afternoon despatched to the Sulphuret mine to learn the truth regarding the reported heavy flow of water encountered on the 500-foot level. Arriving at the hoisting works he found the 50 gallon bucket ascending and descending with great regularity and a small creek was flowing into the gulch. A score marked up on an adjacent post recorded the fact that 92 buckets (about 4,600 gallons of water) had been hoisted during the "shift," from 7 a. m. until 3 p. m., while from the latter hour until the time of the reporter's visit, (5 o'clock) 22 buckets had been hoisted. Superintendent Farrel shortly after emerged, by no means dry, from the shaft, and stated in response to inquiries that it is yet too early to determine the nature of the "strike." The flow was about one thousand gallons per hour and had been encountered while sinking the main shaft at a point 20 feet below the 500-foot level. Mr. Farrell declined to express any opinion regarding the matter until further time should elapse, but seemed inclined to regard the event as more of an ultimate benefit than otherwise. Several mining men of experience were interviewed regarding the matter, but none of them seemed willing to hazard an opinion as to the permanency of the flow, though they were unanimous in regarding it as a great benefit to the camp in many ways should it prove to be permanent.—(March 26, 1881.)

The water, which was expected to be the greatest blessing the camp could know, began to present serious difficulties in 1882, but still the year was to be the richest in the history of the town. The total production of the mines went up to $5,202,000 and a twenty-stamp mill was erected.

One year later the water forced the rich Contention and Grand Central mines to suspend until they could install pumping machinery, and production dropped 50 per cent.

Prospects again looked good in 1884. Contention and Grand Central mines were back in production and were handling the water encountered in the shafts, stopes, and drifts. But that year the miners stopped work in the spring when their demand for an increase from $3 to $4 a day was refused. The strike lasted four months and was a failure. That year the production fell to $1,381,000—another drop of 50 per cent.

Fate struck savagely once more on May 12, 1886, when fire destroyed the Grand Central pump house and hoisting works. That left only the Contention pumps and they were inadequate. Both mines now suspended operations.

This was the blow which ruined the camp. The scenes that followed have been described by many writers but their reports cannot be checked against the *Epitaph* file because the issues are missing.

Only the oldest residents of Tombstone can recall that fateful period. One of them is Mrs. J. H. Macia, pioneer club woman and now historian of the town.

"We heard the fire whistles early one morning," Mrs. Macia

recalls, "and hurried out of the house. Some of the people were screaming and pointing to the hill. Others just stood in the deep dust of the streets or gathered on the rock hillside. Some wept. All were helpless.

"I remember how the draft from the shaft blew a column of flame and smoke high in the air. You could hear it roar.

"After that the town just fell apart and blew away. The people vanished by the thousands. The bank failed. Business houses went bankrupt. Homes and furnishing were almost given away and some were abandoned. Saloons and gambling houses boarded up their doors and windows.

"The great silver boom was over and all but a few stout souls—and the *Epitaph*—admitted this was the end."

Six years later the big Contention hoist was also burned and this report by the *Epitaph* is preserved. As usual, the tale is told chronologically, but the picture is clear.

Contention Hoist Razed by Early Morning Fire
Idle After Grand Central Pumps Burned; Produced Almost $4,000,000

At about 1 o'clock Sunday morning a small blaze was seen by a few persons in town whose attention was drawn toward Contention Hill. At first it was thought that a small cabin was on fire and it was not known to be in the magnificent hoisting works of the Contention mine. The alarm was sounded at the three houses of the fire department in the city, but no assistance could be given by dragging the hose carts up there, a mile distant.

A throng of people, however, went to the scene at once to render what assistance they could to save adjacent property, and to their efforts is due the preservation of many of the surrounding buildings. It was 45 minutes before the immense structure was enveloped in flame from ground to apex of the main building. The picture was sublime as well as awful to contemplate. Nothing could be done to stop the progress of the flames. There was no fire protection with the exception of an inch pipe in the building, which the cold weather had rendered useless.

Hundred Foot Flame

The draught from the shaft was an aid to the grandeur of the scene as it carried the flames high into the air, after the timbers in the shaft had been ignited by the burning embers which fell into it. It belched forth a flame a hundred feet in the air, resembling the burning of gas over a natural gas well.

The Engine company's cart was taken up about 3 o'clock but no connection could be made, and the only stream running in the shaft is an inch one from a stand pipe close to it. It has but little effect, however, as the shaft still gives evidence of being afire. Timbers of the underground workings of the Contention are a vast network, and how long the fire will burn is only conjectured.

For fourteen years Tombstone lay in a coma, with no serious efforts being made to work the mines on a large scale. Then E. B. Gage, a noted mining engineer, and Frank M. Murphy, a prominent financier, took advantage of the depression of the nineties to attempt consolidation of the largest mines in the district.

The *Epitaph,* itself, was close to death in those days but it was not so weak that it couldn't pick up a hot tip on the glorious future. It found such a tip in February, 1900, and the editor was so excited that his metaphor was rather confusing. The paper reported.

The darkest hours of the night are those which immediately precede the dawn. We believe the time is not far distant when our grand old camp will rise from the waves and shake her crested head aloft with pride as of yore.

Two months later the *Epitaph* again hinted that good news was on the way. This time the readers must have been extremely confused by the editor's phraseology in his one long sentence. It is interesting to note, however, that, although the grammatical construction leaves something to be desired, the meaning is astonishingly clear.

That the residents of Tombstone are justified in the knowledge of unmistakable evidence of action looking to the opening of the big mines are being quietly prosecuted by those who have the enterprise in hand, and with the work under way the hope that the prosperity of the palmy days of Tombstone will be reenacted is confidently looked for.

The task of promoting and financing the revival of deep mining met with obstacles and was, apparently, carried on quietly, for the *Epitaph* printed nothing more about it for six months. Then it published this.

Distinguished Visitors

A party of distinguished arrivals were in Tombstone today, and their presence gave rise to the general hope that the dark murky clouds that have long hovered over Tombstone's industrial atmosphere would rise and reveal a luminous silver lining. Such hopes in the minds of Tombstone's residents are pardonable. Whispers, murmers and rumors of the opening of the Tombstone mines under a consolidated management, would, if consummated bring about a dawn of prosperity never equalled hereabouts and the sunshine of consequent good times would start the sluggish commercial blood into the renewed activity and vigor of halcyon days. That some steps are being taken to bring about this condition is evident, but time and much patience are required to accomplish the good work. There are many interests to consult and naturally many phases, difficulties and obstacles to overcome, but a start has been made and it is believed that the controlling influences, heretofore at loggerheads are inclined to join in the contemplated work providing satisfactory arrangements are entered into.

Mr. E. Gage, principal owner and manager of the Grand Central here, now likewise connected with the Congress company; Mr. F. M. Murphy, brother of Gov. Murphy, and president of the Prescott and Phoenix R. R., also one of the heaviest capitalists in Arizona, and Mr. F. M. Staunton, former superintendent of the Toughnut mines here, now superintendent of the Congress, arrived last evening and spent the day in Tombstone. The party were here on a brief visit to take a drive over the Tombstone mines and otherwise acquaint themselves with the preliminary steps in what may develop in the reopening of the big mines here. Mr. Gage is thoroughly familiar with the Tombstone mining district, is one of the most successful mining operators in the U. S., has the utmost confidence in the merits and development of the Tombstone mines, and the guidance of such a mammoth enterprise, if undertaken, could not be in more capable hands. Mr. Murphy, who is also interested and doubtless will turn his attention to the great opportunity offered here, recognizes its worth and his association would be of incalculable benefit to the undertaking. Mr. Staunton is a most competent and capable mining expert of experience, whose judgment and knowledge of Tombstone's mineral ground will prove of much value. The party were in charge of Supt. Grow of the Tranquility company, who has taken a great interest in the rehabilitation of this famous district, and is instrumental in bringing about the results thus far attained.

A reporter interviewed Mr. Gage today and the veteran mining man gave the cordial assurance that he would lend whatever aid possible to bring about the desired boom and it is hopeful that such will be among the early possibilities. Steps now taken were preliminary, much was yet to be looked after and unless serious obstacles or opposition is met with the outlook might be regarded as encouraging. The party left this afternoon for Fairbank where the special car of Mr. Murphy is in waiting.—(Oct. 21, 1900.)

Another year passed, and one September day an important figure appeared again on the streets of Tombstone. The *Epitaph* really went all out over the second coming of E. B. Gage.

It would, however, have done a better job of reporting if it had been more factual and less hysterical. Gage was in Tombstone because he had finally succeeded in organizing the Tombstone Consolidated Mines Company. He was now ready to make the long awaited effort to work the old Contention and Grand Central mines.

Gage's engineering plan called for the sinking of a shaft to the one-thousand-foot level. Pumping stations were to be cut in solid rock at the six-hundred-foot, seven-hundred-foot, eight-hundred-foot and one-thousand-foot levels. By working huge pumps at these points Gage and his engineers believed they could handle all the water they would find.

The project was tremendous but success seemed so certain that the El Paso & Southwestern Railroad decided to build a branch to Tombstone. The "dawn of the new day" did seem at hand. The *Epitaph* could see the first flush of the morning sun coming up behind the mountains to flood with light the great city of which it had dreamed so long.

Considering the state of mind of the editor, it is not too hard to understand why engineering details may have seemed unimportant as he wrote this story.

E. B. Gage Is in the City

The familiar figure of E. B. Gage is seen on the streets of Tombstone today. Mr. Gage is a welcome visitor to the camp, not that through his exertions and enterprise the famous old mines promise soon again to become producers, but that while general manager of the Grand Central mines he was thoroughly identified with every interest of Tombstone that would make of it an ideal city, and to its past, as well as to its future, will the people revert, and look forward to, the future of the great camp, the success of, and an abiding faith in which, is predicated upon the wise judgment of the man who comes to steer us out of the wilderness —as it were.

While Mr. Gage displayed unrelenting confidence in the future of the camp his sagacity was shared in by numerous people who chlorided and dug out a handsome competence. There were no shrieking whistles to awake the midnight dreamer, black smoke from lofty stacks did not obscure the horizon, but they worked and waited and bided their time but not in vain.

The mines will again be in operation. Prosperity has superseded depression. The steam whistles awaken the slumberer, darkening smokes waft lazily over the erstwhile dreamy city casting upon the earth portentious shadows of future prosperity—a silhouette of the past—there are no laggards here. E. B. Gage has returned.— (Sept. 18, 1901.)

Late the next year the new shaft was down to the six-hundred-foot level, and engineers lowered rebuilt pumps from the Contention mine to the new underground station. Here is the *Epitaph's* report of the important event.

BIG PUMP AT WORK

The big pumps of the Consolidated Mines Company have been started and the first water was thrown to the surface by the big Prescott pump from the 600 foot level yesterday. The pumps were not run steady as yet as the volume of water thus far encountered is not sufficient to keep them running.

The men in the shaft are now down to a depth of 640 feet and the volume of water is rapidly increasing but it is not sufficient to keep even the six inch sinking pump to its full capacity of 500 gallons per minute. The latter pump is running at about one third of its capacity which is sufficient to keep the water down at present.

When one stops to figure up the number of gallons of water that can be handled every twenty four hours by the big pump it seems marvelous. At the rate of 1,800 gallons per minute it will throw 108,000 gallons per hour or 2,592,000 gallons every twenty four hours.— (Nov. 22, 1902.)

The year 1903 arrived and the *Epitaph* trumpeted a greeting in which it promised "continued prosperity and phenomenal growth." All was going well, it said, "with the unwatering of the lower depths."

In February it made a report of progress, in which it furnished details on the size of the new pumps.

During the past week the Consolidated Mines company has received another large pump of the same character as the one now at work on the 600 foot level which has been at work for the past month or two and which is now throwing from 900,000 to 1,000,000 gallons of water to the surface every twenty-four hours.

The company now has three pumps of the same character, one to go on the 800 and the last one received to be placed on the 1,000 foot level. The pumps are all of the Prescott make and are duplex, triple expansion condensing type, two with cylinders 15, 23 and 39 inches and 13 inch plungers with 24 inch stroke, and two with the same size of steam cylinders and stroke, but 9¼ inch plungers.— (Feb. 3, 1903.)

Work on the big shaft went on steadily. The seven-hundred-foot level was reached before the year ended, and two fifteen-hundred-gallon pumps were lowered and installed. The *Epitaph* reported as follows.

Work on the Hill

Everything moves smoothly on the hill and to the satisfaction of the Consolidated Mines Co. The big shaft has reached a depth of 717 feet and sinking continues without any hindrance, the water being under thorough subjection, the pumps working admirably and hoisting the usual average having raised to the surface yesterday 1,300,000 gallons.

The drift on the 700 foot level is now heading for a connection with the 600 foot level for air, the heat being almost insufferable, which is intensified by the hot air generated by the pumps.

To illustrate that the management has much to contend with while unwatering the mines, it is sufficient to state that up to January 1, 1904, 675,000,000 gallons of water had been raised to the surface the time being something less than a year. The company has now demonstrated that this subterranean reservoir, which wiseacres contended was fed by a flowing underground stream, can be emptied and caused to remain empty. The main shaft is now below the old working of the old Grand Central or the Contention in whose shafts an uncontrollable body of water contributed materially to their abandonment in the early 80's.

Shipments continue as usual, about 40 carloads of ore per month going from the big shaft and from 10 to 20 carloads from other workings, making an average of about two carloads of ore per day, not counting the Lucky Cuss Dumps, from which shipments of 100 tons a day are being made.

The West Side, the Emerald, the Comet, the Tranquility and the Silver Thread are working the usual quota of miners and are constantly getting the old workings in shape for more active operations later on.—(Jan. 23, 1904.)

In 1905, the underground crews were still drilling and blasting, and the *Epitaph* reported on the fuel consumption.

The Tombstone Consolidated Company are now using a car of oil a day for fuel to keep the pumps and hoist running at the big shaft. They are shipping from four to six cars per week from this shaft.—(Jan. 12, 1906.)

The following day the *Epitaph* announced that two pumps were being placed on the eight-hundred-foot level. It also mentioned very briefly that the water had risen during a temporary shutdown. It did not, however, anticipate any further difficulties.

At the BIG SHAFT of the T. C. M. Co., everything is progressing smoothly. Two new sinking pumps are now being put into the shaft and will be used in throwing water from the present water level to the pumps on the 600. The sinking pumps on the 800 will be used to throw water to the 700 and with the station and Dow pumps, it is expected that the work of lowering the water below the 800 which rose during the temporary shutdown will be accomplished within a week or ten days.—(Jan. 13, 1906.)

The *Epitaph* had reason for its confidence. The Tombstone Consolidated Mines completed a forty-stamp mill early in 1906, and proceeded to process one hundred tons of ore daily.

This was roast beef and potatoes to a paper which had lived on crumbs of hope, and the editor promptly raised his estimate of the Tombstone of the future. This was his new dream.

When the old camp shall have again resumed its wanton [sic] activities—and indications mark the day not far distant—it is freely prophesized that a hundred smokestacks will adorn that many hills; shrill whistles will awaken you at noon, comfort you at eve, and the music of the constantly dropping stamps will lull you to a gentle repose and sweet contentment. Tombstone will be itself again.—(Feb. 7, 1906.)

New equipment for the mines kept rolling in and the *Epitaph* reported each shipment. Now and then, between the lines, one reads a few words which raise a question as to whether all was going as well as reported. This is such a story.

The three new 200 horsepower boilers that have been expected by the Tombstone Consolidated company for some time arrived during the past week. They will be installed directly in front of the others which will then give the company a battery of seven 200 horsepower boilers, besides the two small boilers that have been used for the hoisting engines. When the steam is turned on in the new boilers the battle with the water now in the lower levels of the Tombstone Consolidated Mines will be renewed, and it is safe to announce that the pumps will now have no trouble in lowering the water.—(June 23, 1906.)

It took five years for the engineers and crews to reach their goal at the one-thousand-foot level. They then began cutting out the pumping station and placing the last pumps. The *Epitaph* carried a brief, but clear, description of the work on the lowest level in this news story.

Big Pumps to be Installed

The work of cutting out the station on the 1000 foot level of the Big Shaft is progressing rapidly and will be completed within a few weeks. The station is no small affair and will be 100 feet long by 30 wide. A sump reaches some 20 feet below the present level and further sinking is stopped for the present. The big pumps, similar to those on the 600 foot level are already on hand and ready to be put in place. They have 14-inch plungers and are capable of handling 4,000,000 gallons of water every 24 hours. These with the sinkers are expected to handle all the water encountered in the work.

On the 1000 foot level are strong indications of proximity to an ore body and the management feel highly encouraged. It is believed by many miners that copper will be encountered in the lower levels of this district and progress will be watched with keen interest.—(Jan. 17, 1907.)

The stamp mill had now reached its maximum capacity of 225 tons, keeping time with the rhythm of the pumps on the hill. Production was averaging $500,000 a year. But it wasn't enough, nor were the operators satisfied they had solved the water problem. One reads their fears into an *Epitaph* story and thinks again of the tourists who ask so casually, "Why don't they pump out the mines?"

Good Outlook For Tombstone

Although the water is under thorough control, it is the intention of the company to immediately install another pump on the 1,000-foot level, add another column and increase the pumping capacity from 5,000,000 to 10,000,000 gallons per 24 hours. The pump will be of the more modern design and is at the same time an economic move permitting of not alone unwatering the mines but guarding against a possible increasing flow. And with the aid of this monster pumping plant the lower levels may be kept comparatively dry and the contiguous territory penetrated by drifts and made to relinquish its grasp upon the riches known to exist below the water level.—(Sept. 30, 1907.)

Here let the *Epitaph* tell the story of 1908 chronologically and without interruption.

Work on the Hill

The first consignment of new pumps that are to be installed on the 1,000 foot level of the Big Shaft of the Tombstone Consolidated Company, consisting of three cars, arrived here today. . . . When the new pumps are in operation the company will be in condition to handle 10,000,000 gallons every twenty four hours if occasion should demand it. . . . The operation of the company's various shafts has continued uninterrupted and the mill continues to crush over 200 tons daily with good results.—(March 7, 1908.)

Marks New Era

This week has witnessed the installation and starting of the large pumps on the 1000 foot level of the Tombstone Consolidated Co., and with a total pumping capacity of 10,000,000 gallons every 24 hours, should occasion demand it, the company are in a position to thoroughly drain the district which means that the ore bodies known to exist below will shortly be opened up and their values turned into the commercial marts. . . . Victory is now in sight and the company will in time be richly repaid for their money and time invested in the opinion of all who are familiar with the formation and character of the ore bodies in the Tombstone district. . . . Drifting has already been started on the 1000 foot level and will be crowded as fast as possible under the direction of Supt. E. W. Walker and Assistant Bert Macia.—(June 27, 1908.)

An idea of the magnitude of one day's pumping operations at the T C M Co mines may be gained from the fact that yesterday's record of pumping reached the total of 6,671,321 gallons.

This enormous volume of water forms a veritable river. The two water columns from the 1000-foot level of the big shaft send out a little over 5,000 gallons a minute, and the huge pumps are kept going night and day.

Despite the heavy expense involved in this operation the

general plans as heretofore outlined will be adhered to nor is the company in any wise discouraged by the difficulties confronting them, nor do they falter one moment in their determination to reach the ultimate goal.—(Nov. 21, 1908.)

The low price at which silver was selling became of great concern to mining interests in 1908 but if the *Epitaph* felt any alarms it hid them and whistled bravely in the dark. Its only comment was an assurance that whenever silver went down it eventually went up again. Silver was then bringing 53 cents* although the *Epitaph* did not mention the price in this story.

The Silver Prices

Well-informed Eastern holders of shares in silver mines are not alarmed by the low price of the metal, knowing as they do that there must be from time to time streaks of lean and then streaks of fat. It is the opinion of the best informed bullion dealers that the metal will go down to the low level of 1902, when it touched 47 cents per ounce. In the same year it rose to 61-4c an ounce and then moved slowly upward until it was active at 71 cents in 1906. In 1907 the highest price was 70½ cents. In the same year silver sold as low as 53⅞ cents.—(Dec. 28, 1908.)

In its farewell to the year which had seen a supreme effort to recapture the mines, the *Epitaph* revealed for the first time that there had been serious delays and great obstacles. But, true to the policy set in John Clum's "First Trumpet," it sounded another fanfare of faith in the future in this New Year editorial.

The Old Year and The New

And so at the passing of the old year, Tombstone, DEAR Old Tombstone, takes on new heart and courage and turns her eyes to where is breaking the dawn of a greater prosperity than she ever enjoyed before. Proud queen of the richest county in Arizona, the wealth of her own mines surpass that of any other camp and although the gallant men who spending talent, time and fortune with lavish hand to bring the old camp up to its former stage of productiveness, have in the past year especially been

* University of Arizona Bulletin: "Geology and Ore Deposits of the Tombstone District, Arizona."

> beset by vexatious delays and obstacles almost unsurmountable, they never faltered in their determination nor wearied in their labors and the assurance is almost positive that before 1909 shall have spun its circle Tombstone will be hailed as it once was, the greatest mining camp of the west.—(Dec. 31, 1908.)

There must have been times when the flame burned low in the *Epitaph's* lamp of faith and the year 1909 could well have been one of them.

In the year of 1909 it seemed as if success were about to crown eight years of effort. But it turned out to be the worst period the camp had ever known.

The Arizona Bureau of Mines report says: "The year 1909 proved to be disastrous. On June 1, due to a defect in the fuel supply for the boilers the 1,000 foot level pumps were submerged. Despite efforts to retrieve them by the aid of eight sinkers, the water raised to the 900 foot level. Due to overloading, the six boilers of the power plant went out simultaneously."

Fantastic as it may seem, a tank car of what was supposed to be fuel for the boilers, turned out to be salt water.

One searches the *Epitaph* in vain for this news. True to what it thought was the best interest of the town it avoided the unpleasant facts. Its explanation of what transpired is a masterpiece of evasion as well as being a month late.

> The company has met with unforeseen difficulties but not in the least daunted are proceeding with the energy and determination that has always characterized the men who are at the head of affairs of this great enterprise.
>
> The pumping operations at the T C M will in the future be handled from the 800 foot level, the management having concluded that the process of unwatering the mine can be carried on to better advantage from that station.
>
> In drifting from the big shaft a rich body of ore was recently encountered in the old Contention ground. It is an important strike the ore running high in gold and silver.
>
> The water problem will be attacked in earnest and early in the new year rapid inroads are expected to be made in the shaft to overcome the setback from the recent historic and costly acci-

dent that flooded the lower levels. The year 1910 indeed presents a vista of golden promise.—(July 10, 1909.)

But the *Epitaph's* prophecy was wrong again. Far from being a "vista of golden promise," the year 1910 turned out to be worse than 1909. The mines ordered new boilers but the pumps did not begin to operate at capacity until July, and the total yield of the mines for the twelve-month period was a mere $102,000. This was a sad comparison with the years when the big wagons hauled $5,000,000 in rich ore down Allen Street.

At least the *Epitaph* had good company. It would not give up and neither would the mine operators. They installed eleven steam boilers with a capacity of 2,480 horsepower and hauled a trainload of equipment up the hill to the shaft.

Let the *Epitaph* tell the story from this point.

Much progress is being made at the pump shaft of the Tombstone Consolidated Mines company and the recovery of the 1,000 foot level is in sight.—(July 23, 1910.)

Within the next two or three weeks the whole mine will be completely unwatered so that very extensive mining will be carried on. We feel that the good old days of Tombstone are about to come soon on a vaster scale than ever before and with far more permanency.—(August 30, 1910.)

After one year of vexatious trouble when the lower levels of the Tombstone Consolidated Mines were deluged by seemingly a large body of water not to be coped with, the 1,000 foot level has been reached, the submerged pumps, sinkers and other paraphernalia have been reached and everything is again in working order and the management has no fear that a similar mishap will occur in the future.—(Sept. 3, 1910.)

The mine is now pumping 6,500,000 gallons a day.—(Oct. 22, 1910.)

Pumps are now operating at 6,800,000 gallons a day. Progress at the T. C. M. mines continues uninterruptedly.—(Nov. 12, 1910.)

Two weeks before Christmas, the *Epitaph* reported the Tombstone Mining Company had filed notice of an amendment to its articles of incorporation which would enable it to borrow $6,000,000. This was double its established limit.

The editor also explained that it had been decided the pumping operations might as well be reduced. This must have been a sad Christmas present to a town which knew its future depended on holding the water at the one-thousand-foot level. Even the *Epitaph's* inevitable word of hope sounds empty here.

> It is not necessary to use the full capacity of the pumps in order to hold the water down to a point where every nook and corner of the big mine can be advantageously worked and now that more finances are on the way we can look for the heralding of the long looked for strikes on the hill—resulting in the return of the life and activities of the first boom days—but more substantial and lasting.

This was to be the last dream of a return to the yesterdays when silver streams poured from every shaft on the hill, and the lights burned all night in the bistros and bordellos on the streets below.

It was a dream that was to be shattered in a few days, for, early in January, 1911, the editor said that there would be a reorganization of the big mining company and hinted it was in financial difficulties. Then, with what must have been a very heavy heart, he wrote this final paragraph.

> What is undoubtedly the climax of the arrangements is the order to arrange for practical closing of the property; the bulkheading of the 1,000 foot level pump station and provision for unwatering the mine at a future time by having the pipes and expensive underground machinery protected and ready for resumption on short notice. The fact that the underground machinery has not been ordered brought to the surface shows no abandonment is considered.

Efforts to refinance, however, proved futile and the company gave up. No one could be interested in a mining venture in which every ton of ore was brought out at a loss.

So they left the pumps in their stations, where they are today. They had spent millions. They had worked engineering miracles in the depths. But the water beat them in the end.

And that it why they don't try to pump out the water.

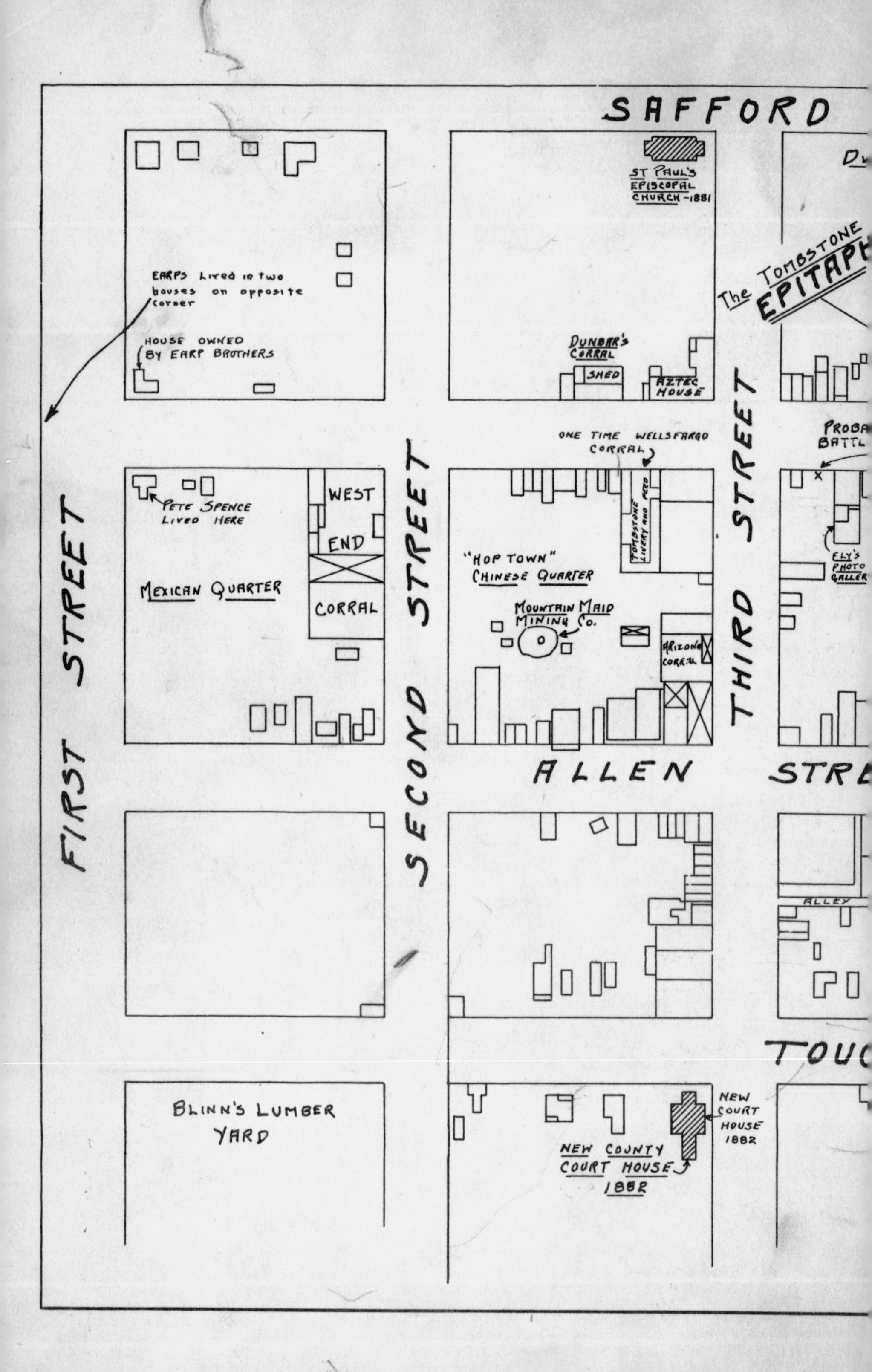
SAFFORD
ST PAUL'S EPISCOPAL CHURCH - 1881
The TOMBSTONE EPITAPH
EARPS Lived in two houses on opposite corner
HOUSE OWNED BY EARP BROTHERS
DUNBAR'S CORRAL
SHED
AZTEC HOUSE
ONE TIME WELLSFARGO CORRAL
TOMBSTONE LIVERY AND FEED
PETE SPENCE LIVED HERE
WEST END CORRAL
MEXICAN QUARTER
"HOP TOWN" CHINESE QUARTER
MOUNTAIN MAID MINING Co.
ARIZONA CORRAL
FLY'S PHOTO GALLERY
FIRST STREET
SECOND STREET
THIRD STREET
ALLEN
STRE
ALLEY
TOUC
BLINN'S LUMBER YARD
NEW COUNTY COURT HOUSE 1882
NEW COURT HOUSE 1882